The Legends of Saints Agatha and Lucy
in Medieval Castilian Literature

Juan de la Cuesta—Hispanic Monographs

FOUNDING EDITOR
Tom Lathrop
University of Delaware, Emeritus

EDITOR
Michael J. McGrath
Georgia Southern University

EDITORIAL BOARD
Samuel G. Armistead
University of California, Davis

Annette G. Cash
Georgia State University

Mark P. Del Mastro
College of Charleston

Vincent Barletta
Stanford University

Juan F. Egea
University of Wisconsin-Madison

Steven D. Kirby
Eastern Michigan University

Vincent Martin
University of Delaware

Mariselle Meléndez
University of Illinois at Urbana-Champaign

Eyda Merediz
University of Maryland

Dayle Seidenspinner-Núñez
University of Notre Dame

Noël Valis
Yale University

Amy Williamsen
University of Arizona

The Severed Breast:
The Legends of Saints Agatha and Lucy in Medieval Castilian Literature

by

Andrew M. Beresford

Juan de la Cuesta
Newark, Delaware

Front cover paintings: Francisco de Zurbarán (1598–1664)
Cover design by Michael Bolan

Copyright © 2010 by Juan de la Cuesta-Hispanic Monographs
An imprint of LinguaText, Ltd.
270 Indian Road
Newark, Delaware 19711-5204 USA

(302) 453-8695
Fax: (302) 453-8601

www.JuandelaCuesta.com

Manufactured in the United States of America

ISBN: 978-1-58871-183-0

Table of Contents

Preface 11

1 Compilation A
Introduction 15
Agatha and Lucy: Manuscript Versions 21
Editorial Questions 25

2 Agatha and Lucy in Compilation A
Introduction 31
The *Istoria de la bienaventurada Santa Ágata* 33
The *Pasión de Santa Luzía* 46

3 Compilation B
Introduction 59
Biblioteca Menéndez Pelayo 8 and
    Biblioteca Menéndez Pelayo 9 60
Fundación Lázaro Galdiano 419 67
Escorial K-II-12 72
Escorial h-I-14 and Escorial M-II-6 78

4 Agatha and Lucy in Compilation B
Introduction 85
Agatha 86
Lucy 99

5 Agatha and Lucy in Context
The Critical Legacy 113
Torture, the Breast, and the Castilian Context 121

  Sex, Torture, and Gender 130
  Dichotomies of Gender and Transformation 140

6 Rereading Agatha and Lucy
  Corporeality and Rhetoric 151
  Torture, Sexualization, and the Breast 170

7 Critical Editions
  Editorial Procedure 183
  The *Istoria de la bienaventurada Santa Ágata* 185
  The *Pasión de Santa Luzía* 193
  The *Passión de Santa Águeda* 199
  The *Vida de Santa Lucía* 209
  The *Vida de Santa Águeda* 217
  The *Vida e passión de Santa Lucía* 223
  The *Vida de la virgen señora Santa Águeda* 227

Appendixes
  Jacobus de Voragine's *De sancta Agatha virgine* 233
  Jacobus de Voragine's *De Sancta Lucia virgine* 239
  A Checklist of Manuscript Filiations
    in Compilation B 243

Works Cited 251

*Dedicated to ANNA,
who slept in my arms as I typed*

Acknowledgments

Sections of this book were read as conference presentations at the Universities of Aberdeen, Durham, Liverpool, Western Michigan, and Queen Mary, London. I should like to thank all those who offered comments and suggestions, and to express a particular debt of gratitude to my colleagues in the Centre for Medieval and Renaissance Studies at the University of Durham. I should also like to thank Mike McGrath, Tom Lathrop, and the editorial team at Juan de la Cuesta for their diligent and professional assistance.

The completion of the book was made possible by a research grant awarded by the Arts and Humanities Research Council.

Preface

Accounting to popular tradition, the Sicilian virgin martyr, Agatha, died in Catania at the height of the Decian persecutions (250-53). Desired by Quintianus, the low-born Roman consul, she spurned his advances and was imprisoned in a brothel, where its keeper, the appropriately named Aphrodisia, was charged with the responsibility of shattering her sexual resolve. When the attempt at coercion failed, Agatha was summoned once again before Quintianus, and after further interrogation, was subjected to a series of gruesome tortures—the most infamous being the severing of her breast. That night, while suffering in prison, Saint Peter appeared before her, and, in a miraculous act of intervention, healed her wounds and restored her breast. The following day, humiliated and enraged, Quintianus inflicted further pains upon her, and having borne her suffering with exemplary courage and steadfast devotion, she eventually yielded up her soul.

Agatha's fame spread far and wide, but is most notable in relation to a second Sicilian saint, Lucy of Syracuse, who, inspired by her example, prayed at her tomb and received a cure for her mother's illness. Taking advantage of the situation, Lucy persuaded her mother to disburse her fortune amongst the poor, but was denounced by her fiancé to the Roman consul, Paschasius, who tried her for being a Christian. Confronted by threats and intimidation, Lucy refused to renounce her faith and was condemned to suffer the ignominy of prostitution. Paschasius, employing various stratagems, attempted to have her moved, but found in each instance that she had been made immobile. In desperation, he had her basted and burned, but was forced eventually to have her put to the sword. Her martyrdom, which is believed to have taken place during the Diocletian persecution of 302, is commonly celebrated on 13 December, several weeks in advance of Agatha's feast, which falls on 5 February.

The legends of Agatha and Lucy circulated in various forms before they were incorporated into Jacobus de Voragine *Legenda aurea* (ca. 1260), a compendium of 182 religious feasts arranged according to their position in the liturgical-sanctoral calendar. Voragine's collection, which is the most important and influential of all of the great medieval hagiographic anthologies, devotes some of its attention to Christ and Mary, but is most notable for its explorations of male sanctity. Female saints are comparatively few in number, and in contrast to the diverse roles and occupations of their male equivalents, they have traditionally been classified according to the application of simplistic parameters based largely on questions of social function, sexual status, or relationship to men. Martha and Mary Magdalene, for instance, are famed for their dealings with Christ, while Petronilla is Saint Peter's daughter. Sophia and Julitta, on the other hand, are the mothers of saintly offspring, while Paula and Elizabeth fall into the category of the pious widow. A third group, including penitent whores such as Thaïs and Mary of Egypt, and transvestites such as Margaret and Eugenia, offer more sensationalized accounts of the female religious experience. Yet the dominant category, accounting for more than half of Voragine's forays into the realm of female sanctity, is that of the virgin martyr. These legends share a good deal of common ground and are developed in similar ways; acts of borrowing are frequent—notably in formulaic descriptions of torture and resistance—but despite this, they remain self-contained. The major exceptions are those of Agatha and Lucy, which are linked not simply at the level of character, but in the elaboration of theme. Surprisingly, however, despite the uniqueness of their status, the relationship between them has not yet been subjected to scrutiny.

The *Legenda aurea* was reworked twice into Castilian in the fourteenth century in the form of anthologies that have come to be known as Compilations A and B. The former, which is studied in Chapters 1-2, provides comprehensive coverage of the liturgical-sanctoral cycle by interpolating a significant number of additional materials garnered from alternative sources. Its treatment of Voragine's Latin suggests that some of its sections were designed to be delivered orally, possibly in the context of sermons celebrating individual feast days, or to clerics as they sat in the refectory. This can be seen most clearly in the adoption of a refined and eloquent register, a relative absence of syntactic complexity, and the inclusion of oral formulas. Its treatment of Agatha and Lucy (whose legends are preserved in an identical sequence of manuscripts) shows that its texts were constructed according to the application of an identical methodology of translation, for in each instance the emphasis falls on clarity, economy, and precision. This is accompanied by a tendency towards sensationalism, notably with regard to the representation of the bond between the virgin martyr and her celestial spouse and its corresponding impact on the sexualization of the female religious experience.

This characteristic can also be seen in Compilation B, which is studied in Chapters 3-4, with an appraisal of context followed by source studies of the extant Castilian recensions. The analysis shows that the texts of the Compilation can be found in six medieval manuscripts, which, unlike those of its counterpart, display a significant degree of internal adaptation and development. This could in part be regarded as the product of a tendency towards linguistic modernization, with the earliest extant versions dating from the late fourteenth century, and others, the latter portion of the fifteenth. The process of development, however, also extends to syntax and expression (which are by no means as polished or eloquent as they are in Compilation A) and the representation of sanctity, which appears in certain instances to have been tailored to suit the demands or requirements of differing audiences. A further significant factor is a tendency towards simplification, with a reduction in the overall number of narratives and the omission of many of the more flowery elements of Voragine's style. The result is that the legends of Agatha and Lucy can be found in a series of recensions, which despite in some ways departing relatively little from another, deserve nonetheless to be read in their own right.

The discussion of the two Compilations and the distinction between them provides a foundation for the thematic analysis offered in Chapters 5-6. The point of departure is an evaluation of recent critical treatments of Agatha and Lucy, which have done much to shed light on the conceptual density of the two legends, particularly from the point of view of the gendering and sexualization of the female religious experience, the relationship between torturer and tortured subject, and the symbolic connotations of the breast. A consideration of this work is used as a means with which to offer a detailed exploration of the Castilian Compilations, as Agatha's legend is read first in relation to a number of her most conspicuous female counterparts, and then, more broadly, the construction of gender and the sexualization of torture in the legends of comparable male saints. This leads to reevaluation of the dichotomy of gender and transformation, which shows that as Agatha's breast is severed and restored, the representation of saintly identity becomes subject to significant modification and development.

Chapter 6 offers a re-reading of the legends of Agatha and Lucy, which deal with questions of corporeality in remarkably similar ways, and a discussion of the gendering of torture and its impact on the representation of female sanctity. It concludes with a consideration of the uniquely female, life-giving, and yet simultaneously erotic quality of the breast, arguing that the torture inflicted on Agatha should be understood not as an act of defeminization or ungendering, but as one that reflects most significantly on traditional representations of nurture and spiritual development. The ultimate effect is most noticeable in relation to the cognate representation of sanctity in Lucy's legend, which focuses on questions of female empathy, and in so doing, offers a powerful exploration of the paradox of womanhood.

The study is completed in Chapter 7 by critical editions of the legends of the two saints supported by a full critical apparatus.

I

Compilation A

INTRODUCTION

IN 1986-87 BILLY BUSSELL THOMPSON and John K. Walsh published a brief but far-reaching article that provided the first systematic attempt to describe and catalogue relationships between the various medieval Castilian hagiographic manuscript collections. Their work, admirable for its erudition and the clarity of its methodology, showed that the collections should not be classified merely as translations of Jacobus de Voragine's *Legenda aurea*, but works that deserve to be read in their own right.

Although most of the manuscripts, as Thompson and Walsh conceded, took Voragine's work as their principal source or frame-text, the uses to which it was put were varied: some omitted a good number of its constituent sections, while in other instances his accounts were replaced by different (usually longer) readings, several of which have been shown by recent scholarship to be more authoritative.[1] A third

---

[1] Compare, for example, the *Istoria de la vida de Santa Ynés* (Escorial h-III-22 fols 117rb-24rb and Biblioteca Nacional 12688 fols 214vb-21vb), which is derived largely from Pseudo-Ambrose, and the *Vida e passión de Santa Ygnés* (Escorial h-I-14 fols 46ra-47va, Escorial K-II-12 fols 40rb-41va, Biblioteca Menéndez Pelayo 9 fol. 12^{rv}, and Fundación Lázaro Galdiano 419 fols 20ra-21ra), which abbreviates the *Legenda aurea* text (see Beresford 2007a: 71-84 and 85-92). The legend of Mary of Egypt, on the other hand, can be found in five manuscripts derived from Jacobus de Voragine (Escorial h-I-14 fols 87rb-88vb, Escorial K-II-12 fols 69rb-70vb, Escorial M-II-6 fols 37^{r}-39^{r}, Biblioteca Menéndez Pelayo 8 fols 14vb-16ra, and Fundación Lázaro Galdiano 419 fols 42ra-43rb), and a more substantial version, the *Vida de Santa María Egipçiaca* (Biblioteca Nacional 780 fols 25vb-39ra and Escorial h-III-22 fols 359rb-74rb), reworked from Paul the Deacon (see Thompson & Walsh 1977: 3-31 and 35-46, and Scarbor-

salient characteristic was a preference for the interpolation of readings for Franciscans, such as Claire of Assisi, or national saints—familiar examples being Ildephonsus, Leocadia of Toledo, Dominic of Silos, Toribius of Astorga, Vincent, Justa and Rufina, and the martyrs of Cordoba and Saragossa.² A fourth was a tendency to modify the chronology of the liturgical-sanctoral cycle, with some manuscripts arranging their readings in a more haphazard fashion. The result of this complex process of dissemination was that the relationship between Voragine and the Castilian *santorales* gradually became more tenuous. In some, the incorporation of fresh material even came to outweigh that which had been derived from the *Legenda* itself.

In addition to their discussion of formal characteristics, Thompson and Walsh also took the first tentative steps towards an authoritative system of classification, dividing the manuscripts into Compilations A and B. The second, which is discussed in a footnote, is comprised of a series of five medieval manuscripts (Escorial h-I-14, Escorial K-II-12, Fundación Lázaro Galdiano 419, Biblioteca Menéndez Pelayo 8, and Biblioteca Menéndez Pelayo 9) along with an eighteenth-century copy (Biblioteca Nacional 5548) of Fundación Lázaro Galdiano 419. (Un-

---

ough 1994). A third text, the *Estoria de Santa María Egiçiaca* (see Walker 1977 and Moore 2008: 25-39), is included in Escorial h-I-13, a manuscript that lies on the generic borderground between hagiography and romance.

2 For a discussion of the Franciscans, see Webster 1993: 260-89. Amongst other activities, she assesses the function of literature and the expectation that friars should familiarize themselves with hagiographic preaching aids as part of their educational programme (267-68). The output for this material, she maintains, came in the festivals of the liturgical calendar, and often included dramatized sermons (269-71). For further information, see Jeffrey 1975, Fleming 1977, Sticca 1988, and in relation to Spain, Castro 1973 and Surtz 1983. Studies of Spanish saints are few, and the most notable lacuna is the absence of a book-length analysis of their impact on popular faith and religious practice. For Ildephonsus, see Romero Tobar 1978-80 and 1984, and Walsh 1992a, and for Leocadia, Gaiffier 1953 and Díaz y Díaz 1990; Toribius of Astorga, in contrast, has been discussed by Walsh & Thompson 1987 and Walsh 1992b, and Dominic, by Ruffinatto 1978: 268-74. The paucity of critical studies stands in opposition to discussions of poetic works (such as those of Gonzalo de Berceo), which have been numerous. For further information see the online bibliography (http://web.uniovedo.es/CEHC/entrada.htm) prepared by Fernando Baños Vallejo.

accountably, a sixth medieval codex, Escorial M-II-6, is overlooked.) They also noted the existence of two further manuscript compilations, Biblioteca Nacional 10252 and Biblioteca Nacional 7098, which are independent.³

The main focus of their article, however, was Compilation A, the *Gran flos sanctorum*, which they identified as appearing in a family of five medieval manuscripts: Biblioteca Nacional 780, Biblioteca Nacional 12688, Biblioteca National 12689, Escorial h-II-18, and Escorial h-III-22.⁴ These are fifteenth-century copies of earlier originals and contain just under half of the readings of the complete compilation. Entries for some saints can be found in two of the manuscripts, and some in three, but no saint can be found in all five. Equally noticeable is that while BNM 12688, BNM 12689, and Escorial h-II-18 adopt a precise sequence that observes the liturgical-sanctoral calendar, BNM 780 and Escorial h-III-22 observe the cycle in part but incorporate other readings in a more random fashion (1986-87: 18).

The dating of the Compilation is by no means easy to ascertain, but in view of the fact that the five extant manuscripts include materials reworked from the writings of the Franciscan priest, Francesc Eiximenis (*ca.* 1340-1409), Thompson and Walsh argued that 'the earliest

---

3 BNM 7098 is a three-volume collection dating from the sixteenth century, and that as such, falls outside the chronological scope of this discussion. BNM 10252, on the other hand, is an important source of fourteenth-century hagiography, offering twenty-four legends arranged not according to their position in the liturgical-sanctoral cycle, but subject matter (effectively, apostles and biblical saints followed by martyrs). Its most distinctive feature is that its table of contents does not correspond to that of the manuscript, and, as Deyermond (1990: 143) has shown, it could be that almost half its content has been lost. This affects the readings for Agatha (listed as Chapter 33) and Lucy (Chapter 44). For editions of the sections on Blaise, James (miracles), Lawrence, and George, see Schiff 1905: 252-58, Connolly 1990, Prince 1993, and Buxton in preparation and for an overview of content, Schiff 1905: 247-51, Walsh & Thompson 1986: 26 (nos. 36-47), and Baños Vallejo 2003: 103.

4 Thompson and Walsh count BNM 12688 and 12689 as one manuscript rather than two, arguing that the latter (in terms of its treatment of the liturgical-sanctoral calendar) is a continuation of the former. It is, however, worth noting that as neither manuscript provides coverage of the period from April to July, the relationship between them is not as close as it first appears.

date for such a translation would have to be around the second half of the fourteenth century' (1986-87: 19). This, however, was subsequently qualified by a caveat, as they noted that:

> the problem is whether the project was begun and all translations were undertaken (perhaps by a single translator-compiler) in the second half of the fourteenth century or later, or whether the compilation represents a collection of readings that evolved and was expanded upon over a long period of time, with some translations (perhaps a large portion of the text) dating back as early as the last part of the thirteenth century. (1986-87: 20)

This, to some extent, is a tenable assumption, but in view of the tendency within the manuscripts towards evolution and amplification, it could be that the Castilian reworkings of Eiximenis were added at a later date. Until such time as they become the subject of sustained academic enquiry, however, it will be difficult to form a more balanced judgement.[5]

In view of the relationship between the manuscripts, Thompson and Walsh devoted the central portion of their study to a hypothetical reconstruction of the archetype from which they were derived. The starting point for their analysis was the prefatory statement that appears in the interpolated index to BNM 780, which they read as a 'precaution against or guide to the haphazard ordering of materials' (1986-87: 18):[6]

> El que trasladare este libro pare mientes con diligencia a esta tabla e escrívala por la orden que ella lieva, e non por la orden que está escripto en el libro, e fallará las ystorias a los cuentos de las fojas que están escriptas en ella. (fol. 1ra)

---

[5] For discussions of (and further references to) the influence and impact of Francesc Eiximenis, see amongst others Montoliu 1959, Viera 1980, Martín 2003, and Hughes 2008.

[6] Manuscript citations are reproduced throughout in accordance with the procedures outlined in Chapter 7.

In the table of contents that follows (fols 1ra-4vb), references are given to some 268 readings which are arranged according to their position in the liturgical-sanctoral calendar. These are accompanied by references to the volume in which they would have been found (for example: 'de Sant Saturn*ino* en la tercera, de Sant Andrés en la *prime*ra, de Santa Biviana en la tercera, de Santa Bárvara en la segu*n*da, de Sant Saba en la q*ua*rta', fol. 1ra). The process of identification continues until the lower portion of fol. 2vb, when the medieval indexer generally fails to indicate the volume in which the texts would have been found. This initial index, however, is followed by a second, which begins on the next folio and is prefaced by the words: 'Estas son las fiestas que están en esta segu*n*da parte del Flor s*a*n*c*toru*m*, las qual*es* son las que se syguen' (fol. 5va). The readings given here (which is where the manuscript originally began) correspond to those that are listed as belonging to the second volume of the compilation in the interpolated index. However, as none of the extant manuscripts (Biblioteca Nacional 12688, Biblioteca Nacional 12689, Escorial h-II-18, or Escorial h-III-22) can be identified as a section of the same four-part compendium, there is good reason to assume that three of the four original volumes have been lost. Those that remain, on the other hand, are separate compilations of the texts mentioned in the interpolated index and often contain duplicate copies of the materials in BNM 780 (1986-87: 18-19).

The index of the four-part sanctoral, as Thompson and Walsh point out, provides an insight into the method of compilation in each of its original parts. The first was a complete and precise translation of Voragine's text running from the start of the liturgical-sanctoral calendar in Advent through until at least Secundus (1 March) and probably Philip the Apostle (1 May). This, by implication, is the volume in which the archetypes of the legends of Lucy (13 December) and Agatha (5 February) would have appeared. The second, which is now conserved as BNM 780, contains readings drawn from the *Legenda aurea* from 1 May (Phillip) until 24 July (Christina), but also includes national saints, prominent examples being Leocadia of Toledo (fols 97ra-98ra), Eulalia of Merida (fols 98ra-102vb), Eulalia of Barcelona (fols 149rb-51vb), Dominic of Silos (fols 102vb-07vb), Leander of Seville (fols 132rb-34rb),

Isidore of Seville (fols 136vb-41ra), and Toribius of Astorga (fols 258rb-61vb). It also offers readings for the archangel Gabriel (fols 134va-36vb), Thomas Aquinas (146vb-49rb), and a series of portions derived from Francesc Eiximenis's *Vita Christi*.[7] The third part, which is now lost, was chiefly a translation of the *Legenda aurea* from James the Greater (25 July) through to Bartholomew (24 August), although it must also have included a number of additional feasts. Finally, the fourth part probably contained readings drawn from the *Legenda aurea* from 25 August until the end of the liturgical-sanctoral year on 29 November, along with the supplementary lives of the Fathers of the Desert and readings for Barlaam and Josaphat, the Dedication of a Church, and Pelagius (otherwise known as the History of the Lombards).[8]

This hypothetical reconstruction, as Thompson and Walsh maintain, 'outlines the process of synthesis and interpolation that entered into the project' (1986-87: 19). In view of this, it becomes possible to see that while later copyists, such as those who collaborated on BNM 12688, BNM 12689, and Escorial h-II-18, consulted the index of BNM 780 to make complete copies in proper sequence, Escorial h-III-22 retained some of the sequence but chose mainly to make random samplings of important readings (1986-87: 19).

---

7 See, for example, the Nativity (fols 52va-69va), the Circumcision (fols 69va-87rb), the Epiphany (fols 107vb-20va), the Holy Innocents (fols 129rb-32rb), the Purification of the Virgin Mary (fols 120va-29rb), and the Ascension (fols 163vb-71ra). Readings for the Passion and Resurrection, on the other hand, are conspicuous by their absence. The feast of the deaconess and martyr, Apollonia of Alexandria, falls on 9 February but is included by Voragine between his accounts of Phillip (24 July) and James (25 July). Reasons for her exclusion from the Castilian reworking have been advanced by Thompson 1990 and Beresford 2001, but it is also possible, in the light of Thompson and Walsh's conjectural reconstruction (1986-87), that her legend was overlooked in the transition between volumes two and three of the four-part original.

8 The lives of the Fathers of the Desert (Pastor, John, Moses, Arsenius, and Agathon) do not form part of the standard sequence of the *Legenda aurea* and can be found as Chapters 175-79 as an addendum. For Compilation A, see BNM 12689 fols 214vb-19ra and Escorial h-II-18 fols 262vb-67ra, and for Pelagius, BNM 12689 fols 226ra-33vb (which is incomplete) and Escorial h-II-18 fols 273vb-84vb. With the exception of a version in Latin of a reading for Pelagius (FLG 419 fols. 211vb-12rb), entitled 'Sant Pelayo en Latín', equivalents do not appear in Compilation B.

Agatha and Lucy: Manuscript Versions

An analysis of Compilation A reveals that the legends of Agatha and Lucy can be found in Escorial h-III-22 and Biblioteca Nacional 12688.[9] The first manuscript dates from the middle of the fifteenth century and contains 542 folios, mostly of paper but with some of parchment. The text is formed in a gothic hand typical of the mid-fifteenth century, and its numeration jumps from fol. 460 to fol. 465 (in a portion of Francesc Eiximenis's *Vita Christi*) although no text is missing. Its cover title ('En el nombre de la Santa Trenidat, Padre e Fijo e Spíritu Santo, aquí comiença el libro que es llamado Flor de los Santos que conpuso el onrrado varón don Diego de Verágine') does not provide an adequate reflection of content, as it offers readings for a number of saints not included in the *Legenda aurea* (see also Thompson & Walsh 1977: xxvii). A supplementary title written inside the front cover in an italic hand from a much later period is broadly consistent, with 'Flos sanctorum' followed by 'Vidas de Christo y otros santos por Jacobo de Vorágine' (fol. 1^r). A third can be seen in the first words of its table of contents, which has 'Aquí comiença la tabla de la primera parte del libro que se llama flor sanctorum' (fol. 3ra).

The ordering of the initial portion of the manuscript is modified by the inclusion of a version of the legend of Saturninus (30 October), which was bound in at a later date and is not mentioned in the table of contents (fols 3ra-8rb). This is followed by Voragine's Prologue and the first three of his readings (Advent, Andrew, and Nicholas), before the sequence is modified by the insertion of a chapter on Ambrose, which follows the date of his translation (7 December) rather than the April feast of Voragine's original (see his Chapter 57). A substantial portion is then given over to forty-four consecutive readings (Chapters 4-47

---

9 For Escorial h-III-22, see Zarco Cuevas 1924-29: I, 231 & III, 211-12, Thompson & Walsh 1977: xxvi-xxviii, Baños Vallejo & Uría Maqua 2000: 64, and Baños Vallejo 2003: 105; and for BNM 12688, Castro 1973: no. 479, Thompson & Walsh 1977: xxviii, Baños Vallejo & Uría Maqua 2000: 63, and Baños Vallejo 2003: 105. For online information, see http://sunsite.berkeley.edu/PhiloBiblon/phhm.html (maintained by Charles B. Faulhaber).

of Voragine's original) which move through the liturgical-sanctoral calendar from Lucy (13 December) to Longinus (15 March).

This is broken by the omission of the legend of Sophia and her Daughters (which cannot be found in Castilian), but is resumed by the incorporation of readings for Benedict, Patrick, and the Annunciation.[10] A subsequent omission is Timothy (Voragine's Chapter 52), before the manuscript proceeds to offer a series of sections on the Passion and Resurrection, supplementing Voragine's original with material derived from Francesc Eiximenis's *Vita Christi* (see Calveras 1944b). The sequence of hagiographic materials resumes with an interpolated reading for the archangel Gabriel (24 March), followed by treatments of Secundus and Mary of Egypt (29 March and 2 April respectively). It then interpolates a reading for Isidore (4 April) before completing the cycle of April feasts with consecutive treatments of George, Mark, Marcellinus, Vitalis, the Virgin of Antioch, and Peter Martyr (Chapters 58-63).

The most curious feature of the manuscript is that its final portion returns to the initial part of the cycle with the incorporation of twenty hagiographic readings (many of them dealing with figures of national interest) with feast days from December through to March.[11] The in-

---

10 Sophia's legend offers a barbaric (if not fanatical) account of sanctity in which her daughters (Faith, Hope, and Charity) are martyred in a series of brutal ways. The tale could have been excluded on grounds of taste (Apollonia is a parallel example—see Thompson 1990 and Beresford 2001), but it could be that the version of the Latin that circulated in the Peninsula was subtly different from the text edited by Graesse in 1846. Some evidence for this can be seen in the fact that it is one of several accounts—including Timothy (52), Apollonia (66), and Boniface (61)—also to have been cut from the thirteenth-century Catalan reworking, the *Vides de sants rosselloneses* (see Maneikis Kniazzeh & Neugaard 1977). The situation, however, is complicated by the fact that five other readings (Fabian, John Chrysostom, Fursey, the Four Crowned Martyrs, and Elizabeth of Hungary), although absent in Catalan, appear nonetheless in Compilation A.

11 Vivian (2 December), Barbara (4 December), Sabas (5 December), the Conception of the Virgin (8 December), Leocadia (9 December), Eulalia of Merida (10 December), Damasus (11 December), Dominic of Silos (20 December), Martina (2-5 January?), Maurus (15 January), Prisca (18 January), Marius (19 January), Anastasius (22 January), Ildephonsus (23 January), Cyrus and John (31 January), Eulalia of Barcelona (12 February), Augustine (28 February), Thomas Aquinas (7 March), the

clusion of this material confirms Thompson and Walsh's assumption (1986-87) that the manuscript was designed to provide comprehensive coverage of a specific part of the liturgical-sanctoral cycle—even at the expense of introducing an unorthodox structure. Further evidence can be seen in the inclusion of several further readings drawn from Francesc Eiximenis, with treatments of the Nativity (fols 441vb-58vb), the Holy Innocents (fols 458vb-66ra), the Circumcision (fols 466ra-85ra), the Epiphany (fols 488ra-502rb), and the Purification (fols 516rb-26rb).

The second manuscript, Biblioteca Nacional 12688, has much in common with Escorial h-III-22, and appears to be a contemporary of it, dating, on the basis of watermarks, from between 1440 and 1460. The codex contains 439 folios and is written on parchment in a standard gothic hand.[12] A title, 'Santoral', appears on its spine, and it is believed that it once belonged to Pedro Fernández de Velasco, first Count of Haro (see Lawrance 1984). The initial section of the text has been lost, and so it now commences on fol. 37ra with an incomplete account of the Conception of the Virgin Mary. This leads, from fol. 47ra onwards, to four December feasts of national significance: Leocadia (9 December), Eulalia of Merida (10 December), Damasus (11 December), and Dominic of Silos (20 December).

This sequence, which is punctuated by Lucy (13 December), is followed by nine consecutive readings drawn from Voragine (Chapters 5-13). Two of these, the Holy Innocents (fols 110va-14rb) and the Cir-

---

Forty Martyrs of Sebaste (10 March), and Leander (13 March).

12   The fact that Escorial h-III-22 consists mainly of paper, while BNM 12688 is written on parchment could suggest a qualitative distinction. However, as Anthony Pym notes: 'It is easy enough to assume that paper was simply cheaper to make than parchment. Yet production costs depend on a range of contingent factors like the availability of raw material, the use of series-production technology such as paper mills, the physical distance between the places of production and consumption, and the political and cultural borders to be crossed [...]. If paper was indeed cheaper to make in one place [...] this does not mean that it was necessarily cheaper to use elsewhere in Hispania [...]. If skins and hides were more readily available, as was presumably the case in the north of Europe, imported paper may have had virtually no relative advantages. Or again, if commercial relations between Christian Hispania were interrupted by war, which was periodically the case, paper may have been more expensive because of short supplies' (1998: 60). See also Constable 1994: 234-35.

cumcision (fols 136vb-57vb) are supplemented once again by material derived from Francesc Eiximenis's *Vita Christi*. It then resumes, after the interpolation of Basil (whose feast is restored to its traditional position on 1 January) and Martina (celebrated not on 30 January, but between 2-5 January, as is the case in Escorial h-III-22), with treatments of the Epiphany (6 January) and Paul the Hermit (10 January). Readings for January then continue with Hilary of Poitiers, Macarius, Felix in Pincis (Chapter 17-19), Maurus (15 January), Marcellus, and Antony of Egypt (Chapters 20-21).

At this point there is a lacuna affecting fols 208-13. The reading for Antony of Egypt, which concludes on fol. 207vb, is followed by the words 'Aquí comiença la istoria', but the manuscript thereafter resumes on fol. 214ra with an incomplete treatment of Sebastian. The content of this section cannot be ascertained with certainty, but in view of the manuscript's adherence to the cycle, it is likely that it followed the pattern adopted by Voragine, with chapters on Antony of Egypt (Chapter 21) followed by Fabian (Chapter 22) and Sebastian (Chapter 23). The problem, however, is that the reading for Fabian is short, and so it becomes necessary to take other factors into account.

The most significant is the correlation between the manuscripts and the feast days of the saints concerned. Escorial h-III-22, as we have seen, returns to a portion of the cycle by appending readings for saints not included by Voragine to its final section. The series of sixteen (Leocadia, Eulalia of Merida, Damasus, Dominic of Silos, Martina, Maurus, Prisca, Marius, Anastasius, Ildephonsus, Cryus and John, Eulalia of Barcelona, Augustine, Thomas Aquinas, the Forty Martyrs of Sebaste, and Leander) does not appear as a discrete entity in BNM 12688, but is fully integrated into a single and almost perfectly coherent cycle. Significantly, the only exceptions are Prisca and Marius, whose feasts (18 January and 19 January) fall between those of Antony of Egypt (17 January) and Fabian and Sebastian (both 20 January).

The correlation between the manuscripts in this respect is not coincidental: the incorporation in BNM 12688 of fourteen from sixteen possible additional readings, with the only two that are absent falling into a section in the cycle affected by a lacuna, provides reason enough to assume that the incomplete treatment Sebastian would have been preceded not only by an account of Fabian, but by readings for Prisca and Marius.[13]

The section after the lacuna continues Voragine's sequence by offering readings for Agnes and Vincent (Chapters 24-25) followed by interpolated accounts of Anastasius and Ildephonsus, whose feasts fall respectively on 22 and 23 January. It resumes with John the Almsgiver, the Conversion of Saint Paul, Paula, and Julian (Chapters 27-30), before continuing with the incorporation of Cyrus and John (31 January). It then returns to Voragine's original sequence with fifteen readings, punctuated only by the interpolation of Eulalia of Barcelona (12 February), before offering an account of the translation Augustine's relics, an event traditionally celebrated on 28 February, six months in advance of his main feast on 28 August.

The final hagiographic section gives a selection of March feasts, with interpolated readings for Thomas Aquinas (7 March), the Forty Martyrs of Sebaste (10 March), Leander (13 March), and Gabriel (24 March) included amongst texts dealing with Gregory (Chapter 46), Longinus (Chapter 47), Benedict (Chapter 49), and Patrick (Chapter 40). Of this group, it is noticeable that Leander's feast is placed according to its position in local tradition (as opposed to its official celebration on 27 February), while the ordering of Gabriel, Benedict, and Patrick is uncharacteristically inverted. The manuscript concludes with a series of texts reworked from Francesc Eiximenis focusing on the Passion and the Resurrection (fols 321ra-439vb) followed by the first few lines of a reading for Saint Secundus (29 March), the majority of which been lost.

Editorial Questions

The two copies of the *Istoria de la bienaventurada Santa Ágata* (Escorial h-III-22 fols 171ra-74vb and Biblioteca Nacional 12688 fols 272va-76ra) differ only in a number of minor respects.[14] The Escorial copy contains

---

13 For a discussion and tentative catalogue of lost hagiography in Spanish, see Deyermond 1990.

14 The title is derived from the incipit to Escorial h-III-22, which has 'Aquí

a limited number of errors, and most can be corrected in relation to the other version. Some, such as the misspelling of 'blasas' (fol. 173vb) as 'brasas' (BNM 12688 fol. 275ra), are purely orthographic, while elsewhere there is a tendency to interpolate spurious words—a good example being 'en el año de la su encarnación de dozientos e treynta e tres [años]' (fol. 174rb). A related feature is the omission of words necessary for comprehension, which can be seen in the rendering of 'dexaron la puerta abierta' (fol. 274vb) as 'dexáronla abierta' (fol. 173va). A fourth difficulty is created by unnecessary lexical substitutions that skew the emphasis of the narrative, the most striking example being 'e apartaste el mi coraçón de todo ensuziamiento' (fol. 174ra) for 'e apartaste el mi cuerpo de todo ensuziamiento' (fol. 275rb).[15] Finally, on a limited number of occasions there are problems with grammatical agreement, notably with the rendering of 'ponga a mis guardas en tribulación e angustia de las sus ánimas' (fol. 274vb) as 'ponga a mis guardas en tribulación e angustia de la su ánima' (fol. 173va).

The most significant problem with the Escorial manuscript, however, is its treatment of the initial portrait of the Roman consul, Quintianus, a section that is also garbled in the other copy, suggesting that the error was derived either from the archetype or an intermediate manuscript from which the extant versions were copied. If not, the texts must have introduced the errors independently, which seems unlikely:

> E Quinciano, un cónsul que era en Cecilia, era de vil linaje e luxurioso e avariento e adorador de los ýdolos, e deseava mucho prender a Santa Ágata. Por que fuese temido, aunque era de baxo linaje, prendiendo a muger tan noble e de tan alto linaje, e cobdiciando

---

comiença la istoria de la bienaventurada Santa Ágata' (fol. 171ra). BNM 12688, in contrast, has two rubrics. The first ('Declaración del nonbre de Santa Ágatha', fol. 272va) appearing before the discussion of etymology, and the second ('Síguese su istoria', fol. 272vb) immediately after. The manuscript in this way marks a tangible distinction between the prefatory discussion of etymology and the beginning of the legend proper.

15 Voragine's original has 'qui corpus meum a pollutione servasti' (109). Quotations from his treatments of Agatha and Lucy are from Appendixes I and II, and are identified throughout by line number only.

mucho conplir con ella su luxuria porque era donzella de grant fermosura, e deseando aver sus riq*ue*zas sy non quisiese adorar los ýdolos. (fol. 171^{rb-va})

This passage can be punctuated in various ways, but even when taken in conjunction with its source, there does not appear to be an easy way of making it intelligible.[16] BNM 12688 registers two differences, with the omission of the conjunction that precedes 'cobdiciando' and the use of 'tanta' rather than 'grant' in the discussion of the saint's beauty. A further point to bear in mind is that the Escorial copy adds 'mucho' in the left-hand margin, suggesting the scribe had realized that something was amiss and was prepared to correct his copy—even if its content (one must assume) was not wholly intelligible to him. As the texts of Compilation B opt for a different formulation, the least unsatisfactory solution here is to emend the verbal structure of the passage, rendering 'prendiendo' as 'quería prender', 'cobdiciando' as 'cobdiciava', and 'deseando' as 'deseava'.[17]

With the overwhelming majority of other discrepancies, Escorial h-III-22 is more reliable. This can be seen in the Madrid manuscript's tendency to interpolate unnecessary words, two of the most notable examples being: 'E cat*án*dose Santa Ágatha, fallóse toda sana [e santa] e tornada la teta a los pechos' (fol. 274vb) and 'E los gentiles descendie-

---

16 'Quintianus autem consularis Siciliae, cum esset ignobilis, libidinosus, avarus et ydolis deditus, beatam Agatham comprehendere nitebatur, ut quia erat ignobilis, comprehendendo nobilem timeretur, quia libidinosus, ejus pulchritudine frueretur, quia avarus, ejus divitias raperet, quia ydololatra, Diis eam faceret immolare' (13-18)

17 This is not the only occasion when the manuscripts are unable to produce a satisfactory reading. In the discussion of divinity, for instance, Agatha's criticism of Quintianus is expressed ungrammatically when she exclaims: 'Mucho me maravillo de ty, que te tienes por onbre sabio e creer ser ynjuriado porque te digo que agora fueses tal como aquel a quien te ynclinas a adorar' (fol. 172rb). BNM 12688 is also problematic at this point, with 'creerte' (fol. 273vb). In this instance, the most plausible solution is to reject 'creer' and 'creerte', and select 'te crees' on grounds of intelligibility. A similar problem affects posthumous events, with the copies opting not for 'del día', but 'a un año el día que fue' (fol. 174va; fol. 275vb), which also requires emendation.

ro*n* del monte e fueron al sepulcro de Santa Ágatha, e tomaro*n* el paño que estava sob*re* el sepulcro [de Santa Ágatha] e pusiéronlo contra el fuego' (fol. 275vb). On other occasions it fails to include words necessary for comprehension. This is the case with 'Ágatha quiere dezir 'deesa sin t*ie*rra'; co*n*viene saber, ['syn amor', fol. 171ra] de las cosas terrenales' (fol. 272vb) and 'diola a guardar a una mala muger que avía no*n*bre Afrodisa, que tenía nueve fijas ['que eran', fol. 171va] todas malas mugeres' (fol. 273ra).

Similar examples are not hard to find, but equally noticeable is the way in which it introduces unnecessary lexical modifications and substitutions, rendering '¿De qué condición eres tú?' (fol. 171vb) as '¿De qué condiciones er*es* tú?' (fol. 273rb), 'Muéstrome tener p*er*sona de sierva' (fol. 172ra) as 'Muéstrome temer persona de sierba' (fol. 273va), and 'ca lo confondía por palabras' (fol. 172va) as 'ca lo ofendía por palabras' (fol. 274ra). The result, in view of this, is that Escorial h-III-22 becomes most suitable for selection as a base text.

The two copies of the *Pasión de Santa Luzía* (Escorial h-III-22 fols 36rb-39ra and Biblioteca Nacional 12688 fols 53vb-56va) confirm the pattern of relationships established in their treatment of Agatha, for once again, the Escorial copy, although differing only marginally from its counterpart, is most suitable for selection as a base text. The regularity of the manuscripts in this respect has implications for future research, for although at present only a minuscule sampling has been subjected to scrutiny, it may be that the relative prioritization of Escorial h-III-22 over BNM 12688 holds for the Compilation as a whole.[18]

---

18 The title is derived from the incipit to Escorial h-III-22, which has 'De la pasió*n* de Santa Luzía' (fol. 36rb). BNM 12688, in contrast, has 'Aquí comiença la istoria de la bienaventurada Santa Luzía, virgen' followed by 'declaración de su non-bre' (fol. 53vb). A difference in this instance, however, is that the discussion of etymology is not followed by an incipit designed to detach it from the legend proper. The orthography of 'Luzía' is not standard usage in either manuscript, although as it appears in both rubrics, it is likely to be consistent with the formulation of the archetype. In his posthumous edition of the *Istoria de Sant Alifonso, arçobispo de Toledo*, John K. Walsh adopts BNM 12688 as a base text with variants from Escorial h-III-22 included in a critical apparatus (1992a: 135-44). Unfortunately, as his work is not accompanied by a rationale, it becomes difficult to determine the validity of this decision.

With regard to minor problems, Escorial h-III-22 is notable for the fact that it omits the closing prayer or colophon: 'Aquí acaba la vida de la bienaventurada Santa Lucía a honrra e gloria del Nuestro Salvador, el qual con el Padre e con el Spíritu Santo bive e regna un Dios por todos los siglos. Amén' (BNM 12688 fol. 56ᵛᵃ). This peculiarity of style frames the text as if it were a prayer or solemn reading, and in view of its inclusion in BNM 12688, there is good reason to incorporate it into a critical edition.

With this exception, the remaining problems are relatively trivial. Some, such as the misspelling of 'suzidat' (fol. 36ᵛᵃ), can be corrected in relation to BNM 12688 ('suziedat', fol. 54ʳᵃ), while others have grammatical functions. Notable in this respect is the use of the indicative 'estiende' (fol. 36ᵛᵃ) in a passage that requires the subjunctive form 'estienda' (fol. 53ᵛᵇ). Elsewhere, there is a minor problem of agreement, for while the Escorial text has 'E como no la pudiese mover' (fol. 38ᵛᵃ), BNM 12688 follows the discussion of men, oxen, and spells with the third-person plural 'pudiesen' (fol. 56ʳᵃ). A final problem can be seen in minor omissions, a notable example being the rendering of 'soror mea Lucia' (23) not as 'Hermana mía Lucía' (fol. 54ʳᵇ), as is the case in BNM 12688, but more plainly as 'Hermana Lucía' (fol. 36ᵛᵇ).

With the majority of other discrepancies, the Madrid manuscript is problematic, particularly with regard to its omissions. Typical examples include: 'sienpre delante' (fol. 54ʳᵇ) for 'sienpre presente delante' (fol. 36ᵛᵇ), 'non só Dios' (fol. 55ʳᵇ) for 'non só yo Dios' (fol. 37ᵛᵇ), and 'por hermana' (fol. 56ʳᵇ) for 'por mi hermana' (fol. 38ᵛᵇ). On a different occasion it omits a sentence present in the Latin ('longissimam lineam divinae operationis sine negligentiae tarditate', 9), thereby abbreviating the prefatory discussion of etymology by failing to include the following: 'E aun ovo luengo rayo de obra continua e buena sin tardança de nigligiencia' (Escorial h-III-22 fol. 36ᵛᵃ). This stands alongside a tendency towards spurious interpolation, the most potentially confusing examples of which are 'sin algund torcimiento [de coraçón]' (fol. 54ʳᵃ) for 'sin algunt torcimiento' (fol. 36ᵛᵃ) and 'as despendido tu patrimonio con los amadores de tu [coraçón e] corrupción' (fol. 55ʳᵃ) for 'has despendido tu patrimonio con los amadores de tu corrupción' (fol. 37va).

A final series of readings can be rejected either on semantic or grammatical grounds. These include the misuse of grammatical gender, with 'el ama' (fol. 54vb) for 'la ama' (fol. 37rb), an implausible use of the subjunctive, with 'oyeran dezir que robara toda la tierra' (fol. 56rb) for 'robava' (fol. 38va), and a risible misapplication of ideas in relation to the pagan consul's eventual state of mental agitation, with 'santiguaba' (fol. 56ra) used in place of 'ensangustiava' (fol. 38vb).

2

Agatha and Lucy in Compilation A

Introduction

The texts of Compilation A are scholarly reworkings of Jacobus de Voragine's Latin originals, most notable for their clarity, precision, and rhythmic elegance. These characteristics, which are indicative of learned origin, point to the spiritual requirements of the lower ranks of the clergy, particularly lay brothers or nuns, where the provision of pious readings in the vernacular would have been of benefit. The context in which they were disseminated cannot be adduced from paratextual evidence, as not one of them is prefaced by an explicit declaration of purpose or a consideration of the procedures and methodologies of translation. The decision to assemble such a vast and impressive corpus, however, was not one that was taken lightly, or indeed, without a sense of purpose in mind.[1]

It becomes important, it view of this, to focus on internal evidence, looking specifically at finite nuances of language and expression. This, of course, is vital when assessing the transition from Latin to Castilian, as the languages are intimately related, particularly with regard to the question of lexical formulation and the way in which common religious and cultural assumptions are encoded into their respective semantic frames of reference. In this respect it becomes difficult to as-

---

[1] For studies of the translation of texts for lay brothers and nuns, see Taylor 1989, McAllister 1989, Connolly 1994, Renevey 1998, Selman 1998, and Pezzini 2003, and for cognate studies of literacy and bilingualism, St-Jacques 1989: 135-36, Wright 1997, and Lusignan 1997.

cribe even minor modifications or variations of emphasis to problems of compatibility.[2]

More likely, in fact, is that departures from the source text are indicative of the influence of a series of deeper underlying factors. These, of course, are numerous, and are in many ways difficult to isolate. Yet while in some respects the texts present modified conceptions of sanctity (which are, in part, a product of the gradual but inexorable evolution of spiritual rhetoric), we need also to bear in mind that they were intended for different purposes and were disseminated in different ways.[3]

A reliable impression of the Compilation is unlikely to emerge until a greater number of sections have been edited and subjected to analysis. A reading of the legends of Agatha and Lucy, however, provides evidence with which to assume that they were designed to be delivered orally—possibly in the context of sermons, but perhaps also to clerics as they sat in the refectory, tempering the potentially corrupting properties of food by ingesting words of spiritual nourishment.[4]

---

2 Jeannette Beer notes that 'the translators' assumptions usually remain implicit, but their lack of theoretical exposition must not be equated with a lack of theoretical principles [...]. The medieval translator required no arguments to justify either his authority or his activities' (1989: 2). Robert Stanton arrives at a similar conclusion, noting that 'It is a truism that medieval translators do not talk much about what they do, they simply do it [...]. But we must not be afraid of importing theory that is anachronistic, or nothing will get done. A lack of explicit translation theory is not the same as an absence of theoretical principles. It is the responsibility of the modern critic of translation to formulate theory that does justice to the text being studied: to extrapolate, as it were, from practice to theory' (1997: 35-36). See also Pratt 1991.

3 In their treatment of Bible translation, Nida and Taber 1969 (see also Nida 1964) establish a distinction between 'literal' and 'dynamic equivalence' in which 'correctness' can be defined not according to traditional issues of fidelity and accuracy, but 'the extent to which the average reader for which a translation is intended will be likely to understand it correctly' (1969: 1). Their work, which has sometimes been poorly received (see, for instance, Gavronsky 1977), has implications for the establishment of a theoretical approach to the reworking of the *Legenda aurea*, as it focuses not just on the translation of language, but broad cultural, spiritual, and ethical concepts. See also Graham 1981, Ross 1981, Prickett 1993, Zelechow 1993, Robyns 1994, Tymoczko 1995: 13, Cloud 2001, Kirk 2005, and Long 2005.

4 Oral delivery has long been the subject of debate. For general or theoretical

The *Istoria de la bienaventurada Santa Ágata*

The introductory section of the *Istoria* provides an engaging context in which to examine the validity of this hypothesis, as it is here that Voragine's often idiosyncratic approach to narrative is at its most impenetrable. The popularizing texts of Compilation B (analysed in Chapters 3-4) pass over this material and instead proceed to offer a more direct account of Agatha's significance. The *Istoria*, however, adopts a more judicious and scholarly approach, omitting lexical derivations in Greek and Latin while introducing clarifying modifications and adjustments in rhetorical and syntactic emphasis. The extent of the difference can be seen when the texts are arranged in parallel, with strikethrough indicating phrases omitted in the vernacular, and underline, its adjustments:[5]

Agatha dicitur ab agios, quod est sanctus, et theos Deus, quasi sancta Dei. Tria enim sunt, sicut dicit Chrysostomus, quae sanctum faciunt, et illa perfecte fuerunt in ea, scilicet cordis munditia, spiritus sancti praesentia, bonorum	Ágata quiere dezir 'santa de Dios'. E segunt dize <u>Sant</u> Crisóstomo, tres cosas fazen al onbre santo: <u>conviene saber</u>, la linpieza del coraçón e la presencia del Spíritu Santo e la muchedunbre de las buenas obras. <u>E todas estas tres co-</u>

---

contributions, see Crosby 1936 and 1938, Chaytor 1945, Lord 1960, Ahern 1981, Ong 1982, Zumthor 1984, Green 1990, Connolly 1994, and Pezzini 2003; and for Castilian, Michael 1961, Gybbon-Monypenny 1965, Walker 1971, Harvey 1974, Deyermond 1982, Gurza 1986, and Seniff 1987. An assessment of the relationship between hagiography and the sermon is overdue, particularly as there are overlaps (see Viera 1991, Sánchez Sánchez 1999: 196-97 and 691-93, and Beresford in press—on Mary Magdalene, Michael, and Julian respectively). For the sermon in Spanish, see Lomax 1969, Chapman 1970, Deyermond 1974, 1979-80, and 1984, Burke 1980-81, Cátedra 1981, 1983-84, 1986, and 1994, Álvarez Pellitero 1991, and Morreale 1996, and for background, Owst 1926, Bataillon 1980, and Muessig 2002. For the relationship between translation and codicology, see Pym 1998, Taylor 1989, McAllister 1989, Tymoczko 1998: 17-18, and Connolly 2003: 20-21.

  5 For studies of Voragine's etymologies, see Reames 1985, Girolami Cheney 1996: 3, and Vitz 1991: 104-05.

operum affluentia. Vel dicitur ~~ab a, quod est sine, et *geos* terra, et *theos* Deus, quasi~~ Dea sine terra, id est, sine amore terrenorum. Vel ~~ab aga, quod est loquens, et *thau* consummatio, quasi~~ consummate et perfecte loquens, quod patet in suis responsis. Vel ~~ab *agath*, quod est servitus, et *thaas* superior, quasi~~ servitus superior: et hoc propter illud quod dixit: summa ingenuitas est ista etc. Vel ~~ab *aga*, quod est solemnis, et *thau*, consummatio, quasi~~ solemniter consummata, id est sepulta, quod patet in angelis, qui eam sepelierunt. (1-11)

sas fueron conplidamente en Santa Ágata. E aun Ágata quiere dezir 'deesa sin tierra'; conviene saber, syn amor de las cosas terrenales. E aun Ágata quiere dezir 'fabladora conplida e acabada'. E aquesto paresce asaz claramente en sus respuestas. E aun Ágata quiere dezir 'servidunbre mayor'. E aquesto paresce asaz claramente en la respuesta que dio a Quinciano, diziendo: 'Aquella es grant nobleza en la qual es provada la servidunbre de Jhesu Christo.' E aun Ágata quiere dezir 'acabada solepnemente'. E esto paresce asaz claramente en el su enterramiento, que fue acabado de los ángeles. (1-13)

The modifications introduced in the prefatory section alter the emphasis of Voragine's original, with a text ideally suited to individual reading and reflection (accessible in particular to those with a knowledge of classical morphology) reworked into a more streamlined account, remarkable for its clarity, precision, and readability. The omission of references to Greek and Latin accelerates the pace of the narrative while partially diminishing the impression of scholarly *gravitas*. The most important point to note, however, is that the elimination presupposes the fact that its target audience could function only in the vernacular and that its interests would be served by a greater degree of attention to detail in other areas. Striking in this respect is the development of a delicately cadenced rhetorical structure that lends itself perfectly to the demands of oral delivery, whether it be from lectern or pulpit.

Equally noticeable, however, is the decision to interpolate references to its main protagonists, with Quintianus's name now given once, and Agatha's, on five additional occasions. This technique could be dismissed as heavy-handed, but while repetition is fundamental to the development of an effective strategy for oral delivery (Crosby 1936 and 1938), it is noticeable that it functions in conjunction with several further adjustments. These include the restructuring of the narrator's comments about Agatha's saintly perfection (which are transferred to a more syntactically advantageous position) and the interpolation of a reference to her spiritual enslavement to Christ. The second of these is the most telling, for by alluding to a subsequent section of the narrative, it shows that its content must already have been familiar to the reworker and that his endeavour could not, therefore, have been undertaken slavishly. This point should not be underestimated: with other saints the architects of Compilation A replaced Voragine's accounts with readings that they considered to be more reliable, effective, or stimulating—familiar examples being Agnes and Mary of Egypt. Here, in contrast, his version has not only been adopted, but read and interpreted before being reworked into Castilian.

The early portion of the narrative characterizes Agatha as a model of sanctity, first as the interpolated epithet 'aquesta santa virgen' is repeated for emphasis (14 and 16), and then with the deployment of a modified cliché, as 'ingenua et corpore pulcherrima' (12) is expanded to become 'noble e fermosa por linaje e por cuerpo, mas mucho más noble e fermosa por alma' (14-16). This expression, founded on the *meollo* versus *corteza* distinction, presents her as a noble and upright figure whose body and soul are fused in the expression of Christian service.[6]

---

6 The *meollo* versus *corteza* distinction is employed by Gonzalo de Berceo in the *Milagros de Nuestra Señora* as the speaker establishes a distinction between surface impression and inner meaning: 'tolgamos la corteza, al meollo entremos, / prendamos lo de dentro, lo de fuera dessemos' (Bayo & Michael 2006: 93; st. 16cd). The Compilation A version of the legend of Saint Agnes, on the other hand, describes her as 'niña de días e vieja de entendimiento, fermosa en el cuerpo e más fermosa en el ánima' (Beresford 2007a: 85).

Quintianus, in contrast, suffers an inversely symmetrical diminution, falling from his elevated position as 'consularis Siciliae' (14) to become 'un cónsul que era en Cecilia' (17). This provides an effective link into a modified account of his motivation, which presents him in a more negative light:

ut quia erat ignobilis, comprehendendo nobilem timeretur, quia libidinosus, ejus pulchritudine frueretur, quia avarus, ejus divitias raperet, quia ydololatra, Diis eam faceret immolare (15-18)	Por que fuese temido, aunque era de baxo linaje, quería prender a muger tan noble e de tan alto linaje, e cobdiciava mucho conplir con ella su luxuria porque era donzella de grant fermosura, e deseava aver sus riquezas sy non quisiese adorar los ýdolos. (19-22)

Voragine's Latin is founded on a symmetrical structure in which we are invited to consider four aspects of Quintianus's motivation: social inadequacy satisfied by the possession of a noblewoman, lust by beauty, avarice by wealth, and paganism by sacrifice. The *Istoria* appears initially to adopt the same sequence, but while the first and second accusations are expanded, the third and fourth are amalgamated, making the invitation to sacrifice a mere pretext to embezzlement. The text in this way presents him in a more despotic light, with his faith in pagan icons now linked to his lust for wealth. The appeal of this transformation, particularly to a clerical audience accustomed to receiving detailed instruction on the domino-like dangers of sin, is self-evident.

As Agatha is summoned to court, the underlying impression of possession and entrapment is enhanced as 'fecitque eam ad se adduci' (18) is reworked as 'E fízola prender e traer delante sý' (23), a turn of phrase that echoes the twofold use of *prender* in the preceding description (18 and 19). The attempt at coercion, however, is a failure, and so she is turned over to the brothel-keeper, Aphrodisia, and her nine harlot daughters. The *Istoria*, with characteristic clarity, emphasizes the saint's resolve through tautology, as 'immovible' (19) is rendered as 'muy firme e non movible' (23-24). This is accompanied by the fourfold repetition of Aphrodisia's name (25, 27, 31, and 39), which is given only twice in Voragine's original.[7]

A more significant transformation can be seen in the task she is assigned, as 'ejus animum immutarent' (21-22) is reworked as 'por que mudase el su coraçón de la entinción de la christiandat e la ynclinase a aver ayuntamiento con él' (26-27). This development fuses notions of sexual conquest and religious service, making the renunciation of faith a prerequisite in the corruption of Agatha's corporeal integrity. It also transfers the source of her resolve from soul to heart, a feature equally apparent in the rendering of 'Mens mea' (24) as 'El mi coraçón' (31) and 'ipsam immobilem permanere' (28-29) as 'la fortaleza del su coraçón' (39).

Agatha's triumph is in this way made emotional rather than cerebral, and affective rather than cognitive, and it is perhaps unsurprising in view of this that there are parallel developments in religious terminology, first as 'Christo' (24) becomes 'Jhesu Christo, fijo de Dios bivo' (32-33), and then more tellingly, as 'orabat' (27) is rendered as 'rogava al Señor que conpliese el su deseo' (37-38). This phrase, which echoes the earlier discussion of carnal union, underlines the extent to which the text has been brought up to date with developments in sexualized rhetoric, for in common with works dealing specifically with the female religious experience—notably Fray Martín de Córdoba's *Jardín de nobles donzellas* and Álvaro de Luna's *Libro de las virtuosas e claras mugeres*—it presents virginity not as a denial of sexuality, but a sublimated form of desire predicated on Christ.[8]

---

7 For the relationship between tautology and orality, see Crosby 1936 and 1938, and for tautology as a linguistic and sociological device, Emmet 1962, Hutchings 1964, and Turner & Edgley 1980. The Castilian text translates 'meretrici' (20) as 'mala muger' (24), while the thirteenth-century Catalan version included in the *Vides de sants rosselloneses* (which reworks the same Latin original), is equally unambiguous with 'bagassa' (11, 261), a noun adopted by Berceo in his *Milagros de Nuestra Señora* (see Bayo & Michael 2006: 140n161d). For a thought-provoking analysis of loan words in Anglo-Norman (with partial reference to the rhetoric of prostitution), see Trotter 1998: 23.

8 For an edition of the *Jardín*, see Goldberg 1974, and for the *Libro*, Menén-

The chronology of Agatha's return from the brothel is made clearer in the *Iſtoria* as it interpolates a reference to the time she ſpends within its walls: 'pasados los treynta días' (40). A parallel adjuſtment can be seen in the firſt of two interpolated references to the consul's seat of judgement ('asentóse en su silla', 43-44), as this develops a more robuſt approach to the representation of worldly power. The moſt significant transformation, however, is the reſtruéturing of the debate that follows, where exchanges between the two charaéters are introduced in a formulaic manner, with 'E reſpondióle Santa Ágata e dixo' and 'E díxole Quinciano' used in place of a number of phrases in the Latin. Although this could potentially be dismissed as an aſpeét of scribal habit (in each inſtance the translation is semantically legitimate), the use of such repetitive and prediétable *verba dicendi* seems out of place in a text notable for the vibrancy of its rhetoric and polished lexical sophiſtication. This, of course, gives further credence to the assumption that it was designed to be delivered orally, as its ponderous rhythmic prediétability would have been of benefit to an audience not only in guiding them through the ebb and flow of debate, but allowing them to focus on content rather than the mechanics associated with changes of ſpeaker.[9]

In the early portion of the debate Agatha is presented as the voice of orthodoxy, with 'Chriſti' (36 and 38) rendered as 'Jhesu Chriſto, fijo de Dios bivo' (49-50) and 'Jhesu Chriſto, criador del syglo' (52-53). The interpolation of traditional epithets plays partly on the gendered bond between virgin martyr and celeſtial ſpouse, and it is perhaps for

---

dez y Pelayo 1891, Caſtillo 1908, and Vélez-Sainz 2009. Surprisingly, the gendering and sexualization of religious discourse is a topic that has seldom received the attention that it deserves. For brief discussions, see Demerson 1984, Boyer 1988, Weiss 1991, Coria-Sánchez 1998, Vélez-Sainz 2002, Hernández-Amez 2002-03, and Beresford 2007a: 41-44.

9 The formula 'Reſpondióle Santa Ágata e dixo' (44-45, 48, 51-52, 55, 58-59, 69, 104-05, 108, 113-14, 128, 132, and 134) is used in place of 'Cui illa' (33), 'Illa reſpondit' (35 and 37-38), 'Cui Agatha' (40, 76, 79), 'Agatha reſpondit' (43 and 49), and Agatha dixit' (99). On a further occasion 'Cui Agatha' (64-65) is reworked more plainly as 'díxole Santa Ágata' (91). 'E díxole Quincianio' (47, 50, 53, 62, 131, 133, and 136), on the other hand, replaces 'Cui Quintianus' (84) and 'Quintianus dixit' (37, 39, 47, 97, 96, and 100).

this reason that the subsequent discussion of pagan emulation ('Sit talis uxor tua, qualis Venus Dea tua, et tu talis sis, qualis fuit Deus tuus Jupiter', 40-41) is truncated, with the text omitting all reference to the gendering of roles: '¡Tales seades tú e tu muger qual fue el tu dios Júpiter!' (56). This leads to a further development, as Agatha offers a detailed musing on the relationship between individual and divine:

Miror te virum prudentem ad tantam ſtultitiam devolutum, ut illos dicas Deos tuos esse, quorum vitam non cupias tum conjugem vel te imitari, ut dicas tibi injuriam fieri, si eorum vivas exemplo. Nam si Dei tui sunt boni, bonum tibi optavi, si autem exsecraris eorum consortia, mecum sentis. (43-47)

Mucho me maravillo de ty, que te tienes por onbre sabio e te crees ser ynjuriado porque te digo que agora fueses tal como aquél a quien te ynclinas a adorar. E si tú e tu muger non deseades remedar la vida de aquél que adorades por dios, ¿en qué manera te ynclinas a le sacreficar e onrrar? Ca si Júpiter es tu dios, non te desee mal mas bien, conviene saber que fueses semejable a él. E si aborresces de le semejar, ¿por qué me coſtriñes a lo adorar? Ca sy aborresces la su conpañía, eso mesmo sientes que yo siento, e non deves querer que yo le ofresca encienso. (59-67)

The *Iſtoria* interpolates rhetorical queſtions along with references to physical objeƈts such as incense—a technique that adds depth while confirming the extent to which Agatha is able to remain calm and rational under pressure. The adroit manipulation of rhetoric provides a further indication of clerical involvement, but perhaps the moſt important point to note is that deſpite partially deintelleƈtualizing the saint elsewhere by transferring the source of her resolve from soul to heart, she is here accredited with genuine cognitive ability, confronting the consul with a strain of intellectual logic that he is unable to comprehend.

When the altercation resumes, the opposition between pagan and Christian is emphasized by the expansion of 'Abnega Christum et adora Deos' (56-57) into 'Niega a Jhesu Christo crucificado e adora a los dioses muy altos' (80). A more intriguing development, however, comes in the threat of torture on the rack, as 'jussit eam in equuleum suspendi et torqueri' (57) is rendered as 'mandóla atormentar muy gravemente en un tormento que era llamado cavallejo' (81-82). This transformation sheds further light on the approach to translation, as 'equuleum' is reworked in a morphologically plausible (although semantically unorthodox) manner, leading to the use of 'cavallejo' in place of the more logical 'potro'. What emerges is a dogged determination to render Latin into Castilian without tarnishing its theological or semantic validity, for despite departing from its original (notably by omitting reference to the fact that the saint is suspended), it succeeds in conveying a coherent meaning.[10]

After the torture, the interpolation of 'E desque fue cortada' (90-91) establishes a firmer impression of chronology. This reflects in part on Quintianus's ruthlessness, but it also prepares the audience for a

---

10   D. A Trotter argues that translations 'are by definition not "natural language" production. In the Middle Ages in particular, they are generated in close proximity to, and are often patterned closely on, documents written in another language. Many medieval translations are transparently *un*natural, often to the point of being unreadable or (at worst) incomprehensible without the aid, paradoxically enough, of the original' (1998: 29). Maria Tymoczko offers a similar perspective, noting that it 'has become a commonplace these days to say that literary language is defamiliarized language—but it is also generally agreed that if language becomes too strange or defamiliarized, it cannot be comprehended. The information load becomes too heavy for comprehension, and, in the case of translations, the receiving audience cannot understand the translated text' (1995: 13). Jeannette Beer, on the other hand, notes that 'Demonstrable need in a target language for technical terminologies, whether social, scientific, or philosophical, precipitates direct imports or closely calqued approximations. One hazard is, of course, incomprehensibility, as one unrecognizable term is substituted for or "cloned" on another. The process is nevertheless an essential part of the translative process whenever the translator is faced with lexical superiority in a source text' (1989: 4).

revised version of Agatha's reaction, as its temporal frame of reference ('Ego habeo mamillas integras in anima mea, ex quibus nutrio omnes sensus meos, quas ab infantia domino consecravi', 66-68) is expanded in order to present her predicament as the culmination of a lifetime of cognitive ambition: 'Yo he otras tetas entregas en la mi alma que consagré al Señor desde la mi niñez, e con ellas dó yo a los mis sesos fartura de leche' (93-94).[11]

A deeper insight, however, is provided by Saint Peter, whose opening address is also modified:

Licet consularis insanus tormentis te afflixerit, tu eum tuis responsis amplius afflixisti et licet ubera tua torserit, sed illius ubertas in amaritudinem convertetur (72-75)	Aqueste cónsul loco, Quinciano, te ha mucho atormentado, mas más atormentaste tú a él con tus respuestas sabias e enseñadas. E aunque él te fizo cortar la teta, la su alegría se le tornará en amargura e tristeza. (99-102)

The Istoria reworks 'amplius' and 'amaritudinem' as 'sabias e enseñadas' and 'amargura e tristeza', a twofold use of tautology that suggests that the text was designed to be read aloud, with its ponderous and sermonizing tone ideally suited to the demands of oral delivery.

---

11   Curiously, the Catalan text preserved in the *Vides de sants rosselloneses*, which reworks the same Latin original, affirms that Agatha loses both breasts: 'Per què adoncs En Quincià fo molt irat, e manà que om li tortorés les mameles; e quant om les li auria ben tortes, que les li talés om' (Maneikis Kniazzeh & Neugaard 1977: II, 264). Agatha's words confirm this ('Sàpies que eu é mameles entires dins en la mia ànima, de les quals eu noyresc tots los meus sens, que eu é consegratz al Seyor meu en ma enfantesa', II, 264), as do those of Peter: 'e jasia aysò que les tues mameles t'aja tortes' (II, 264). However, the phasing of the restoration produces ambiguity: 'e trobà la sua mamela garida en lo pitz' (II, 265). Maneikis Kniazzeh and Neugaard offer the following clarification: '*mamela* sembla tenir valor de plural, potser per analogia amb el plural neutre en *-a*' (II, 265n94). It may be, however, that the scribe decided initially to rework his original, but returned unconsciously to the content of the Latin, in the process introducing inconsistency.

An equally noticeable development comes in the discussion of medicine and the claim that Agatha's flesh has been protected not by her own hand, but 'por la gracia divinal' (106-07). This transformation, which diminishes the extent of her independence, is related not only to the words of Saint Peter, as he reinforces notions of gendered subservience by rendering 'ego apostolus ejus sum' (86) as 'yo, fija, el su apóstol só' (117) but the restoration, where a single section of Voragine's original ('Et procidens beata Agatha gratias agens invenit se undique sanatam et mamillam suam pectori restitutam', 87-89) is expanded to produce two sentences, with Agatha first examining herself ('E catándose Santa Ágata, fallóse toda sana e tornada la teta a los pechos', 119-20), and then falling deferentially to the ground in prayer: 'E derribóse en tierra, faziendo gracias al señor Jhesu Christo e al apóstol Sant Pedro' (120-21). A further impression of hierarchy is established in relation to the prison guards, as Agatha emphasizes the extent of their fear by rendering 'et custodes meos tribulationibus tradam' (92) as 'e ponga a mis guardas en tribulación e angustia de las sus ánimas' (124-25).

When the altercation resumes, Agatha draws attention to Quintianus's stupidity by rendering 'Miser sine intellectu' (95) as 'mezquino syn seso e sin entendimiento' (130).[12] His residence, on the other hand, is downgraded from 'palatium' (104) to 'casa' (139), while his subjects complain tautologously about his 'agravios e tormentos syn justicia' (142), in this way building on a reference in the Latin merely to 'cruciatum' (106). Agatha, in contrast, grows in dignity and stature in a modified version of her prayer:

---

12 The fact that the Catalan text preserved in the *Vides de sants rosselloneses* adopts an all but identical turn of phrase ('O home mesquí, sens sen e senes enteniment!', II, 265) could potentially suggest that both vernacular texts were derived from a copy of the Latin that differed slightly from the version edited by Graesse in 1846. Alternatively, it could be seen as a purely fortuitous point of contact in the application of two significantly differing methodologies of translation.

| Domine Jesu Christe, qui me creasti et ab infantia custodisti, qui corpus meum a pollutione servasti et a me amorem saeculi abstulisti, et qui tormenta me vincere fecisti et in iis virtutem patientiae tribuisti, accipe spiritum meum et jube me ad tuam misericordiam pervenire. (108-13) | Señor Jhesu Christo, que me criaste e me guardaste desde la mi niñez, e me feziste trabajar varonilmente en la mi mancebía, e quitaste de mí el amor del siglo, e apartaste el mi cuerpo de todo ensuziamiento, e me feziste vencer los tormentos de los carniceros (el fierro e las prisiones e el fuego), e me diste virtud de paciencia entre los tormentos, ruégote que rescibas agora el mi espíritu, ca tienpo es, Señor, que me mandes dexar aqueste siglo e yr a la tu misericordia. (146-53) |

In this instance, interpolations such as 'ca tienpo es, Señor' and 'dexar aqueste siglo' (152-53) add vibrancy and immediacy, while 'varonilmente' (148) impacts on the configuration of gender roles, showing that Agatha has risen above the limitations of her sex and vanquished a seasoned male opponent.[13] This is followed by an inversion of clauses and an interpolated parenthetic enumeration of the torments to which she has been subjected, the combined effect of which is to introduce a greater element of realism.

Parallel developments can be seen in the accompanying description, first as 'Haec cum orasset, cum ingenti voce spiritum tradidit' (112-13) is expanded to become 'E como ella dixiese aquestas cosas con grant devoción e con grant voz, dio el spíritu al Señor' (153-54), and then as its dating is made more specific, with 'annum Domini CCLIII sub Daciano imperatore' (112-13) rendered as 'en el año de la su encar-

---

13 The same adverb is used in Compilation A in relation to Agnes: 'E porque la fee non peresce con la muerte, aun fasta el día de oy veen muchas vírgenes Romanas a la bienaventurada Santa Ynés, asý como sy biviese en el cuerpo e perseveran entregas varonilmente por el su enxienplo, creyendo syn alguna dubda que alcançarán el gualardón de la corona perdurable si en la su entreguedat perseveraren' (Beresford 2007a: 79-80).

nación de dozientos e treynta e tres, a cinco días de febrero, seyendo Decio enperador' (154-56). A third development appears in the simplification of the wording of the marble tablet placed at the saint's head:

Erat autem in praedicta tabula scriptum: 'Mentem sanctam, spontaneam, honorem, Deo et patriae liberationem'. Quod sic intelligitur: 'Mentem sanctam habuit, spontaneam se obtulit, honorem Deo dedit et patriae liberationem fecit.' (118-22)	una tabla de mármol pequeña en que estava escripto: 'Aquesta donzella avía alma santa e voluntaria, e dio a Dios onrra e a la tierra libramiento.' (162)

The stilted and repetitive wording of Voragine's Latin (which makes it ideally suited to personal reading and reflection) is in this instance replaced by a pithier treatment, remarkable for its simplicity. This provides an effective lead into a reinterpretation of the significance of the visitation, as a single phrase ('ab oculis omnium statim disparuit', 118) is replaced by a more substantial appreciation of events: 'E estovo allí fasta que fue cerrado el sepulcro con toda diligiencia. E fuése luego dende, e non paresció más en toda aquella tierra. E sin alguna dubda es de creer que fue el su ángel' (164-67). The incorporation of this material marks a fresh departure, for in contrast to the emphasis of Voragine's original, the identification of the celestial figure as Agatha's angel guardian partially diminishes the importance of her status as *sponsa Christi*.

The events surrounding Quintianus's demise are also modified. The interpolation of 'E después de aquesto' (170) establishes a clearer impression of chronology, while the description of his motivation ('dum ad ejus investigandas divitias pergeret', 124) is rendered in more black-and-white terms, with the threat of violence and imprisonment spiralling out of control and extending to Agatha's kinsfolk: 'yva Quinciano a buscar e tomar la riqueza de Santa Ágata e a prender a todos sus parientes' (170-71). A symbolic development can be seen in the fact that his death takes place on a bridge ('E pasando por una puente', 171-72), as this brings to mind notions of liminality, with the crossing over water providing a perfect image of the transition between states of being.[14] This is accompanied by a fourth modification, with 'afogóse luego' (174) developing a detail implied but by no means confirmed by Voragine's original. The cumulative effect is the reinforcement of an underlying textual equation in which saintly virtue and celestial reward are pitted against pagan vice and worldly punishment.

A similar degree of rethinking can be seen in the volcanic eruption, first as 'Revoluto anno circa diem natalis ejus' (128) is reworked more concretely as 'dende a un año del día que fue martiriada Santa Ágata' (175), and then as the emphasis of the description falls on destructive power rather than speed, with lava flowing from the summit not with 'magno impetu' (130-31), but 'llama muy brava' (178). The progress of the eruption is halted in both versions by the saint's pall, but a difference thereafter is that the *Istoria* continues to avoid figurative expression, omitting a reworking of 'in die natalis ipsius virginis' (133-34) so as to proceed directly to the paraphrase of Ambrose's *De virginibus*:

O illustris et gloriosa gemino illustrata decore, quae inter tormenta aspera cunctis praelata miraculis et mistico pollens suffragio apostoli meruit visitatione curari. (137-39)	Aquésta es santa clara e gloriosa, ennoblecida de dos fermosuras de grant prescio, porque entre la aspereza e graveza de los tormentos meresció ser vesitada e sanada del apóstol Sant Pedro. (184-87)

Although both texts praise Agatha's twofold glory, the *Istoria* says nothing of her miracles, focusing instead on the fact that she was visited and cured by Saint Peter. This prepares the audience for the interpolation of 'su esposo e medianero' (187-88) and the replacement of 'Sic

---

14   The image of crossing over water is associated with Christopher, who carried Christ on his shoulders (see Buxton 2006), and Mary of Egypt, who crosses the river Jordan and is reborn into a life of spiritual purity. For further information, see Foster 1967 and 1970, Kassier 1972-73, Cortina 1972 and 1980, Sargent 1977, Wyatt 1983, Solomon 1995, Scarborough 1995 and 1998, Weiss 2006: 82-95, and Beresford 2007b: 44-53.

nuptam Christo susceperunt aethera' (139-40) by a reference to celestial marriage ('E subió al cielo a casar con Jhesu Christo', 187).

These developments draw attention to the strength of the bond between Christ and the virgin martyr (which, by implication mirrors the relationship between Christians and the Church), laying the foundations for an interpolated colophon, which although formulaic, is unique to the Castilian version, framing it as if it were a solemn moral lesson. This, of course, can be taken as an indication of purpose, as the final word ('Amén', 193) binds reader and audience in a blessing designed not simply to laud Agatha's memory, but celebrate a common ethos capable of uniting Christians in the never-ending battle against iniquity.[15]

The *Pasión de Santa Luzía*

The second Compilation A text, the *Pasión de Santa Luzía*, displays many of the same characteristics. There are few major omissions or interpolations, its adjustments and departures from the Latin add clarity and emphasis (not just in rhetorical and syntactic structure, but also in the representation of the interaction between virtue and vice), while its polished eloquence and rhythmic clarity once again make it suitable for oral delivery. These features can be seen clearly in the prefatory discussion of etymology, which departs only very slightly from Voragine's original. This could in part be due to the fact that his text does not in this instance offer lexical derivations in Greek and Latin, but it could also be seen as the product of a more sustained focus, with the properties of light dealt with from a largely scientific and theoretical perspective.

One of few noticeable modifications in this respect is the amalgamation of the narrator's observations on the beauty and cleanliness of light, which form a single syntactic unit (2-5), and the corresponding

---

15   William MacBain notes that although some hagiographic texts were reworked into the vernacular, they nonetheless included final prayers or blessings in Latin designed to unite reader and audience (1989: 45). As the texts of Compilation A do not adopt this formula, we must assume that they were directed at an audience that could function only in the vernacular. For a study of the 'folly' of using Latin in a translated work designed for lay readers, see Connolly 2003.

interpolation of a third reference to pollution ('sobre algunas cosas suzias', 5) complementing the twofold use of *ensuziar* in the preceding clause (4). A parallel reworking can be seen with 'Rectum incessum sine curvitate' (4-5), which repeats the subject of the sentence in the interests of clarity: 'E aun de la natura de la luz es enderesçar los sus rayos sin torcer' (5-6). These developments bring the contrast between light and polluting forces into sharper focus and in this way anticipate the confrontation between Lucy and Paschasius and the series of feverish but futile attempts to have her defiled. The most significant transformations, however, appear towards the end of the passage, first as 'beata virgo Lucia' (6) is standardized as 'Santa Lucía' (7), and then as 'diffusionem caritatis' (7) is reworked as 'derramamiento de la su claridad' (8-9), a development that reinterprets a central lesson of the legend, with the emphasis now falling not on charity (the disbursal of Lucy's fortune amongst the poor) but her clarity of purpose and conviction.[16]

The early stages of the *Pasión* enliven the narrative through the interpolation of details that add emphasis and clarity. This can be seen in the expansion of 'Lucia virgo Syracusana' (11) into 'E esta santa virgen fue natural de Çaragoça de Cecilia' (13), and in the reception of Euthicia, whose ailment ('annis quatour fluxum sanguinis incurabiliter', 13) is presented in a more vivid light, with physicians creating an impression of industrious but futile activity in their attempt to find a cure: 'avía quatro años que tenía fluxo de sangre e non podía sanar por mucho

---

16   The transition from 'caritatis' to 'claridad' could potentially be regarded as a product of scribal error, although the emphasis of the text militates against this. A possible analogue can be seen in the orthography of 'Çaragoça', which could have led to confusion and is not sustained. Compare, for instance, with Lucy's final speech, where she claims: 'asý será anparada por mí aquesta cibdat Ciracusana' (122). The thirteenth-century Catalan version in the *Vides de sants rosselloneses* makes a similar orthographic transition, but is more consistent, with 'Lúcia, verge de Saragossa' (11, 51) followed by 'e enaxí con la sor mia, Senta Àgata, és donada a la ciutat de Catània per defenedora, enaxí són eu donada per defenedora a la ciutat de Saragossa per so que eu per aquela cuitat prec Nostre Seyor' (11, 54). An all but identical orthographic transition in Álvaro de Luna's *Libro de las virtuosas e claras mugeres* shows that it is related to the textual tradition of the *Legenda aurea* in Spain (see Menéndez y Pelayo 1891: 304). See also González Palencia 1942: 20.

que los físicos travajavan por la remediar' (15-17). It can also be seen in the tale of woman with a haemorrhage ('in quo dominus mulierem ab hac passione sanasse narratur', 15), which uses references to Scripture to amplify its source: 'que dize de cómo sanó el Señor a la muger que tenía fluxo de sangre doze años avía' (18-19). The text in this way builds on the opposition between secular and spiritual healing, which as we shall see in Chapters 5-6, provides a robust thematic and conceptual link between the legends of the two saints.[17]

The experiences of Lucy and Euthicia are framed in Voragine's original by descriptions of their journeys to and from church. In the *Pasión*, however, their arrival is abbreviated, as the Latin ('Inter ipsa igitur missarum solemnia contigit, ut illud evangelium legeretur', 14-15) is reworked more plainly as 'E como a la misa se leyese el evangelio' (17-18). This modification, which sees a reduction from two verbs to one and the omission of the largely redundant adjective 'solemnia', allows the text to focus on Agatha's tomb not as a distant adjunct, but the core of holiness on which the church is founded. It is matched by a parallel development at the end of Mass, as a short phrase ('Igitur recedentibus cunctis et matre et filia juxta sepulchrum in oratione', 20-21) is expanded to provide a fuller account of the decision to petition Agatha for a cure: 'E desque se fueron todos los que ende estavan, quedaron allí Santa Lucía e su madre, Euticia, e ynclináronse a orar amas al sepulcro de Santa Ágata' (24-26). This transformation produces a more vibrant visual picture, for while the Latin vaguely discusses the actions of mother and daughter, in the *Pasión* Lucy and Euthicia wait patiently until the sizeable congregation has drifted away. It is only then that they make a decision to visit Agatha's tomb (rather than one without name) to solicit a cure. A final distinction can be seen in the display of hierarchical deference, as they kneel in ritualized submission before her tomb.

An insistence on the standardization of names and titles dominates the early portion of the narrative, as Lucy (19, 24-25, and 30) and Agatha (14, 20, and 26) are identified specifically as figures of saintly standing. A related transformation is in Lucy's advice to Euthicia, where a

---

17 See Matthew 9:20-22, Mark 5:25-34, and Luke 8:43-48.

mechanical introduction to direct speech ('Tunc Lucia matri dixit', 16) is modified by the interpolation of a possessive pronoun: 'Madre mía, sy creyes a estas cosas' (19-20). This brings the bond between mother and daughter into sharper focus and is paralleled by the precise rendering of 'Soror mea' (22-23) and 'Mater mea' (25) as 'Hermana mía' (28) and 'Madre mía' (31). A fourth instance of personal and homely affection can be seen as Lucy counsels her mother on the futility of posthumous possession, rendering complex theological notions in everyday terms:[18]

Quod moriens das, ideo das, quia ferre tecum non potes: da mihi, dum vivis, et mercedem habebis. (29-31)

Madre mía, lo que dieres después de la muerte, non lo darás si non porque non lo podrás contigo levar. E por ende dalo mientra bives e has sanidat por que ayas gualardón en el regno celestial. (36-39)

The interpolation of a personal pronoun ('madre mía') can be read in conjunction with several other modifications as part of a strategy of reworking designed to make the text more intelligible to its audience. A threefold use of negation adds rhetorical intensity, while the linking of statements with a simple conjunction enhances the relationship between cause and effect. This leads to an interpolated reference to health ('has sanidat') and a phrase that concretizes the abstract notion of heaven in the form of a celestial kingdom ('regno celestial'). The cumulative effect is the evolution of a passage of scholarly Latin suitable for personal reading and private reflection into a more familiar and rhetorically cadenced aspect of dogma ideally suited to the demands of oral delivery.[19]

---

18   Equally noticeable is the interpolation of an emotional reference to the bond between mother and daughter ('por amor de', 31) and a revised statement of acceptance, with the dryness of the Latin ('Tege prius oculos meos et quidquid volueris, de facultatibus facito', 28-29) replaced by a vibrant retort, notable for the interpolation of an affective tag and a reference to the inevitability of death: 'Fija, cubre primero mis ojos e después faz lo que quisieres de todo lo que quedare después de mi muerte' (34-36).

19   A related transformation is in Agatha's celestial visitation, where she is pre-

As Lucy and Euthicia return from church, the rendering of 'Cum ergo rediissent' (32) as 'E como se tornasen para su casa' (40) strengthens the sense of spatial location, while the interpolation of a second adverb ('alegremente', 41) into the description of the disbursal of wealth emphasizes the attractiveness of charity and voluntary poverty. A more significant development can be seen in the depiction of Lucy's husband-to-be, for while the Latin offers a factual report of his discovery ('Interea dum patrimonium distribuitor, ad sponsum notitia pervenit', 33-34), the *Pasión* reformulates it so as to include references to his future wife and mother-in-law: 'E oyendo dezir el esposo que su esposa vendía todo lo que su madre avía' (41-42). The result is the establishment of a more personalized and antagonistic atmosphere, with *esposo* and *esposa* functioning not merely as antitheses, but opposing forces representative of rival religions and cultural values.

It also paves the way for a transition from reported to direct speech, with Lucy's wet-nurse prioritizing figurative over literal as she plays on the young man's intellectual limitations:[20]

Respondit ille caute, quod utiliorem possessionem sponsa sua invenisset, quam suo volebat nomine comparare, et ideo videbatur aliquanta distrahere. (34-36)	E ella respondióle sabiamente e díxole: 'Tu esposa ha fallado otra heredat mucho mejor e queríala conprar para sí e en su nonbre, e vende algunas cosas de las de su madre para la poder aver.' (43-46)

---

sented as a figure adorned not merely with precious stones, but 'vestiduras muy fermosas' (27-28). This detail could have been borrowed from the celestial apparition of Agnes to her parents (see Beresford 2007a: 78-79 and 87).

20 A major tactical decision undertaken by the compiler of the Catalan text can be seen in the fact that he eliminates the role of the wet-nurse in order to present the episode as an encounter between mother and potential son-in-law: 'E dementre que·l patremoni tot alienaven, al seu espòs fo dit; per què, querec l'espòs a la mare de Senta Lúcia per qual cosa venia ela lo seu patremoni; per què, ela li respòs sàviament que pus útil possecció ac trobada a vendre la sua esposa, la qual en lo seu nom volia comprar, per la qual cosa volia alcunes coses vendre' (II, 52). This impacts significantly on Lucy's relationship to Agatha, notably with regard to the severing and restoration of her breast and the discussion of breast milk (topics discussed in Chapters 5-6). For a study of transitions between modes of speech and their contextual effect, see Pratt 1989.

By characterizing the wet-nurse's words as wise rather than cautious, the *Pasión* emphasizes the question of intelligence—a topic discussed in greater detail in Chapters 5-6. This timely and judicious adjustment leads more naturally into direct speech, with a fourth female voice complementing those of Lucy, Agatha, and Euthicia. In so doing it contributes to an already heady atmosphere of female complicity, which as a result modifies the way in which the text focuses on questions of male power and authority.

It is perhaps unsurprising, in view of this, that the account should proceed to omit a direct reference to the young man's stupidity, preferring instead to offer an extended portrait of his fundamentally childlike state of ingenuousness:

Credit stultus carnale commercium et coepit auctor esse vendentium. (37-38)	E el esposo, creyendo esto, començó a la ayudar a vender, creyendo ser verdat lo que le dixiera la ama que criara a su esposa, e que quería conprar alguna heredat tenporal. (46-48)

While the repetition of 'creyendo' establishes a robust impression of the extent of the young man's gullibility, the remainder of the passage constitutes an interpolation extrapolated from details implied but not discussed in Voragine's original. The reiteration of references to family bonds and relationships produces binary distinctions between Christian and pagan, on the one hand, and female versus male, on the other, but most noticeable is the young man's abject inability to understand that an estate can be anything other than temporal.

A consequence of the interplay between literal and metaphorical can be seen in the interpolation of references to his realization ('vídose engañado el esposo', 49) and reaction ('quexóse della', 50-51), with his humiliation in this way becoming a more tangible catalyst in the decision to bring Lucy to trial. A related development is a diminution in Paschasius's status, with 'juez' (52) replacing 'consulari' (39), as proceedings are now prefaced by an impression of petty vindictiveness instigated not by the chief representative of state authority, but a minor functionary. The final irony is, of course, implicit, for by having Lucy tried, the young man fails to recoup his lost inheritance and in the process also loses the wife that he once desired. This, perhaps, is something that could be manipulated in performance for comic effect, with the audience's laughter celebrating a common ethos capable of uniting Christian against pagan in the struggle against materialism.

The debate between Lucy and Paschasius follows the pattern set by the *Istoria*, as Voragine's *verba dicendi* are once again synthesized into a pair of instantly recognizable introductions to direct speech. This development imbues the text with a degree of familiarity, allowing the audience to appreciate the movement from argument to counter-argument without being distracted by unnecessary padding.[21]

The initial exchange between the two protagonists is reworked faithfully into Castilian, but as the altercation alights on the subject of loyalty to Empire, Paschasius's boastful (and ultimately untruthful) affirmations of allegiance are modified by tautology, as 'qui principum decreta custodio' (45) is rendered as 'que guardo las leyes e mandamientos de los señores del ynperio' (57-58). This leads to a response in which the grammatical structure of the Latin is altered by the introduction of a hypothetical frame of reference:[22]

Tu principum tuorum decreta custodis et ego Dei mei legem custodiam. Tu principes times et ego Deum timeo. Tu illos offendere non vis, et ego Deum offendere caveo. Tu il-	Si tú guardas las leyes de tus príncipes, así guardo yo la ley del mi Dios. E si tú temes al enperador, yo temo a Dios. E sy tú non quieres ofender a tus señores, yo non quiero ofend-

---

21 'E respondió(le) Santa Lucía e dixo' (53, 58-59, 66, 69-70, 75, 83, 86-87, and 106) is used in place of 'respondit' (41), 'Ad quem Lucia' (46), 'Cui Lucia' (53, 59, 62, and 65), 'Lucia dixit' (55), 'Cui Lucia dixit' (59), and 'Respondit Lucia' (61). 'E díxole don Pascual' (56, 63-64, 68, 74, 76, and 84), in contrast, reworks 'Cui Paschasius' (44, 51, 59-60, and 63), 'respondit Paschasius' (54), and 'Paschasius dixit' (58 and 62).

22 For a study of translated hypothetical 'si' clauses, see Brook 1998.

lis placere desideras et ego ut Christo placeam concupisco. Tu ergo fac quod tibi utile esse cognosces et ego faciam, quod utile mihi esse perspexero. (46-51)	er a mi Señor. E si tú deseas plazer al enperador, yo deseo plazer al mi Salvador. E por ende faz todo lo que quisieres, que yo non faré si non lo que entendiere. (59-63)

The *Pasión* replaces pronouns by nouns while adding variety through the use of near synonyms. The most spectacular modification, however, is the fourfold interpolation of 'si', which in addition to questioning Paschasius's allegiance, imbues the speech with an aggressively independent tone. This quality is carried through into the response, as he equates disloyalty to Empire with corruption and prostitution, rendering 'cum corruptoribus' (51) as 'con los amadores de tu corrupción' (64-65) and 'ideo quasi meretrix loqueris' (52) as 'fablas así como muger pública que non ha vergueña nin temor' (65-66).

As the discussion develops, verbal aggression is replaced by its physical equivalent. Voragine, emphasizing the distinction, establishes a play on words ('Cessabunt verba, cum perventum fuerit ad verbera', 58-59), a figure of speech notoriously difficult to translate. In its place, the *Pasión* opts for amplification, with Paschasius now speaking of whips and wounds: '¡Cesarán las palabras quando viniéramos a los açotes e a las llagas!' (74-75).[23]

Lucy's response follows the Latin closely, but her answer to the next question produces a major act of restructuring, as she glosses a citation that is otherwise taken for granted. In this way she is presented as a figure of greater authority, functioning as the mouthpiece of the Holy Spirit:

---

23 Translation strategies are predictably varied. The medieval Catalan text opts for literal translation ('Adoncs cessaran les tues paraules quant pervenguda seràs als batemens', II, 53) while William Granger Ryan's translation into modern English replaces the pun with a rhyme: 'The sting of the whip will silence your lip!' (1993: I, 28). For a less convincing attempt, see Macías 1982: I, 45. For studies of the translation of puns and wordplay, see Heller 1974, Ulmer 1988, Delabastita 1994 and 1997, Leppihalme 1996, Alexeiva 1997, Davis 1997, and Veisbergs 1997.

Ancilla Dei sum, qui dixit: 'Cum steteritis ante reges et praesides etc. Non enim vos estis etc.' (60-62)	Non só yo Dios, mas só sierva de Dios. E él dixo que quando estioviésemos delante los reyes e de los juezes, non oviésemos cuydado de pensar lo que avíamos de fablar, que él nos diría lo que oviésemos a dezir, e que non seríamos nós los que fablávamos, mas el Spíritu Santo que fablaría en nós. (77-82)

While Voragine takes matters for granted, the *Pasión* leaves nothing to chance, spelling out the content of the passage in full. This development provides further evidence of a distinction in purpose (private reading on the one hand versus public delivery on the other), but the fact that the medieval Catalan reworking of Voragine's original is also partially expanded at this point raises an important methodological consideration, for it may be that they are derived from a version of the Latin that differed slightly from the text edited by Graesse in 1846. Until such time as we are able to learn more about the dissemination of the *Legenda*, however, it will be impossible to arrive at a more nuanced understanding.[24]

In response to Lucy's dexterity, Paschasius acts on the accusation of harlotry and resolves to have her taken to a brothel. The *Pasión*, building on the logical implications of Voragine's original ('Nunquam autem voluntatem meam ad consensum poteris provocare', 67-68), establishes a robust distinction between body and soul: 'E non podrás ynclinar la mi voluntad a consentir a la suziedat, ca tienes en tu mano el mi cuerpo mas non tienes la mi alma en tu poderío' (89-91). This development augments the distinction between spiritual innocence and sexual tyranny, but Paschasius remains undaunted, and instead summons a crowd to perform the deed.

---

24   For studies of the textual dissemination of the *Legenda aurea*, see Calveras 1944a, Seybolt 1946a and 1946b, and Reames 1985.

In the Latin his command is recorded as direct speech ('Invitate ad eam omnem populum et tamdiu illudatur, donec mortua nuntietur', 70-71), but in the *Pasión*, which diminishes his standing, it is given as reported speech: 'fizo venir muchos rufianes e mandóles que conbidasen el pueblo a la su castidat e durmiesen con ella fasta que la dexasen por muerta' (94-96). The phrasing of the text at this point is subtle, for while the evolution of 'dicens' (70) to 'mandóles' (94) characterizes him as a tyrant, 'lenones' (70) is translated not as 'alcahuetes' but 'rufianes' (94 and 96), a word that retains connotations of mindless thuggery. Equally noticeable is the incongruity established by the euphemism 'durmiesen' in a place where one might logically expect an expression such as 'aver ayuntamiento'.[25]

An impression of violence is reinforced in the following section with the interpolation of a series of additional references to bondage and entrapment. This development, which presents Paschasius in a more despotic light, stands alongside a corresponding elevation in Lucy's power, as she shows that she is able to triumph over man and beast alike. A more puzzling modification can be seen in the final attempt to have her moved, for having heard that spells can be undone by washing with urine, her antagonist now speaks only of oil (109). Reasons for this transformation are unclear, but the effect is to create a doubling of tortures, for when the attempt at washing fails, he resolves to have her basted and burned.

His ineptitude in this respect prepares the audience for a modified description of Lucy's death blow, for in contrast to the Latin ('in gutture ejus gladium immerserunt', 87-88), Paschasius now performs the deed at the behest of his friends: 'mandáronle meter una espada por la garganta' (117). This action, which underlines the extent to which his power has progressively ebbed away, provides a final and appropriate humiliation, as he now effectively receives and acts on orders from his

---

25   The opening section of the *Vida de Santa Tays* (Compilation B) opts for the more usual term for a pimp: 'Santa Tays fue muger pública […]. E los amigos, por razón de los alcahuetes entre sí ayuntados, muchas vegadas finchían los unbrales de la su puerta de sangre' (Beresford 2007b: 135). 'Aver ayuntamiento', on the other hand, is used in the *Istoria* in relation to Agatha (27).

own underlings, revealing in so doing that the authority of Rome has crumbled from within.

As Lucy reels from the blow, twin interpolations identify her and Agatha as saints (117 and 121) while the introduction to her words is reworked in the interests of clarity, with 'quae nequaquam loquelam amittens dixit' (88) rendered as 'non perdiendo por esto la fabla, dixo a los que allí estavan' (118). Her speech otherwise follows the Latin, but while a clarifying interpolation identifies Diocletian as 'el emperador' (119-20), her prefatory announcement ('annuntio vobis', 89) is expanded to include a declaration of communal joy: 'Dígovos de donde vós podedes alegrar' (118-19).

Paschasius, in contrast, continues, via a process of inverse proportion, to be presented as a wretched figure, first as the 'ministri Romanorum' (93) are reduced to the level of 'cavalleros romanos' (124), and then as the journey to Caesar in chains ('vinctum ad Caesarem secum ducunt', 94) is replaced by a mundane appearance before the Senate: 'lleváronlo a Roma a los senadores' (124-25). In place of the abstract emphasis of the Latin ('convictus capitali sententia est punitus', 96-97), he is sentenced to an ignominious fate, suffering death by decapitation: 'fue fallado culpado de las acusaciones, e fue mandado descabeçar' (127).

The narrative in this way draws to a conclusion, and it is perhaps in the interests of economy that it omits a reference to the dating of Lucy's martyrdom: 'Passa autem est tempore Constantini et Maxentii circa annos domini CCCX' (101-02). A final development, however, is more telling, for while the Latin concludes with a blessing ('et omnes astantes amen domino responderunt', 99-100), the Castilian text performs a shift from intra- to extra-textual, replacing it with a prayer directed at those who would have listened patiently: 'Aquí acaba la vida de la bienaventurada Santa Lucía a honrra e gloria del Nuestro Salvador, el qual con el Padre e con el Spíritu Santo bive e regna un Dios por todos los siglos. Amén' (133-135). With these words the *Pasión* concludes by establishing a collective Christian ethos, binding reader and audience in commemoration of the achievements of an exemplary figure with a legacy still palpably relevant to the world in which they lived.

The text in this respect appears to be the product of an identical methodology of translation, for as is the case with Agatha, it offers a scholarly reworking designed with the requirements of oral delivery to a captive audience in mind. Striking in this respect are the final blessings, which echo the form and rhetoric of the liturgy, but equally noticeable is the incorporation of oral formulas, notably in the deployment of repetitive and predictable *verba dicendi* along with various other aspects of stylized language, particularly in the form of repetition and tautology. An adroit manipulation of syntax produces an impression of clarity and authority, and although both texts specifically avoid flowery, abstract, or unnecessarily complex aspects of rhetoric, they succeed nonetheless in establishing an impression of scholarly *gravitas* which further emphasizes the relationship between reader and captive audience.

This characteristic—which is underpinned structurally by a penchant for rhythmic and syntactic elegance, and semantically, by a dogged determination to render Latin into Castilian in a vibrant and credible manner—stands alongside a tendency to polarize the distinction between Christian and pagan, often by interpolating additional references to tangible properties or aspects of physical or corporeal imagery. The result is that, in addition to the integration of additional elements of clarity and precision, the language of the legends plays in various passages on traditional developments in the sexualization of religious discourse, notably in relation to the representation of the inviolate bond between virgin martyr and celestial spouse. The combined effect is the production of a series of hagiographic portraits that, as we shall see in Chapters 3-4, differ significantly from those of Compilation B.

3
Compilation B

Introduction

THE PIONEERING WORK OF Billy Bussell Thompson and John K. Walsh (1986-87) provides readers with an insight not only into the formation and scope of the hypothetical archetype of Compilation A, but the content and characteristics of the various manuscript recensions that circulated in Spain during the Middle Ages. An analysis of the legends of Agatha and Lucy, on the other hand, confirms and expands on their understanding, while showing at the same time that there is a good deal of evidence with which to assume that sections of the Compilation were designed for oral delivery—possibly to the lower ranks of the clergy, where literacy in Latin would otherwise have provided an impediment to comprehension.

The overwhelming majority of texts dealing with the two saints, however, can be found in Compilation B, a collection described by Thompson and Walsh only in the broadest possible terms (1986-87: 17n1), and that appears to have undergone a more complex process of formation and development. This, as we shall see, is one that led to several further stages of reworking in the vernacular, with individual manuscripts tailoring their source texts in differing ways. The process is further complicated by questions of chronological development (with the earliest versions dating from around the close of the fourteenth century, and others, almost a hundred years later), and by the fact that the work was undertaken as the manuscripts were produced rather than in annotated intermediate (or working) copies, which would have given a clearer impression of the revisions that had been introduced.

The result is the creation of a sequence of subtly differing representations of sanctity (and of the relationship between Church and society), which although coherent in themselves, can only be fully understood when subjected to detailed comparative analysis. In this respect, Compilation B offers a more conceptually demanding challenge, for while an appreciation of translation methodology in Compilation A involves rigorous scrutiny of the transition from Latin to Castilian, in this instance the process is extended, with the Castilian texts being reworked first from the Latin, and then evolving from one another. It is perhaps for this reason that other than an edition of Biblioteca Menéndez Pelayo 8 (Baños Vallejo & Uría Maqua 2000) and a number of attempts at establishing synoptic (Thompson & Walsh 1977: 35-46) and critical editions (Vega 1991: 83-96, Beresford 2007a: 85-92), little is known about the way in which the manuscripts fit together or how they should be interpreted, particularly with regard to the application of a coherent and watertight methodology. As a result, almost nothing is known about the orientation, reception, or purpose of the Compilation as a whole.[1]

Biblioteca Menéndez Pelayo 8 and Biblioteca Menéndez Pelayo 9

The earliest extant manuscripts in Compilation B are Biblioteca Menéndez Pelayo 8 and Biblioteca Menéndez Pelayo 9, which are fifteenth-century copies of earlier originals. The former, as Fernando Ba-

---

[1] In his discussion of Castilian epic, Alan Deyermond raises a methodological consideration applicable not simply to the distinction between Compilations A and B, but the recensions of the latter: 'it is inadvisable to combine lines or plot elements from several chronicles, as has sometimes been done, since the result would be a text which, however interesting, was a modern construct unrepresentative of the versions which circulated in the Middle Ages. Each chronicle version should therefore be treated independently, and each [...] can safely be regarded as an artistically coherent realization of an epic tradition' (1976: 283). For a discussion of similar problems in relation to Thaïs and Pelagia, see Beresford 2007b: 91, and for the broader Hispano-medieval context, Dagenais 1994. For studies of working copies in the process of translation and revision, see Connolly 1994 and Pezzini 2003.

ños Vallejo and Isabel Uría Maqua have shown (2000: 19-23), contains 73 folios and is written out on paper in twin columns. Blank spaces were left for large coloured initials to mark the beginning of individual sections, but this expensive and time consuming work was not subsequently undertaken. The scribal hand is clear, although some words are difficult to decipher, and a small number of others, all but illegible. This is caused partly by the fact that scribal practice is in a state of transition, with the standard gothic hand revealing cursive characteristics. The only exception can be seen in the three final folios (71-73), which were sewn into the manuscript at a later date.[2]

A short lacuna affects the conclusion of the treatment of Paul and the beginning of the reading for Margaret (known throughout the Compilation as Marina), with the lower portion of fol. 44rb and all of fol. 44^v left blank, presumably so that materials could be filled in at a later date. Equally noticeable is an awkward transition between the two final sections, with the loss of the final part of the reading for the Assumption (which is where the original portion of the manuscript comes to an end) and the truncation of the initial section of the Exaltation of the Holy Cross. There is no attempt at illumination or formal embellishment.[3]

---

2 Baños Vallejo and Uría Maqua note that 'Aunque Artigas [1930] dató todo este manuscrito [BMP 8] como del siglo XIV, tanto el tipo de letra como las diversas filigranas que presentan los primeros setenta folios permiten también pensar en una época más tardía, como comienzos del XV (hasta 1425, aproximadamente)' (2000: 19). On its status as a copy of an earlier original, on the other hand, they cite four arguments: the admixture of Castilian and Leonese, the pattern of variants in the two recensions of the reading for Patrick, the manuscript's calligraphy, and its relationship to BMP 9 (2000: 21-22). See also Baños Vallejo 2000a, 2000b, and 2003: 103.

3 For discussions of the confusion between Margaret and Marina, see Spencer 1889 and 1890, Rodado Ruiz 1990, Drewer 1993, Magennis 1996, and Beresford 2007b: 17-20. Baños Vallejo and Uría Maqua note: 'Al relato de la Asunción, inconcluso, le siguen los tres folios de distinta mano (ff. 71a-73b), que transmiten una parte del capítulo sobre la Exaltación de la Santa Cruz, a la cual le falta el comienzo. De hecho, se ve muy claro, aún hoy, el resto de un folio entre los actuales 70 y 71' (2000: 20-21).

The manuscript's forty-four readings cover the liturgical-sanctoral cycle from the Chair of Saint Peter (22 February) to the Assumption (15 August), with the Exaltation of the Holy Cross (fols 71-73) extending its chronological frame of reference as far as 14 September. The selective nature of its content could potentially indicate that it is an abridged copy, and with a clear but unorthodox six-month cycle, it could have been accompanied by a companion compilation covering the remaining portion of the year from 16 August to 21 February. This, by implication, would have contained copies of the legends of Lucy and Agatha, which fall respectively on 13 December and 5 February.

The fact that the reading for Peter is not preceded by a title, incipit, or table of contents, however, makes it more likely that a substantial portion of the introductory section has been lost. Most notable in this respect is that with the exception of Escorial M-II-6 (which begins *in media res* on fol. 19^r), the other Compilation B manuscripts begin after Advent with readings for Andrew. Whether or not the manuscript continued after its incomplete treatment of the Assumption is a more complex issue, particularly as two of the six extant manuscripts (Escorial M-II-6 and Escorial K-II-12) conclude their cycles on 17 July (Alexis) and 21 September (Matthew) respectively.[4] Equally noticeable is the omission throughout the Compilation of Chapters 175-82 of Voragine's original, which suggests that the process of abbreviation had begun with the archetype and not all of his work was included.[5]

---

4   Escorial K-II-12 offers a treatment of Chrysanthus and Daria (25 October), but this appears out of sequence, placed (along with Barbara) between readings for Andrew and Nicholas. Its treatment of Matthew, on the other hand, lacks the final sentence, and this provides some evidence with which to assume that it could have continued further into the cycle. The same, however, is not true of Escorial M-II-6, which ends prematurely.

5   Baños Vallejo and Uría Maqua offer an illuminating discussion of the original size and scope of the manuscript but take a different view on its concluding stages: 'Por lo general los santorales castellanos omiten muchas vidas de la *Legenda aurea*, pero, aun así, es improbable que la copia del ms. 8, en su origen, fuera tan reducida como la parte que se ha conservado. Parece más bien que lo que tenemos es sólo un fragmento de la copia, pues comienza y termina abruptamente, sin título general, ni índice, ni *incipit*, ni *explicit*. También la adición de los tres últimos folios, aunque probablemente sean un resto de otra copia, refuerza la idea del carácter

The criteria that led to the selection of the manuscript's readings cannot be ascertained with certainty, but in its present form it displays a preference for early Christian and New Testament saints (Mark the Evangelist is an exception) at the expense of popes and theologians, notable examples being Ambrose, Marcellinus, Urban, and Dominic. A third characteristic is the exclusion of prominent martyr narratives, several of them dealing with female saints. The most notable casualty, however, is George, whose legend, despite appearing in all of the other manuscripts of the Compilation, is unaccountably absent.

The only addition, other than a duplication of the reading for Patrick (entered erroneously as 'Patricio' and 'Aparicio'), is Mammes (see Baños Vallejo 1995 and Baños Vallejo & Uría Maqua 2000: 51-58), while elsewhere there are a number of modifications to the ordering of the cycle. The most significant affects Julian, bishop of Le Mans, whose feast, traditionally held on 27 January, is in this instance sandwiched between Gervasius and Potasius (19 June) and the Birth of John the Baptist (24 June). This appears to be the result of confusion, with the date of his celebration advancing through the calendar to occupy that of his namesake, Julian of Tarsus on 21 June. Also worthy of note is a partial restructuring of March feasts, with Gregory (12 March), Longinus (15 March), and Benedict (21 March) falling out of sequence partly as a result of the duplication of entries for Patrick (17 March).[6]

---

fragmentario del ms. 8. Por otro lado, el ms. 9, que es […] una copia hermana de la misma traducción castellana, abarca todo el año litúrgico. Así que cabe pensar que se ha perdido parte de la copia del ms. 8, pues sería raro que el amanuense abitrariamente empezase en febrero y finalizase en agosto' (2000: 29). The eight chapters omitted are: Pastor, John, Moses, Arsenius, Agathon, Barlaam and Josaphat, Pelagius (History of the Lombards), and the Dedication of a Church. For an overview of content, see Appendix III.

6   A further problem is that 21 June corresponds to Julian's feast in the Eastern calendar. For questions of identification, see Gaiffer 1945, Farmer 1997: 279-80, and Beresford in press. Baños Vallejo and Uría Maqua conclude that the formation of BMP 8 is the result of aesthetic taste: 'así que lo único que podemos concluir es que el traductor tomó lo que a él más le interesó, de acuerdo con su devoción e intereses y los de su entorno' (2000: 30). For editions of George, see Buxton 2010 and in preparation.

The second manuscript, Biblioteca Menéndez Pelayo 9, is one of the most problematic, principally because its text has deteriorated to such an extent that in various places it is now all but impossible to decipher. This, for the most part, has been caused by the weathering of its upper and right-hand margins, particularly fols 1-16 and 54-63, where a significant portion of the text has been lost, and fols 36-38 and 47-48, where problems affect the lower right-hand margin. In its present state it contains sixty-three paper folios written out in single (fols 1^r-17^v) and then double columns (fols 18ra-63rb). This curious arrangement suggests that it could have been copied by a novice eager to assemble a hagiographic compendium but with limited experience in book production. Individual sections are indicated by large initials and titles in red ink, but there is no illumination. Curiously, its final folio returns to a single column with the inclusion of an inscription composed in a more recent but virtually illegible hand. This is followed by an unusual line, reminiscent of the opening invocations of *cuaderna vía* poetry: 'En el nombre de Dios y de Santa María, sy Dios me ayudase quería fazer un libro' (fol. 63^v).[7]

The origin of the manuscript is uncertain, but as Baños Vallejo and Uría Maqua have argued (2000: 22-23), it likely to have been produced in a convent or monastery before passing into the library of Alonso Osorio, Marquis of Astorga, where it is documented as being in 1593. It is probably here that it was rebound in white parchment along with Biblioteca Menéndez Pelayo 8 to form a single hagiographic compendium.

In view of the current state of BMP 9, its relationship to the *Legenda aurea* is not easy to ascertain. Its initial portion respects the liturgical-sanctoral cycle with readings for Andrew, Nicholas, and Lucy (Chapters 2-4 of Voragine's original). There is then a jump to Stephen and John the Apostle (8-9), before it returns to Thomas the Apostle and the Nativity (5-6), texts punctuated by an *exemplum* prefaced by

---

7   For further information see Artigas 1930: 18-21 and Baños Vallejo & Uría Maqua 2000: 60-61. The latter notes: 'Según nuestras noticias el ms. 9 permanece enteramente inédito, lo que no es de estrañar, dado que está en un estado muy deteriorado, y hay muchos puntos en los que resulta prácticamente ilegible' (2000: 61).

an incomplete incipit: 'Del obispo que aparesció Jhesu Christo e non le abe[...]' (fol. 8ʳᵛ). It then continues with the Epiphany (14) and Sylvester (12), which appear out of sequence, before moving on to Antony of Egypt (21).[8] This is followed by treatments of Sebastian (23), Agnes (24), Basil (26), the Conversion of Paul (28), and the Purification of the Virgin (37) before there is a problem affecting the content of fols 14 and 15, which are inverted. The result is that the account of the Purification begins on fol. 13ᵛ and continues onto fol. 15ᵛ followed by fol. 15ʳ. Sandwiched between them are readings for Blaise (fol. 15ʳ followed by fol. 14ᵛ and then fol. 14ʳ) and Agatha (fol. 14ʳ), whose legend is incomplete.

At this point the extent of the damage to the sequence becomes apparent, for after the accounts of the Purification, Blaise, and Agatha (Chapters 37-39 of Voragine's original), the next extant folio (16ʳ) offers the final seven lines of a reading for the Ascension (72) followed by the Holy Spirit (73). Although it could be that the scribe of BMP 9 decided, as is the case in BMP 8, to omit a portion of the cycle, there are compelling reasons to assume that the central portion of the manuscript has been lost. The most convincing is that it deals with the most important events in the Christian calendar and would have included accounts of the Passion (53) and Resurrection (54), readings present in all of the other manuscripts of the Compilation (see Appendix III).

A second and more practical reason can be adduced from the process of selection, for although the manuscript overlooks a number of important readings, it does not otherwise make such a substantial omission. In view of this, with the exception of six chapters not present elsewhere (Vaast, Sophia and her Daughters, Timothy, Fabian, Apollonia, and Boniface) and three others that appear out of sequence (Longinus, Ambrose, and George), there is good reason to assume that

---

8   As none of the manuscripts offer reworkings of Chapters 15-20 of Voragine's original (Paul the Hermit, Remy, Hilary of Poitiers, Macarius, Felix in Pincis, and Marcellus), there is no reason to assume that the section is necessarily affected by a lacuna.

in addition to the truncation of the readings for Agatha and the Assumption, twenty-three others have been lost.[9]

After the lacuna, the reading for the Holy Spirit is followed by treatments of Petronilla (78), Peter the Exorcist (79), Primus and Felicianus (80), Barnabas (81), Quiricus and Julitta (83), and Gervasius and Protasius (85). The structure of Voragine's original is then interrupted, as is the case in BMP 8, with the unorthodox positioning of Julian (30). This anomaly shows that the manuscripts are derived from a common ancestor that, as we shall see, is at a stage removed from the archetype (see also Baños Vallejo & Uría Maqua 2000: 19-23). Voragine's sequence then resumes with readings for the Birth of John the Baptist (86), John and Paul (87), Peter the Apostle (89), and the first few lines of a chapter on Paul the Apostle (90).

Here, however, there is another problem, as the section on Paul (fol. 23vb) is followed by another instance of an inverted folio, with the latter stages an incomplete reading for Martha (105) beginning on fol. 24va and concluding on fol. 24ra. The extent of this second lacuna cannot be ascertained with certainty, but with the exception of Praxedes (95), whose legend is not recorded elsewhere in the Compilation, and that of the Seven Sleepers (101), which appears out of sequence, it could be that twelve further readings have been lost.[10]

The incomplete reading for Martha is followed by treatments of Saint Peter in Chains (110), Pope Stephen (111), the Finding of Saint Stephen (112), and Sixtus (114). It then interrupts the cycle of August feasts with the interpolation of Mammes (17 August in the Roman calendar, but 7 August in Spain), a text that provides further evidence

---

9   The potentially lost readings are: Amand (41), Valentine (42), Juliana (43), the Chair of Saint Peter (44), Matthias (45), Gregory (46), Benedict (49), Patrick (50), the Annunciation (51), the Passion (53), the Resurrection (54), Secundus (55), Mary of Egypt (56), Mark (59), Marcellinus (60), Vitalis (61), the Virgin of Antioch (62), Peter Martyr (63), Philip (65), James the Less (67), the Finding of the Holy Cross (68), John before the Latin Gate (69), and the Greater and Lesser Litanies (70).

10 The possible lost texts are: the Seven Brothers, Sons of Saint Felicity (91), Theodora (92), Margaret (93), Alexis (95), Mary Magdalene (96), Apollinaris (97), Christina (98), James the Greater (99), Christopher (100), Nazarius and Celsus (102), Felix (103), and Simplicius and Faustinus (104).

of the relationship between BMP 8 and BMP 9 (see Baños Vallejo 1995 and Baños Vallejo & Uría Maqua 2000: 51-58). With the exception of a chapter on Cornelius and Cyprian (132), which is restored to its traditional position on 14 September, its treatment of feasts from August through to the beginning of November is unproblematic (see Appendix III). A missing folio, however, between fol. 48vb and fol. 49ra truncates the conclusion of the reading for All Souls (163) and the beginning of the section on Martin of Tours (166). It could also potentially have affected the Four Crowned Martyrs (164) and Theodore (165), which are attested elsewhere, although in view of its relationship to other manuscripts (particularly Fundación Lázaro Galdiano 419), this is unlikely to have been the case.[11]

The hagiographic section of BMP 9 concludes with four further readings for November (Brice, Cecilia, Clement, and Catherine) and five others that appear out of sequence: Longinus (47), Ambrose (57), George (58), the Seven Sleepers (101), and Jerome (146). Reasons for this uncharacteristic rupture are far from clear, but it could be that the texts were appended in the interests of comprehensiveness, having been overlooked during the initial process of selection. Most notable in this respect is that they appear in relative sequential order.

The manuscript closes with the incorporation of two sermons of tangential significance. The first, 'Este sermón se deve dezir en el día de Sant Julián o de otros mártires qualesquier o de confesores quien sea uno o más nonbrado' (fol. 62^{ra-vb}), alludes once again to Julian, whose legend appears curiously out of sequence in BMP 8 and BMP 9. The second, 'Aquí comiença el sermón "De invencio Sancti Stephani", que quier dezir "Del fallamiento del cuerpo de Sant Esteban"' (fols 62vb-63ra), provides an account of the translation of the relics of the protomartyr Stephen, a significant portion of which has been badly mutilated.

---

11   The Four Crowned Martyrs can be found in Escorial h-I-14 (fol. 297va), while Theodore appears in Escorial h-I-14 (fols 297va-98ra) and Fundación Lázaro Galdiano 419 (fol. 212^{rb-ra}). The corresponding portion of FLG 419 reveals that some seven columns (from the lower portion of fol. 140ra to the final two thirds of fol. 141vb) have been lost. This equates approximately to the loss of a single folio in BMP 9, which is more compressed.

Fundación Lázaro Galdiano 419

The third manuscript, Fundación Lázaro Galdiano 419, dates from between 1450 and 1475, and was copied onto paper in twin columns. Its 221 folios are preceded by a table of contents (fol. 1^{ra-vb}), prefaced by a large JHS tavoletta (as made popular, for instance, by figures such as Bernardino of Siena) and the words 'Estas son las estorias que son escriptas en este libro e collegio de los santos e a quantas tantas e fojas señaladas' (fol. 1ra). The table of contents gives a generally accurate guide to the scope of the manuscript, but is not without error. Of particular note is an erroneous entry for Bede, which has subsequently been crossed out, and the inversion of entries for Lawrence, Hippolytus, and Mammes. A sequence of three readings in Latin, on the other hand, is abbreviated (Prudentius is listed, while Saturninus and Pelagius are not), while two others become subject to changes of identity, with Peter Martyr listed in place of Peter the Exorcist, and, as is typical of Compilation B, Marina instead of Margaret. The manuscript is written out in a series of semi-gothic hands and has large coloured and decorated initials marking the beginning of individual sections. These are followed by incipits in red ink but there is otherwise no illumination or formal embellishment. A longwinded invocation placed before the reading for Andrew dedicates the collection to the Trinity, the Virgin, and the saints of the celestial court:[12]

> En el nonbre del Padre e del Fijo e del Spíritu Santo que son tres personas e un solo Dios vivo e verdadero que vive e regna agora e por sienpre jamás, e a honrra de la bendita Virgen sin manzilla, madre e fija de aqueste mesmo Señor, e de todos los santos de la corte celestial. Amén. (fol. 2ra)

---

12 The manuscript's numeration produces duplicates of fols 74, 114, 116, and 190. Fol. 215, on the other hand, is numbered as fol. 205, while fol. 207 is omitted. It also contains a final blank folio with ruled margins but no text. For further information see Faulhaber 1976, Romero Tobar 1978-80, Vega 1991: 83-85, Walsh 1992a: 189-95, Baños Vallejo & Uría Maqua 2000: 61-63, and Baños Vallejo 2003: 106. For Bernardino's use of the tavoletta, see Polecritti 2000.

The most distinctive feature of FLG 419 is that it runs twice through the liturgical-sanctoral calendar, initially from Andrew (30 November) to Catherine of Alexandria (25 November), and then from the Nativity (6 January) to James the Dismembered (27 November). This curiously bipartite arrangement, described infamously by John K. Walsh as a 'somewhat mixed pudding' (1992a: 190), raises a number of questions, the most important of which is textual provenance. The initial sequence of 82 readings (fols 2ra-153va) is the most straightforward, for with the exception of Vincent, whose legend must have been garnered from the now lost initial portion of BMP 8 or a misplaced and lost chapter of BMP 9, the other readings in this section are attested by the extant sections of BMP 8 and BMP 9 (see Appendix III).

The correlation between the manuscripts in this respect cannot be dismissed as coincidental, particularly as FLG 419 preserves a series of striking inherited idiosyncrasies. The most significant is that it is the only other manuscript to preserve a copy of the legend of Mammes. Equally noticeable, however, is that several of its other chapters appear out of sequence. These include Longinus (Chapter 47, fol. 31^{ra-rb}) and Gregory (Chapter 46, fols 31rb-34ra), which appear in the same sequential order in BMP 8 (see fols 2vb-3ra and 4ra-6vb), and the Exaltation of the Holy Cross (Chapter 137, fols 123rb-25va) and Cornelius and Cyprian (Chapter 132, fols 125^{va-vb}), which appear in the same sequential order in BMP 9 (see fols 39vb-41rb and 41rb). The most compelling evidence for a link between the three, however, can be seen in their treatment of Julian Le Mans (27 January), whose feast is celebrated on 21 June between those of Gervasius and Protasius (19 June) and the Birth of John the Baptist (24 June).[13]

---

13   Escorial h-I-14 offers a reading for Julian in its traditional position (between the Conversion of Paul and Ignatius), while in Escorial K-II-12 the reading is omitted. This forms a contrast with Escorial M-II-6, which offers two readings, the first dealing with Julian the Hospitaller (fol. 19^r), and the second, Julian of Le Mans, Julian of Auvergne, and Julian, brother of Saint Julius (fol. 55^{r-v}). For further information, see Beresford in press.

The relationship between the three manuscripts makes it possible to advance a conjectural reconstruction of the way in which they were assembled. BMP 8 and BMP 9, as we have seen, are closest to the archetype, and must therefore have been copied from a relatively complete but now lost intermediate manuscript (*Z), which modified the position of Julian and added a reading for Mammes (see figure 1). These anomalies, which are present in BMP 8, BMP 9, and the first part of FLG 419 (but not in any of the other manuscripts of the Compilation), provide evidence not only of a direct line of textual descent, but of the fact that BMP 8 and BMP 9 must already have lost a good number of folios by the time they were adopted and used as an amalgamated foundation for the first part of FLG 419.

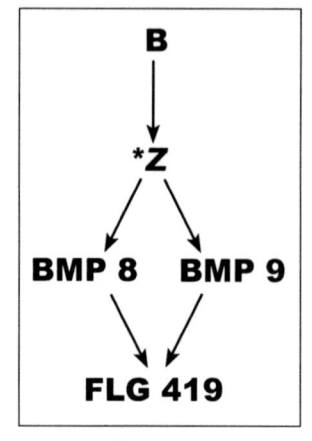

Figure 1

A reading of the BMP 9 and FLG 419 accounts of Agatha and Lucy gives credence to this hypothesis, as there are only a limited number of differences between them. One of the most significant is the use of the archaic -*ié* imperfect, which is replaced in FLG 419 on all but one occasion by the equivalent -*ía* form. Typical examples include 'corría' (fol. 28vb) for 'corrié' (fol. 14^{r}), 'podía' (fol. 27ra) for 'podié' (fol. 14^{r}), and 'sirvía' (fol. 26vb) for 'sirvié' (fol. 14^{r}). This distinction, which can be read as an aspect of linguistic modernization typical of the late fifteenth-century (Penny 1991: 168), stands alongside a series of parallel adjustments in lexis, with archaic forms such as 'asmar' and 'semejar' (fol. 14^{r}) replaced by 'querer' and 'parecer' (fol. 26vb).

A third characteristic is a tendency to introduce modifications, a good example being the rendering of '¿por qué te muestras e te das por villana en tus costunbres?' (fol. 14^{r}) as '¿por qué te muestras e te das por villana en tus fechos?' (fol. 27ra). This reading, which is not attested elsewhere, is matched by a series of others in which the modifications are more substantial. Two striking examples from the early portion Agatha's legend are the interpolation of 'non enbargante que él era villano' (fol. 26vb) into the description of Quintianus's motivation, and 'ca está afirmado sobre piedra' (fol. 27ra) into Aphrodisia's discussion of the power of the saint's resolve.

The extent to which the relationship between BMP 8, BMP 9, and the first part of FLG 419 holds for the manuscripts as a whole will not be determined with certainty until a greater number of sections have been edited and subjected to analysis. In the interim, however, the most logical editorial procedure is to combine them in a critical edition. Unfortunately, in view of the fact that the BMP 8 copies of Agatha and Lucy have been lost, while those of BMP 9 contain lacunae, the only complete versions are in FLG 419. These, of course, were copied long after their originals, and are in parts inauthentic, but other than the establishment of an experimental edition based on the fragmentary accounts offered by BMP 9 and completed with reference to later manuscripts, it is difficult to see that there is an alternative.

The problem that remains concerns the origin of the second part of FLG 419 (fols 153va-217rb) and the 54 readings that constitute a second abbreviated sanctoral cycle (see Appendix III). This material was collated from more than one source, with the scribes, having completed their work on BMP 8 and BMP 9, amplifying their collection by seeking out additional materials. An exception is a treatment of the Nativity (fols 153va-54va) garnered from BMP 9 (fols 7^{v}-8^{v}) that must have been overlooked during the initial process of selection. This is followed by two further works taken from the same source, the 'Enxenplo del obispo que bivía deleitosamente' (fols 154va-55rb), which draws from the *exemplum* tradition (see Lacarra 1996), and a version of the sermon on Saint Julian: 'Declaración deste evangelio en la fiesta de Sant Jullián e dízelo Sant Juan Limosnero' (fols 155rb-56rb).

This change of focus appears to be indicative of a moment of uncertainty, as the scribes cast around for suitable materials but were only partially able to achieve their objectives. At this point, however, they encountered three further sources. The most curious is a reading for Ildephonsus, 'La vida de Sant Alifonsso por metros' (fols 165vb-72va), a prose version of a poetic source that is not attested elsewhere in the Compilation (see Romero Tobar 1978-80 and Walsh 1992a). This is accompanied by three short sections in Latin dealing with Prudentius, Saturninus, and Pelagius (fols 209va-12rb), which show that although the scribes had the ability to copy Latin, they lacked either the dexterity or the inclination to rework it into the vernacular in the interests of homogeneity.

The most significant additional source, however, is a corpus of 52 Castilian readings arranged broadly in chronological order. A partial restructuring of September feasts can be seen with Gorgonius and Dorotheus (135) and Adrian (134), on the one hand, and Euphemia (139) and Lambert (133), on the other. The first is insignificant and could be dismissed either as a decision to modify the order of two feasts celebrated on the same day (16 September) or an error in sampling, with the scribe remedying the omission of Adrian by copying his passion into the next available place. The second, however, is significant, as the chronological rationalization of readings for Euphemia (16 September) and Lambert (17 September) is attested also by Escorial K-II-12 and Escorial h-I-14. An equally telling anomaly can be seen slightly later, as the inclusion of a reading for Barbara (sandwiched in this instance between Saturninus and James the Dismembered) provides corroborating evidence of a relationship between the three.

Escorial K-II-12

The manuscript with the closest textual affinity to the second part of FLG 419 is Escorial K-II-12, a compilation consisting of 201 folios written out on paper and parchment in dual columns in a well formed gothic hand. The initial folio of the reading for Andrew is highly decorated, but other than large coloured initials and section titles in red ink, there is no formal embellishment or even an introductory table of contents or incipit. An anomaly can be seen in the treatment of Basil, with fol. 29^v left blank, while elsewhere there are discrepancies between incipits and the texts that they are supposed to describe. The most notable examples are 'de los Ynocentes' (fol. 13ra), which deals with Eulalia of Merida, and 'de los tres Herodes' (fol. 24va), which takes its title from the opening sections of the reading for the Holy Innocents. Pancratius, in contrast, is confused with Patrick ('de Sant

Patricio', fol. 94vb), while the Seven Brothers (Sons of Felicity) are confused with the Seven Sleepers of Ephesus ('de los siete dormientes', fol. 110va). Equally noticeable is a problem with Mamertinus (129) on fol. 181vb, with the scribe initially offering the first three lines of a reading for Giles (130) before striking them out and returning to the sequence.

The manuscript once belonged to Gaspar de Guzmán, Conde-Duque de Olivares, but little is known about provenance or dating. Its final folio, which offers the latter stages of a reading for Matthew, contains a note in an italic hand recording an important aspect of its subsequent fortunes: 'Costóme este libro de la almoneda de Juan Collados 24, res. en Madrid a 20 de julio de el año de 1616' (fol. 201^v). Its date of composition, however, remains uncertain, and while Julián Zarco Cuevas (1924-29: II, 164-65 and III, 217-18) has suggested that it was produced between 1400 and 1500, one suspects (on the basis of language and orthography) that it was copied from an earlier original, possibly at some point during the second quarter of the century (see also Baños Vallejo & Uría Maqua 2000: 63 and Baños Vallejo 2003: 105-06).

Escorial K-II-12 runs through the cycle from Andrew (30 November) to Matthew (21 September), initially somewhat erratically, but then with greater coherence. Anomalies are present immediately after Andrew, first with the repositioning of Chrysanthus and Daria (25 October), and then the interpolation of Barbara (4 December). This is followed by Nicholas (6 December) and interpolated versions of two national saints, Leocadia of Toledo (9 December) and Eulalia of Merida (10 December), neither of which is attested elsewhere. The sequence then resumes with Lucy (4 December) and Thomas (21 December) before there is a development in relation to the Nativity (25 December), with a supplementary reading ('de Nuestro Señor Jhesu Christo', fols 18ra-20rb) placed before the account recorded elsewhere by BMP 9 and FLG 419: 'de la natividat de Nuestro Señor Jhesu Christo' (fols 20rb-21va).[14] The manuscript then offers four readings in sequential order (Stephen, John the Apostle, the Holy Innocents, and Sylvester) before moving backwards to include a chapter on Anastasia (25 De-

---

[14] The reading preserved by Escorial h-1-14 (fols 24va-29rb) is different, and is in many ways closer to the content of Voragine's original.

cember). It then moves forward once again to Basil (1 January) and John the Almsgiver (23 January), before returning to the earlier part of the month with an account of the Circumcision (1 January).

From this point onwards the manuscript reverts to an orthodox sequence, progressing without further digression through 99 consecutive readings from the Epiphany (6 January) to the Birth of the Virgin (8 September). Its idiosyncratic treatment of September feasts, however, provides an indication of its position in the Compilation. The first adjustment is the feast of Cornelius and Cyprian (132), which is restored to its traditional position on 14 September along with the Exaltation of the Holy Cross (137). As this development is attested also by BMP 9, the first part of FLG 419, and Escorial h-I-14 (the extant portions of BMP 8 and Escorial M-II-6 do not cover this part of the calendar), there is good reason to assume that it was present in the archetype of Compilation B. A second adjustment can be seen in the treatment of Lambert (133), whose feast (17 September) falls out of sequence in Voragine's original and is in this instance placed after that of Euphemia (139) on 16 September, as is the case in Escorial h-I-14 and FLG 419.

A final point of contact can be seen in the interpolation of an additional group of readings which appear in the correct sequential order: Brigit (1 February), Toribius of Astorga (16 April), Anthony of Padua (13 June), and Antoninus (2 September). The incorporation of this material raises the number of additional readings to seven, which is by far the highest in the Compilation. Its treatments of Leocadia of Toledo, Eulalia of Merida, Toribius of Astorga, and Anthony of Padua are not attested elsewhere, and must, by implication, have been garnered from an additional source. Versions of the legend of Barbara, however, can also be found in FLG 419 and Escorial h-I-14, while supplementary readings for Antoninus and Brigit appear respectively in Escorial h-I-14 (fols 241vb-45rb) and Escorial M-II-6 (fols 55^v-59^v).

The significance of these relationships, particularly in the absence of corroborating textual studies, is open to interpretation, but it becomes possible, nonetheless, to postulate more detailed lines of textual descent. The addition of Barbara and the chronological reordering of readings for Euphemia and Lambert gives good reason to assume

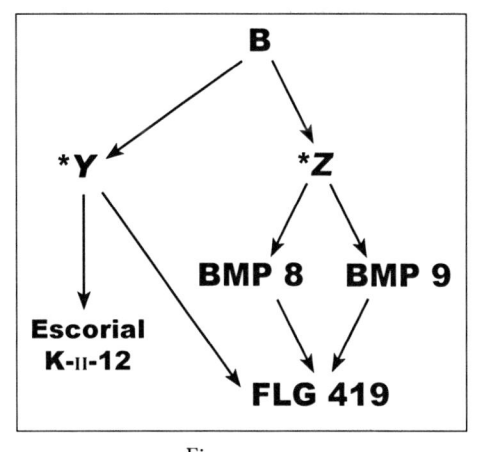

Figure 2

that Escorial K-II-12, Escorial h-I-14, and the second part of FLG 419 were derived ultimately from an ancestor (*Y) related to the archetype but not otherwise to BMP 8 or BMP 9. (Escorial M-II-6 does not cover this part of the cycle but belongs within this line of textual descent.) The now lost manuscript, *Y, was the immediate source of Escorial K-II-12 and the second part of FLG 419, with all but one of the latter's vernacular hagiographic readings (Ildephonsus on fols 165vb-72va) included also in Escorial K-II-12 before its premature conclusion with Matthew.[15]

The strength of this relationship suggests not only that *Y must have been relatively complete, but that the scribes who assembled the second part of FLG 419 had set themselves a difficult but achievable target and were working with a clear sense of selection and design. This can be seen in the fact that readings drawn from *Y are incorporated into the final work not only in the correct sequential order, but without duplicating feasts present in the earlier cycle. It can also be seen in the rejection of others, preserved in turn as they were copied by Escorial K-II-12, that did not suit their requirements.[16]

---

15   The reading for Matthew was either abbreviated to make it fit into the space provided by the final folio, or continued into a section (potentially along with several others) that has now been lost. Evidence of its truncation can be seen in the omission of the concluding sentence preserved by FLG 419: 'pues que tales gra*ci*as e tan grandes dones ovieron tales pecadores como éstos' (127ra). As the second part of FLG 419 gives thirteen readings after this point, the following chapters could have been included: Maurice (141), Justina (142), Cosmas and Damian (143), Remy (147), Leger (148), Margaret (151), Dionysius, Rusticus, and Eleutherius (153), Leonard (155), Ursula and the Eleven Thousand Virgins (158), Theodore (165), Chrysogonus (171), Saturninus (173), and James the Dismembered (174).

16   Other than interpolated feasts, ten readings present in Escorial K-II-12 are not recorded in FLG 419: Anastasia (7), the Holy Innocents (10), the Circumcision

In its treatment of Agatha and Lucy, Escorial K-II-12 raises a number of complex textual questions, as there are a number of notable distinctions in rhetorical and syntactic emphasis. The relationship between BMP 9 and the initial portion of FLG 419 is not entirely stable in this respect, with the later manuscript introducing a partial process of modernization. With Escorial K-II-12, however, the distinction between recensions is more pronounced, with some of its readings suggesting that it was reworked from its immediate ancestor, and others, that a parallel process of reworking took place in BMP 9 (and thus, in the first part of FLG 419), making this manuscript in some respects a more authentic copy of the archetype.

A telling example can be seen when Lucy is summoned before Paschasius: 'Venditis autem omnibus et pauperibus erogatis sponsus trahit eam coram Paschasio consulari, dicens eam christianam esse et contra leges agere Augustorum' (38-40). BMP 9 offers a plausible but abbreviated account ('E después *que* fue todo vendido e dado a pobres, su esposo *qu*ando lo sopo, adúxola a juyzio d*e*lante el alcalde P*a*scu*al*', fol. 4ʳ) which is further abbreviated in FLG 419: 'E después que fue todo vendido e dado a pobres, su esposo adúxola a juyzio antel alc*a*lde Pascual' (fol. 9ʳᵃ). Escorial K-II-12, however, echoes some of the wording of these versions but is closer to the Latin: 'E después q*ue* fue vendido e dado todo a pobres, adúxola ant*e*l alcal*de* don Pascual su esposo en juyzio. E acusóla q*ue* era *christi*ana e q*ue* yva contra la ley de los enp*e*radores' (fol. 14ᵛᵃ). The fact that an almost identical reading is preserved by Escorial h-I-14 ('E después q*ue* fue todo vendido e dado a los pobres, su esposo tráxola a juyzio ante el alcal*de* don Pascual. E acusóla como era *christi*ana e fazía cont*ra* la ley de los emp*e*radores', fol. 12ᵛᵇ) could theoretically indicate that that the additional phrase was added in *Y, but the balance of evidence suggests that this is unlikely.

With most of its other readings, however, Escorial K-II-12 is defective. An example can be seen in the discussion of Agatha's sojourn in the brothel, with the text of BMP 9 ('Mandóla dar a una mala muger q*ue* dizién Afrodisa, q*ue* avié nueve fijas tan malas como ella', fol. 14ʳ)

---

(13), Secundus (55), Gordianus and Epimachus (74), Nereus and Achilleus (75), Pancratius (76), Urban (77), Christina (98), and Symphorian (122).

partially revised in FLG 419 ('E mandóla dar a una mala muger que dizían Afrodisa, que avía nueve fijas tan malas como ella', fol. 26vb), but expressed quite differently in Escorial K-II-12: 'Mandóla dar a una mala muger que dizían Estodisa, e a diez fijas suyas que eran tan malas como ella' (fol. 48vb). The addition of tenth daughter is not attested by Escorial h-I-14 ('E mandóla dar a una mala muger que dizían Efrodizia; avía nueve fijas que eran tan malas como ella', fol. 61rb), which suggests that the modification must have been introduced by Escorial K-II-12. Some doubt in this respect is raised by Escorial M-II-6, which claims that Aphrodisia has ten sons: 'E mandóla dar a una mala muger que llamavan Frodisia, e avía diez fijos que eran tan malos como ella' (fol. 24^{r}). The most likely explanation, however, is that while the texts of BMP 9 and FLG 419 are close to the archetype, Escorial K-II-12 and Escorial M-II-6 introduced modifications independently. Alternatively, the only possible explanation is that the adjustment was introduced in *Y, but was subsequently corrected in isolation by Escorial h-I-14. Some evidence for this can be seen in the fact that the three Escorial manuscripts include an additional verbal clause ('que eran'), but this alone does not give grounds with which to assume that *Y also provided a modified description of Aphrodisia's offspring.

Further examples are not hard to find, and in some instances it is clear that the scribe of Escorial K-II-12 was not paying attention. When Paschasius is summoned to Rome, for instance, he is accused not of having 'robado toda la provincia', but of having 'robado la tierra e toda la cibdat de Provincia' (fol. 15rb). This reading, which is impossible to defend (see, for instance, BMP 9 fol. 4^{v}, FLG 419 fol. 9vb, and Escorial h-I-14 fol. 13va), is followed by an interpolated and misspelled reference to Roman senators ('sañadores', fol. 15rb) and a garbled discussion of Lucy's final moments. In this instance the other extant manuscripts offer an identical formulation ('non se movió del logar do la firieron', BMP 9 fol. 4^{v}, FLG 419 fol. 9vb, and Escorial h-I-14 fol. 13vb), while Escorial K-II-12 provides a meaningless and eccentric account: 'non se movió de los logares do lo fezieron' (fol. 15rb).

These errors, which are of the scribe's creation, are matched by some inherited from *Y, its immediate ancestor. One of the most striking appears in the discussion of the Holy Spirit. With the exception of a minor lacuna, BMP 9 and FLG 419 are identical at this point, following Lucy's contention about the domain of the Holy Spirit ('Vos sodes casa de Sp*írit*u San*t*o') with the question '¿El Sp*í*ritu San*t*o es en ti?' (fol. 9rb; see also BMP 9, fol. 4[r]). Escorial K-II-12, however, inherits a classic palaeographic blunder, with the scribe of *Y jumping from the first mention of the Holy Spirit to the second. The result, 'Vos sodes casa de Sp*írit*u Santo es en ty' (fol. 14vb) is meaningless, and suggests either that the scribe of Escorial K-II-12 was too lazy to correct an obvious error, or that he was copying too mechanically to notice that something was amiss. This stands in contrast to the treatment of the section in Escorial h-I-14, which remedies the problem by deleting the exchange and advancing to the discussion of imprisonment in a brothel. The result is the creation of a cleaner and crisper narrative, albeit one that lacks some of the theological intensity of its forebears.

In view of its uneven treatment, Escorial K-II-12 is the most problematic manuscript of the Compilation. Its texts are carelessly copied and contain striking errors and anomalies. They are also inelegant in their use of language. On other occasions, however, they preserve a limited number of readings that are not only beneficial in establishing lines of textual descent, but more reliable that those preserved by BMP 9 or FLG 419. Although a good deal of work remains to be done on its standing in the Compilation, its treatment of Agatha and Lucy shows that it stands at a paradoxical position (see also Beresford 2007a: 34-39). As a discrete entity it does not provide readers with texts sufficiently different from those of BMP 9 or FLG 419 to be edited separately; nor does it display the quality or authenticity to be adopted as the base text of a critical edition. It is, however, a useful guide to the content of the archetype, and therefore cannot be dismissed out of hand. In this instance the most practical solution is to use it, along with BMP 9, as a supplement to a critical edition based on FLG 419. This, of course, is a relationship that may not hold for all of its readings, and could potentially be inverted in relation the second part of FLG 419, which was copied not from BMP 8 or BMP 9, but (along with Escorial K-II-12) from *Y, albeit at a later date.

Escorial h-I-14 and Escorial M-II-6

The final Compilation B manuscripts are Escorial h-I-14 and Escorial M-II-6, which offer modified versions of the legends of the two saints. The earlier of the two, Escorial h-I-14, contains 324 folios (11 + 322) and is written out on paper in twin columns in a gothic hand. An initial table of contents is prefaced by the words 'Aquí comiença la tabla de los capítulos de la vida de los santos' (fol. 1ra), and with the exception of a misplaced entry for John the Apostle, it provides an accurate guide until it concludes prematurely with the virgin martyr Justina. Entries for the remaining 31 chapters, from Cosmas and Damian through to Hilarion, appear on a second unnumbered folio sandwiched between fols 12^v and 13^r in the context of the reading for Lucy; the only anomaly is the inversion of entries for Clement and Chrysogonus.

The beginning of the sanctoral proper is marked by a traditional invocation in Latin 'Sancti spiritus adsit nobis gratia amen' and the words: 'Aquí comiençan las vidas de todos los santos e las sus passiones' (fol. 1ra). An inscription on its final folio dates the copy to 1427 ('Este libro fue fecho e acabado en el año del Señor de mill e quatrocientos e veynte e siete años', fol. 322vb), but other than the possibility that it could have been compiled in the Capilla Real in Granada, little is known about its origin, and it has not so far been subjected to adequate critical scrutiny. Most alarming in this respect is that with 151 extant readings, it is the most comprehensive of the Compilation (see Zarco Cuevas 1924-29: I, 189-90 and III, 206-08, Baños Vallejo & Uría Maqua 2000: 63).

The second manuscript, Escorial M-II-6, is one of the least extensive, consisting of 102 folios written out on paper in single columns in a late gothic hand. Its date is uncertain, but while Julián Zarco Cuevas (1924-29: I, 189-90) maintains that it was produced between 1400 and 1500, one suspects, on the basis of language and orthography, that it was assembled during the latter stages of the century. It then passed at a later date (along with Escorial K-II-12) into the collection of Gaspar de Guzmán, Conde-Duque de Olivares.

In its present form the manuscript is incomplete, beginning on fol. 19^r with the concluding stages of a reading for Julian the Hospitaller, the first in a series of 56 extant hagiographic sections. These are followed by two works that are only tangentially related to the textual tradition of the *Legenda aurea*: 'El sermón de la Pasión de Jhesu Christo que predicó frey Vicente en Murcia' (fols 103ᵛ-13ᵛ) and 'Contemplatio divinae pasionis' (fols 113ᵛ-21ᵛ). A distinctive feature can be seen in the concluding stages of the reading for Theodora and the early portion of the chapter on Vincent, with a diagonal tear destroying most of fol. 98ʳᵛ. This may have been the result of censorship, but as the equally (if not more) sensational legend of Mary of Egypt is preserved intact (fols 37ᵛ-39ʳ), there could be other explanations.[17]

In its treatment of the textual sequence of the Compilation, Escorial h-I-14 is relatively unproblematic (see Appendix III). Its readings for Pelagius (fols 145ʳᵇ-49ʳᵇ) and Hilarion (fols 314ʳᵇ-22ᵛᵇ) appear to have been garnered from additional sources, but its other apocryphal sections (Barbara and Antoninus) are attested by other manuscripts and in this way provide firm evidence of textual relationships. The same is true of its treatment of Cornelius and Cyprian, which is restored to its traditional position on 14 September (along with the feast of the Exaltation of the Holy Cross), and the chronological adjustment of readings for Euphemia (139) and Lambert (133), which are celebrated respectively on 16 and 17 September. The significance of two further adjustments, with Basil (26) followed by Vincent (25) and then Saturninus (173) followed by Catherine of Alexandria (172), is less clear, but while the former is reproduced in part in Escorial K-II-12 and Escorial M-II-6, the latter is probably an error in sampling, with the scribe remedying the omission of Catherine by copying her legend into the nearest available place.

A final point of interest is the inclusion of seven chapters not attested elsewhere, with Thomas of Canterbury (28 December) followed later on by six readings from October and early November (Pelagia,

---

17   See Zarco Cuevas 1924-29: II, 283 and III, 219-20, Baños Vallejo & Uría Maqua 2000: 64, and Baños Vallejo 2003: 105-06. The content of the lost section cannot be ascertained with certainty, but in view of the manuscript's relationship to Escorial h-I-14, it could be that thirteen readings have been lost: Andrew, Barbara, Nicholas, Lucy, Thomas the Apostle, the Nativity, Stephen, John the Apostle, the Holy Innocents, Thomas of Canterbury, Antony of Egypt, Sebastian, and Agnes. For the sermon by Vincent Ferrer, see Zarco Cuevas 1927 and Sánchez Sánchez 2000: 790-91.

Thaïs, Callistus, Quentin, Eustace, and the Four Crowned Martyrs). These texts could potentially have been taken from a supplementary source, but in view of the manuscript's position in the Compilation, notably with regard to its relationship to Escorial K-II-12 and Escorial M-II-6 (which do not cover this part of the liturgical-sanctoral cycle), there is reason to assume that they were present in the manuscript from which it was copied.

The clarity of Escorial h-I-14 stands in contrast to Escorial M-II-6, which moves through the cycle erratically from Julian (27 January) to James the Less (1 May), and from Sylvester (31 December) to Alexis (17 July). The result is that the overwhelming majority of feasts fall into the period from January to July, with no coverage from August through to November. The initial sequence, the beginning of which has been lost, divides the reading for Gregory the Great (46) into two sections, with a separate incipit detaching the discussion of John the Deacon (here confused with John of Damascus, 'Sant Juan Damasceno', fol. 33ra) and presenting it as a chapter in its own right. A similar problem can be seen in the reading for the Purification ('Un miraglo de la Virgen María que contesció a una donzella fija dalgo la qual avié grand devoción en la Virgen', fol. 21^v), and more conspicuously in relation to the Annunciation, where the interpolation of additional incipits subdivides the reading into a series of miracles, with 'Un maravilloso miraglo de la Virgen María de un cavallero su devoto el qual era monge de Cistel' (fol. 35^v) followed by 'Un miraglo muy maravilloso de Santa María de un cavallero que morava en un castillo' (fol. 36^r).

The second cycle, in contrast, is more complex, with an interpolated reading for Brigit confirming the manuscript's relationship to Escorial K-II-12, and chronological adjustments affecting Basil (26), who is placed before Marina (84), and Vincent (25), who is placed before Margaret known as Marina (93). These adjustments are separated by more than a dozen folios, but the fact that Basil appears before Vincent in Escorial h-I-14 and Escorial M-II-6 adds weight to the assumption that they share a common ancestor. Equally noticeable is that by advancing the reading for Basil further into the cycle, Escorial M-II-6 displays a degree of sophistication by opting not for the feast of his birth, but his consecration (14 June). A final idiosyncrasy is a division between the various Julians of Voragine's original, with the first cycle offering the conclusion of a reading for Julian the Hospitaller (fol. 19^r), and the second dealing with Julian of Le Mans, Julian of Auvergne, and Julian, brother of Julius (fol. 55^{r-v}). This unusual arrangement, which reveals a sense of selection and design, suggests that far from being an arbitrary creation, the manuscript was assembled according to principles that have not yet been fully understood (see Appendix III).

Although the extant portion of Escorial M-II-6 covers only a small part of the cycle, evidence suggests that it was reworked, along with Escorial h-I-14, from an intermediate but now lost manuscript (*X) that was copied directly from *Y (see figure 3). An example of this relationship can be seen when Agatha returns from the brothel. BMP 9 and FLG 419 offer an identical formulation, with 'Estonce Quinciano fízola adozir ante sí' (fol. 14^r; fol. 27ra). Confirmation that this reading was present in the archetype and *Y is provided by Escorial K-II-12 ('Estonce Quinciano fízola adozir ante sý', fol. 49ra), while Escorial h-I-14 ('Estonces Quinciano fízola traer ante sí', fol. 61va) and Escorial M-II-6 ('E luego Quinciano fízola traher ante sí', fol. 24^v) are subtly different. The replacement of 'Estonces' by 'E luego' in Escorial M-II-6 can be attributed to scribal intervention. However, a common verbal variant, with 'traer' adopted in both manuscripts in place of 'adozir', is

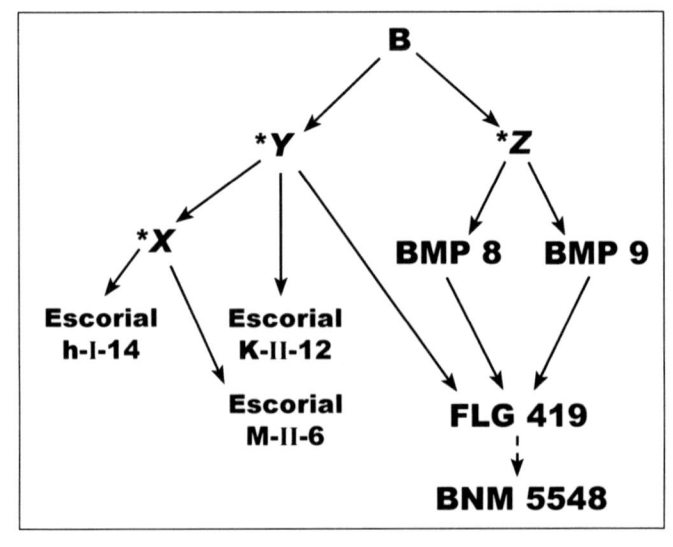

Figure 3

too fortuitous an outcome to be dismissed as coincidental. In view of this, it becomes likely that Escorial h-I-14 and Escorial M-II-6 were derived from a common ancestor (*X) that introduced modifications as it was copied from *Y.

Further evidence of this relationship can be found in the same portion of Agatha's legend. The BMP 9 reading, 'Onrrava e sirvié sie*n*pre a Dios' (fol. 14ʳ), raises questions of authenticity, as the unusual complexity of its treatment of the Latin ('Deum semper in omni sanctitate colebat', 13) suggests that a reworking took place either in BMP 9 or *Z, its immediate ancestor. FLG 419 preserves an abbreviated version of this reading ('Honrrava sienpre a Dios', fol. 26ᵛᵇ), omitting the second of the two verbs so as to avoid tautology, while Escorial K-II-12 either misreads 'onrrava' or introduces a deliberate modification, rendering the sentence as 'Orava sienpre a Dios' (fol. 48ᵛᵇ). This reading, which is not attested elsewhere, suggests that the most reliable copy of the archetype in this instance was *Y. This, however, must have been modified as it was copied by *X, as both Escorial h-I-14 and Escorial M-II-6 offer a different formulation, with the semantically related 'E rogava sienpre a Dios' (fol. 61ʳᵃ; fol. 24ʳ).

A final example confirms the pattern of textual descent. The BMP 9 reading of Agatha's initial summons before Quintianus, 'fecitque eam ad se adduci' (18), is reproduced faithfully by FLG 419 ('E por ende fízola adozir ante sí', fol. 14ʳ, fol. 26ᵛᵇ), while Escorial K-II-12 adopts a slightly different formulation: 'E por ende mandóla adozir ante sý' (fol. 48ᵛᵇ). As Escorial h-I-14 ('E por ende fízola traer ante sí', fol. 61ʳᵇ) and Escorial M-II-6 ('E fízola tra*h*er delante sí', fol. 24ʳ) preserve the initial verb attested by BMP 9 and FLG 419, there is good reason to assume that the reading offered by *Y was close to that of the archetype. The transition in Escorial h-I-14 and Escorial M-II-6 from 'adozir' to 'traer', on the other hand, shows not only that they were derived from a common ancestor (*X), but that the scribe who produced the copy introduced a number of emendations. These are complemented in this instance by a subsequent development in Escorial M-II-6, as 'por ende' is omitted in the interests of economy.

The result of this complex process of textual development is that in the establishment of critical editions it becomes difficult to deal with the manuscripts collectively. BMP 9 is the oldest of the extant versions, but in addition to the fact that it is fragmentary, it appears in certain instances to have been reworked via *Z from the archetype. FLG 419, in contrast, offers a partially modernized copy of BMP 9 and is generally free from error, although some of its readings are abbreviated while in other instances it interpolates fresh material. Escorial K-II-12 is in some ways closer to the archetype, but along with a series of minor modifications inherited from *Y, it transmits elementary scribal errors. The final manuscripts, Escorial h-I-14 and Escorial M-II-6, belong to a more distant line of textual descent, and in addition to modifications inherited from a major act of reworking in *X, they introduce their own adjustments. The result is that they appear to have been tailored to the tastes and demands of a specific audience and transmit differing conceptions of sanctity. In Escorial h-I-14, which is arguably the most accomplished and elegant, the result is the creation of texts that deserve to be edited and read in their own right. The same is true of Escorial M-II-6, which despite sharing a related line of textual descent, preserves an accurate and succinct account, notable for its theological vibrancy.

In view of this, the Compilation B texts edited in Chapter 7 are presented independently: critical editions based on FLG 419, including variants from BMP 9 and Escorial K-II-12, accompanied by supplementary editions of Escorial h-I-14 and Escorial M-II-6. The distinction between the texts and their evolution from the Latin (and one another) is an issue considered in detail in Chapter 4.[18]

---

18   As with Compilation A, titles are derived from the wording of rubrics: *Passión de Santa Águeda* ('La passión de Santa Águeda, virgen e mártir', FLG 419 fol. 26vb), *Vida de Santa Águeda* ('Capítulo XXIII, de la vida de Santa Águeda', Escorial h-I-14 fol. 61ra), *Vida de la virgen señora Santa Águeda* ('La vida de la virgen señora Santa Águeda', Escorial M-II-6 fol. 24^{r}), *Vida de Santa Lucía* ('Santa Lucía, virgen', FLG 419 fol. 8vb), and *Vida e passión de Santa Lucía* ('Capítulo quarto, de la vida e passión de Santa Lucía', Escorial h-I-14 fol. 12rb). An important study of Compilation B (Hernández Amez 2008) came to my attention too late to be considered in this chapter. Our views, although different, are not entirely incompatible, and will be discussed in a forthcoming study.

4
Agatha and Lucy in Compilation B

Introduction

In contrast to the scholarly tone of Compilation A, the texts of Compilation B are most notable for their popularizing tendencies. This can be seen most clearly in the decision to omit reworkings of Jacobus de Voragine's prefatory etymologies, which, one must assume, were considered to be too learned or abstract to be suitable for inclusion. The appeal of these texts, in contrast, is to a different audience, and with their richness of simple detail and their tendency to employ the techniques of popular storytelling, it is likely that they were produced for the benefit of a lay audience, interested more in drawing inspiration from the heroic deeds of the saints of yore than their abstract theological significance.

Although all medieval texts were designed in one way or another to be read aloud, an absence of oral formulas, a certain corresponding complexity of syntax, and a less polished approach to the demands of language and rhetoric, suggest also that they were produced for private enjoyment rather than formal or public recitation. They could, therefore, have been commissioned by pious and literate members of the lay community, whose purchasing power would have gone hand-in-hand with their appetite for religious reading material. Their use in this respect may not, paradoxically, have differed substantially from those of Compilation A, as they would no doubt have been employed in the context of private celebrations and as an instrument of moral education in the families (or perhaps even extended social circles) of an educated minority.[1]

---

[1] By the same token, an absence of costly illumination combined with a tendency to favour paper over parchment shows that funds were not unlimited. For

Agatha

In place of Voragine's abstract introduction, the *Passión de Santa Águeda* (FLG 419), begins with a cliché, as the content of the Latin ('Agatha virgo ingenua et corpore pulcherrima', 12) is expanded to produce a reference to the saint's harmonious equilibrium of inner and outer virtue: 'Santa Águeda, virgen, fue fija dalgo, muy fermosa en el cuerpo e más en el alma' (2-3). This popular although hackneyed turn-of-phrase, founded on the *meollo* versus *corteza* distinction, modifies the corporeal emphasis of the narrative by presenting her as a rounded figure whose soul is equally worthy of admiration.

The extent to which this could be read as part of a strategy designed to inculcate a more balanced conception of sanctity, notably in relation to noble young ladies (who would no doubt have been inspired by a less purely corporeal heroine) is an interesting question, but it is noticeable that it stands alongside several further modifications. The most important of these appear in relation to descriptions of religious service, with Agatha presented as a diligent and exemplary disciple, and Quintianus, a mere idolater. This can be seen in the reworking of 'ydolis deditus' (15) as 'sirvía de grado a los ýdolos' (5) and in the rendering of 'Diis eam faceret immolare' (18) as 'quería que sacrificasse los ýdolos' (9-10).

Further developments take place in the *Vida* (Escorial h-I-14) and the *Vida de la virgen* (Escorial M-II-6), as the abstract notion of religious service ('onrrava sienpre a Dios', 3) is replaced by a tangible reference to prayer: 'rogava sienpre a Dios' (3, 4). Equally notable is the fact that despite being furthest from the archetype, the *Vida de la virgen* is the only text to transmit the correct form of the name of the city in which Agatha lives, for while the *Passión* (FLG 419) has 'Atritanea' (3), in the *Vida* it is given as 'Acatania' (4).

As Agatha is summoned before Quintianus, the image of a house built on rock initially all but disappears, as 'ejus immobile propositum cognovisset' (19) becomes 'él cognosció su talante' (11-12), a phrase

---

studies of the dissemination of vernacular hagiography to lay audiences, see Johnson 1985, Pezzini 1991, and Vitz 1986, 1987, and 1991.

glossed by the subsequent interpolation of 'que non quería fazer nada de lo que él quería' (12). It resurfaces again in Quintianus's instruction to Aphrodisia, although the emphasis is transferred in all three versions from soul ('ejus animum immutarent', 21-22) to heart ('mudasse su coraçón', 14), and thus, by implication, from cerebral to emotional. The result is an element of deintellectualization, with the saint now led by Christological desire rather than cognitive understanding.[2]

Its third appearance is in her speech in the brothel, where it becomes subject to modification:[3]

Mens mea super petram solidata est et in Christo fundata, verba vestra venti sunt, promissiones vestrae pluviae, terrores vestri flumina sunt. Quae quantumvis impugnant, stat fundamentum domus meae, cadere non valebit. (24-27)	La mi voluntad está asý afirmada e raygada en Jhesu Christo, que vuestras palabras non valen nada, e vuestras promissiones son como luvia, e vuestros spantos son como ríos. Ca comoquier que estas cosas lidien contra mí, el cimiento de la mi casa non puede caher, ca está afirmado sobre piedra. (17-21)

Agatha affirms that her will is founded not on rock, but on Christ. The phrasing of this observation points to popular reception and an audience less interested in allusions to Scripture than images of union

---

2   See Matthew 7:24-27. The *Passión* and the *Vida* focus on Quintianus's unrestrained sexual urges while the *Vida de la virgen* considers the possibility of marriage: 'pensó que si él tomasse a Santa Águeda por muger, quel avrían todos miedo como a fidalgo' (7-8). Equally noticeable is the interpolation of a more emphatic reference to idolatry, with the *Passión*'s 'non quería fazer nada de lo que él quería' (12) expanded to become 'non quería adorar los ýdolos nin fazer nada de lo que él asmava' (12-13).

3   The texts differ in their understanding of the brothel scene. The *Passión* claims that Aphrodisia works in isolation from her daughters while in the *Vida* the use of 'mudasen' (13) affirms that their actions are collective. The *Vida de la virgen* follows the *Passión* with regard to Aphrodisia's operational isolation, but claims that she has ten sons. A transformation less easy to understand is the orthography of her name, with the *Passión* adopting 'Afrodisa' (13 and 23), the *Vida* 'Efrodizia' (12) and 'Efrodisia' (21), and the *Vida de la virgen* 'Frodisia' (14) and 'Frodissia' (24).

between virgin martyr and celestial bridegroom. It is perhaps for this reason that the tripartite progression of similes drawn from the natural world is replaced by a more emphatic register, with 'non valen nada' (18) offered in place of 'venti sunt' (25). The result is forceful and direct, but it has a detrimental impact on the legend's structural integrity, with some of the necessary exposition for the volcano episode (where the rocks are indeed rent asunder) partially diminished in intensity. Faced by this problem, the *Passión* appends an additional phrase ('ca está afirmado sobre piedra', 21), and in this way succeeds in bringing an otherwise latent reference to the forefront of the narrative.

Further developments can be seen in the *Vida*, which prefaces the speech with an interpolated rhetorical question ('¿En qué estades?', 16) while omitting a clause ('vuestras palabras non valen nada', 18) that could potentially be dismissed as superfluous. A similar approach is adopted by the *Vida de la virgen*, which introduces the imperative 'Sabed' (18) before replacing 'palabras' by 'amenazas' (19), 'luvia' by 'llama' (20), and more importantly, 'desseando venir a la gloria del martirio' (22 and 20) by 'con grand desseo por venir a la iglesia de Dios' (23). The cumulative effect is the establishment of a modified frame of reference, with the allusion to Matthew 7:24-27 replaced in part by a more spontaneous and popularizing register underpinned by references to Christological devotion.

In the face of such resistance Aphrodisia recognizes that she will be unable to break Agatha's will. The *Passión* follows the Latin closely, but in the *Vida* the interpolation of 'Así dígote que' (22) prefaces her speech with a sense of reluctant inevitability.[4] A more complex transformation can be seen in the words that follow, as the content of the Latin ('Facilius possunt saxa molliri et ferrum in plumbi mollitiem converti, quam ab intentione christiana mens istius puellae converti seu revocari', 29-31) is progressively modified. The *Passión* is the most literal and polished of the three, offering readers a forthright Christological account of Agatha's determination: 'Más de ligero se podrían

---

[4] This parallels the interpolation of a rhetorical question ('¿En qué estades?', 16) into Agatha's announcement to Aphrodisia and can be taken as a hallmark of style in Escorial h-1-14.

amollentar las piedras e el fierro tornarse en plomo blando que trastornar la voluntad desta niña de la fe de Jhesu Christo' (23-25). In the *Vida de la virgen*, in contrast, the tendency is towards simplification, with a reduction in the main clause from two verbs to one and a shift in emphasis from will to heart: 'Más de ligero se podrían tornar las piedras blandas e el fierro plomo que trastornar el coraçón desta niña de la fe de Jhesu Christo' (24-26). The most spectacular transformation, however, is in the *Vida*, where the emphasis falls not on the difficulty of the task, but the destructive force necessary to ensure its completion: 'más de ligero se podrían las piedras e el fierro torrnarse en polvo muy blando ante que trastornar esta niña de la fe de Jhesu Christo' (22-24).

In contrast to the formulaic treatment of direct speech in Compilation A, the texts of Compilation B opt for a flexible approach bearing none of the hallmarks of oral delivery. In the debates between Agatha and her inquisitor, for instance, changes of speaker are indicated by the use of a wide-ranging series of *verba dicendi* that are ideally suited to private reading. The most noticeable distinction can be seen in relation to Agatha, for in contrast to the single ponderous phrase adopted by the *Istoria* ('respondióle Santa Ágata e dixo'), the *Passión* introduces her words in a variety of ways: 'díxole ella' (27), 'respondió ella' (29 and 31-32), 'díxole Águeda' (34, 53, 59, and 89), 'respondió Águeda' (37 and 43-44), and 'dixo Águeda' (93).[5] A similar, although less spectacular, distinction can be seen with Quintianus, as the phrases 'Cui Quintianus' (34), 'Quintianus dixit' (37, 39, 47, 98, and 100), and 'dixit ei Quintianus' (56) are reduced in this instance to two: 'díxole Quinciano' (28, 31, 33, 52, 95, and 98) and 'dixo Quinciano' (42).

The process of evolution continues in the *Vida*, which draws attention to Quintianus's anger ('díxole fuertemente Quinciano', 30) and Agatha's saintly status (26, 34, 37, 44, 54, 61, 93, 97, and 99), and in the *Vida de la virgen*, which adopts a more simplistic approach based on a single verb: 'ella le dixo' (28), 'díxol Quinciano' (29, 32, 34, 41, and

---

5   The diversity of the *Passión* in this respect is almost as great as that of its source: 'Cui illa' (33), 'illa respondit' (35 and 37-38), 'Cui Agatha' (40, 64-65, and 94), 'Agatha respondit' (43 and 49), 'dixitque Agatha' (58), and 'Agatha dixit' (99).

48), 'dixo ella' (30 and 33), 'díxol Águeda' (36, 38-39, 42, 56, 68, 86-87, and 90), 'dixo Águeda' (50 and 69), and 'dixo Quinciano' (83 and 89).

The tendency within the debate is towards simplification. Quintianus's opening question ('Cujus conditionis es?', 32-33), for instance, is made to refer not to social standing, but identity: '¿Quién eres tú?' (26-27). This leads to a modified response in which the rhetorical structure of the Latin ('Non solum ingenua, sed et spectabilis genere', 33-34) is rendered in a more accessible manner: 'Muger fija dalgo e muy noble, segund que dizen mis parientes' (27-28). The emphasis in this way falls on clarity and intelligibility, and it is perhaps for this reason that the prefect's next question ('Si ingenua es, cur moribus te servilem personam habere ostendis?', 34-35) is expanded by twin interpolations that reflect specifically on Agatha's bearing in society: 'Si tú eres fija dalgo, ¿por qué te muestras e te das por villana en tus fechos?' (28-29). This in turn is revised by the *Vida de la virgin* ('Si tú eres muy fija dalgo, ¿por qué te demuestras en tus costunbres en darte por villana?', 29-30), which proceeds thereafter to interpolate fresh material: 'Non ay ninguno que pueda ser libre si primeramente non serviere al mi señor Jhesu Christo' (33-34).

In the face of continued resistance, Quintianus orders Agatha to offer sacrifice. The *Passión* reworks 'Elige quod volueris' (39) as 'Escoje qual más quisieres' (33), but in the *Vida* there is a more noticeable adjustment, as 'De dos cosas faz la una' (32-33) establishes a more aggressive tone.[6] Agatha, however, refuses to acquiesce to his demands, and instead attacks the stupidity of worshipping pagan icons. Most

---

6   In the *Passión* Quintianus orders Agatha to sacrifice to his 'dioses' (34) while in the *Vida* and the *Vida de la virgen* he speaks of mere 'ýdolos' (33, 35). This transformation, which seems implausible in view of the strength of his faith, is consistent in two of the three texts with the subsequent repetition of the order. Compare, for instance, '¡O sacrifica a los dioses o fazerte he matar muy atormentada!' (*Passión*, 42-43), '¡O sacrifica los dioses o fazerte he morir atormentada!' (*Vida*, 43-44), and '¡Sacrifica los ýdolos o muere a tormentos!' (*Vida de la virgen*, 42). The lack of consistency in the *Vida* in this instance is typical of its engaging but uneven quality.

notable is that she questions not whether Quintianus's gods are good, but if they can be considered gods at all:[7]

Miror te virum prudentem ad tantam stultitiam devolutum, ut illos dicas Deos tuos esse, quorum vitam non cupias tuam conjugem vel te imitari, ut dicas tibi injuriam fieri, si eorum vivas exemplo. Nam si Dei tui sunt boni, bonum tibi optavi, si autem exsecraris eorum consortia, mecum sentis. (43-47)	Maravíllome mucho como tan sabio como tú tomeste tan grand locura que digas que aquestos son los mis dioses e non quieres tú nin tu muger semejarles. E dizes que te fago tuerto porque te digo que bivas así como ellos. Ca si son dioses, querrán tu bien; mas pues que aborresces su conpañía, quieras semejar a mí. (37-42)

The *Passión* expands on the syntactic tautness of the Latin, leading Agatha not to the offer of a good wish, but a statement of fact in which the rejection of the notion of imitation is taken as a measure of a latent desire to be like her. The directness of her tone and the homely nature of her logic produce an immediate effect, for now, in addition to the threat of suffering ('Aut sacrifica Diis aut te faciam diversis suppliciis interire', 48-49), Quintianus speaks for the first time of her death: '¡O sacrifica a los dioses o fazerte he matar muy atormentada!' (42-43).

In this respect the Castilian texts display an unmistakable fondness for intensification and exaggeration, characteristics that are equally apparent in Agatha's response:

---

7 The speech is abbreviated in the *Vida de la virgin* ('Maravíllome mucho porque tan sabio como tú tomaste tan grand locura, diziendo que non querías semejar al tu dios e mandas a mí quel adore', 39-41), while the *Vida* expands on its ironic and antagonistic tone: 'Maravíllome mucho porque tan grant sabio como tú, porque conosciste a tan grant locura, que dizes a los maderos que son tus dioses. E dizes que tú e tu muger non queredes semejar a ellos. E dizes que te fablo mal porque digo que bivas así como ellos. Ca si son dioses querán el tu bien, mas aborresces su conpaña; quieras pues semejar a mí' (37-42).

Si feras mihi promittas, audito Christi nomine mansuescunt, si ignem adhibeas, de coelo mihi rorem salvificum angeli ministrabunt, si plagas vel tormenta ingeras, habeo spiritum sanctum, per quem despicio universa. (49-52)

Sy me pusieres entre las bestias crueles, nonbrando a Jhesu Christo fazerse han mansas. E si me metieres en el fuego, los ángeles de Dios enbiarán rocío del cielo e matarlo han. E si me llagares e me atormentares, el Spíritu Santo, por quien desprecio todas las tus amenazas, te confrondrá. (44-48)

In this instance the *Passión* establishes a more vivid impression of space and location. The threat of wild beasts, for instance, is now envisioned as a confrontation, with the specificity of Agatha's words evoking an image of encirclement, as if within the amphitheatre. The prospect of coercion by fire, on the other hand, is reworked as a reference to burning (with the saint's flesh protected by heavenly dew), while the formulaic discussion of plagues and torments evolves into an image of the saint wounded but rescued by the Holy Spirit.[8] These developments, which seem tailored to the tastes of a lay audience interested in drawing inspiration from a gripping narrative, lead to a modified account of Quintianus's reaction, as he sends Agatha to jail not because he has been made to appear foolish in public ('Tunc jussit eam trahi ad carcerem, quia voce eum publice confundebat', 52-53) but because she has been able to mock him at will: 'Entonce mandóla levar a la cárcel porque lo confondía por placer' (48-49).

When the dialogue between Agatha and the prefect resumes, the *Passión* and the *Vida de la virgen* follow the Latin closely, while in the

---

8   The *Vida* focuses on bondage, thereby establishing a link between Agatha and Lucy: 'Si me atares o ligares e me atormentares, sanarme ha el Spíritu Santo, porque desprecio todas tus menazas' (48-49). The *Vida de la virgen*, in contrast, offers a pithier description: 'Si tú me pusieres entre las bestias crueles, yo llamando a Jhesu Christo luego serán mansas. E si me pusieres en el fuego, los ángeles de Dios a matarlo han. E si me llagas e me atormentares, el Spíritu Santo sanarme ha. E por esto non precio nada tus tormentos' (43-46).

Vida the interpolation of 'mandóla traer ante sí' (52) establishes a more noticeable impression of coercive force. When Agatha refuses to offer sacrifice, she is ordered to be racked ('jussit eam in equuleum suspendi et torqueri', 57-58), but as is the case in Compilation A, the formulation of the *Passión* at this point ('mandóla atar e dar torcejones', 51-52) suggests that the translator experienced problems of interpretation, opting in the end to replace racking by the infliction of sharp pains.[9]

An equally noticeable development can be seen in the words that follow, as the *Vida* and the *Vida de la virgen* preface the content of the Latin ('Non enim potest triticum in horreum poni', 60) in differing ways, the former with the passive construction 'Ca saben que' (57), and the latter, an imperative: 'E sabed' (52). This paves the way for the interpolation of additional emphasis ('non pueden poner el trigo en el alfolí o en el orno', *Vida*, 57-58) and the restructuring of Agatha's comments on the destruction of the physical body, as 'nisi diligenter feceris corpus meum a carnificibus attrectari' (62-63) is rendered as 'E assí la mi alma non puede entrar en el Paraýso si non fuesse el mi cuerpo primero menuzado e quebrantado con palma de martirio' (*Vida de la virgen*, 53-55).

Unable to convince Agatha to offer sacrifice, Quintianus orders the severing of her breast. This action is simplified in the *Passión* and the *Vida*, as the content of the Latin ('jussit ejus mamillam torqueri et tortam diutissime jussit abscidi', 63-64) is expressed bluntly as 'mandóle tajar la teta' (59 and 61). In the *Vida de la virgen*, on the other hand, both breasts are severed: 'mandól tajar las tetas' (56). This development is one of the most revealing, as it sheds light on the *Vida de la virgen*'s ability to reach beyond Compilation B and access the earlier tradition.

Agatha's response is equally striking, as the diffuse emphasis of the Latin ('Impie crudelis et dire tyranne, non es confusus amputare

---

9   The *Vida de San Millán de la Cogolla* discusses the devil's 'puntas e torcejones' (Dutton 1992: 193, st. 261d) while in the *Istoria de Sant Mamés* the saint suffers 'torcejones en la cabeça' (Baños Vallejo & Uría Maqua 2000: 259). The *Vida* and the *Vida de la virgen* extend the process of evolution by removing the reference to bondage and replacing it with a second physical torture: 'mandóla aspar e darle torcejones' (54, 49).

in femina, quod ipse in matre suxisti?', 65-66) is expressed in more personal terms, with the saint regarding herself not as an archetype of womankind, but an individual: 'O omne cruel, sin piadat e falsso, ¿non oviste vergüença de tajar en mí lo que tú mameste en tu madre?' (60-61). The phrasing of the text at this point raises questions about the extent to which it could have been reworked with the interests of a female audience in mind, for it is difficult to see how Agatha's more personal reaction could not have inspired feelings of empathy or admiration. This is equally apparent as she continues, as the emphasis of Voragine's original ('Ego habeo mamillas integras in anima mea, ex quibus nutrio omnes sensus meos, quas ab infantia domino consecravi', 66-68) is modified by the claim that the breasts in her soul have nurtured her brain rather than her senses: 'Enpero yo tengo otras tetas enteras de dentro en mi alma de que se crian todos los mis sesos. E los ofrescí a Dios de pequeña' (61-62).[10]

As Agatha is returned to prison, the *Passión* follows the Latin closely. The tenor of Peter's opening address, however, is altered, as the emphasis falls no longer on praise for Agatha's verbal dexterity, but the vilification and humiliation of a pagan tyrant:

| Licet consularis insanus tormentis te afflixerit, tu eum tuis responsis amplius afflixisti et licet ubera tua torserit, sed illius ubertas in amaritudinem convertetur, et quoniam ibi eram, quando hoc patiebaris, vidi, quia mamilla tua potest curam salutis suscipere. (75-79) | Maguer este adelantado loco te quebrantó los mienbros con tormentos, más lo atormentaste tú. Enpero que él te tajó la teta e te atormentó en ella, más es él atormentado e amargado. E porque lo sofriste en paciencia, vy que la tu teta podría muy bien sanar. (66-70) |

---

10   The reference to 'sesos' is omitted in the *Vida*, while in the *Vida de la virgen* it is replaced by 'deseos' (59). A further distinction can be seen in the words that follow, as the *Vida* and the *Vida de la virgen* play on the bond between virgin martyr and celestial spouse, the latter maintaining that her desires have been divinely consecrated ('E los ofrecí de pequeña a Dios', 59), and the former, that the consecration has been of her breasts: 'E las ofrescí de pequeña a Dios' (64). The result is the creation of one of the most obviously sexualized references to celestial union in the early Castilian canon—a topic discussed in detail in Chapters 5-6.

While the Latin praises Agatha's responses, the *Passión* focuses on pain and torment, emphasizing the extent of her suffering through tautology before presenting her (rather than her words) as a force capable of inflicting harm. This leads to a more direct discussion of the severing of the breast, as the Latin's delicate lexical symmetry is reworked as a play on the verb *atormentar* (67-68). A second instance of tautology, with 'amaritudinem' (74) rendered as 'atormentado e amargado' (69), paves the way for a final declaration, as Peter insists not that he was a witness to the torture, but that in view of Agatha's forbearance, the breast can be restored.[11]

Much of the remainder of the conversation follows the Latin closely, although it is noticeable that in the *Vida de la virgen* references to shame are replaced by expressions of fear.[12] A development affecting all three texts is the discussion of Christ's curative ability, as the stilted wording of the original ('Quia habeo dominum Jesum Christum, qui solo verbo curat omnia', 83-84) is replaced by a less figurative turn of phrase: 'Porque el Nuestro Señor Jhesu Christo solamente por la palabra sana todas las coses e las aduze a su estado' (78-79). This is followed by a modified account of the revelation of Peter's identity, as the content of the Latin ('Et ego apostolus ejus sum et ipse me misit ad te', 86) is rendered more concretely as 'Yo soy el apóstol Sant Pedro e él me

---

11 The *Vida* offers an expanded account at this point ('Empero que este adelantado loco te fizo mal e te quebrantó con muchos tormentos, tú más le atormenteste. Empero que él te tajó la tu teta e te atormentó en ella, más él es atormentado e amargo. E porque lo sofriste en grant paciencia, vi que la tu teta podrié bien sanar', 69-72) while the *Vida de la virgin* is more succinct: 'Maguer que este adelantado loco te quebrantó con tormentos, mucho más atormenteste tú a él. E maguer que te tajó las tetas e te amargó, mucho más amargo finca él. E porque lo sofriste en paciencia, só aquí venido por sanar tus tetas' (63-67).

12 In the *Passión* Peter informs Agatha that he is a Christian and urges her not to feel ashamed: 'de mí non ayas ninguna vergüença' (73); Agatha then responds with a question: '¿Por qué avré de ti vergüença, ca eres viejo e anciano, e yo soy tan malamente depedaçada que non ha omne en el mundo que en mí tomasse plazer?' (74-76). In the *Vida de la virgen*, however, the emphasis is modified, with 'e non temas de mí en ninguna cosa' (69) followed by '¿Por qué avría yo te ti miedo, que tú eres viejo e anciano, e yo estó muy fuerte despedaçada que non ha omne en el mundo que de mí tomasse plazer?' (70-72).

enbió a ti' (80-81). The process of evolution continues in the *Vida de la virgen*, which omits the second part of the statement, and in the *Vida*, which fails to identify Peter by name. A reason for this divergence can be seen in the section that follows, as the *Vida* adopts the delaying tactics of popular storytelling by first announcing his departure ('E desaparesció el anciano adesora', 84-85) before then offering his name: 'E éste fue el apóstol Sant Pedro' (85).

The relationship between Christ and Agatha comes into sharper focus in the *Vida* during the incident with the prison guards, as she fears not that she might lose her 'coronam patientiae' (91), but 'la corona que he ganada del mi señor Jhesu Christo' (90). A more symbolic development is noticeable on her return, as the chronology of the Latin becomes vaguer, with the saint now appearing before Quintianus merely on a different day. The shaping of the texts at this point, with Agatha emerging once more from her cell, provides more than a passing reminiscence of the triumph of Christ in rising from the darkness of his tomb. It is perhaps for this reason that the conversation thereafter establishes a vivid distinction between Christianity and paganism—a factor that can be seen in Quintianus's opening retort ('Ut Deos adoraret, ne graviora supplicia sustineret', 93-94), which is reworked into reported speech in the *Passión* ('díxole Quinciano que adorase los dioses en tal que non sufriesse mayores penas', 91-92) but becomes subject to greater modification in the *Vida*, where a reference to the gods is replaced by an allusion to pagan icons: 'dixo Quinciano que adorasse los ýdolos por tal manera que non sufriese mayores penas' (88-89). These transformations, which belittle his beliefs, are followed by a modified version of Agatha's response in which the insulting power of her rejection is reinforced (exactly as it is in Compilation A) through tautology, with 'Miser sine intellectu' (95) reworked as 'Mesquino syn seso e sin entendimiento' (90-91).

This distinction, however, pales into insignificance in comparison with the treatment of the episode in the *Vida de la virgen*, which introduces fresh material:

E dixo Quinciano: 'Águeda, dime quál físico te sanó tan aýna de las llagas.' E díxol Águeda: 'Aquel físico sanó a mí que de la su palabra tan solamente puede sanar e fazer todas las cosas.' E dixo Quinciano: 'Si tú adoras los ýdolos, ya non sofrirás más penas.' E díxol Águeda: '¡Las tus palabras son locas e vanas e ensuzian todo el ayre! O mesquino loco e sin entendimiento, ¿por qué quieres que adore el ayre e las piedras e dexe a Dios del cielo que me sanó?' (83-89)

The reworking of this exchange shows that the *Vida de la virgen* has a unique intellectual and theological integrity and deserves to be read in its own right. Further evidence can be seen in the fact that it chooses not to include a version of Quintianus's final threat ('Nunc videbo, si Christus te curabit', 100-01) which is instead recycled along with a reference to physical torture: 'Estonce asañósse Quinciano e mandó esparzir muchos tiestos quebrados e poner carbones encendidos sobre ellos. E mandó que la enbolviessen en ellos toda fasta en los cabellos por ver si la sanaría Jhesu Christo' (92-95). Curiously, this leaves the *Vida* as the only Castilian version to transmit a reworking of the subsequent portion of Voragine's original ('Quintianus dixit: "Et quis te sanavit?" Cui Agatha: "Christus filius Dei"', 97-98), which is rendered in all but identical form: 'E díxole Quinciano: "¿Quién te sanó?" E díxole Santa Águeda: "Jhesu Christo, el fijo de Dios"' (96-97).

As the walls of the palace come crashing down, the rebellion of Quintianus's subjects is given additional emphasis with a move from reported ('quod propter injustum Agathae cruciatum talia paterentur', 105-06) to direct speech: '¡Tales cosas sofrimos por que fazes mal a Santa Águeda!' (101-02). This transformation, which makes his grip on authority appear more tenuous, prepares the reader for a series of simplifications. The first is the truncation of Agatha's prayer, as a reworking of 'et a me amorem saeculi abstulisti' (109-10) is cut in the interests of economy. The second is the omission of the dating of her martyrdom ('circa annum domini CCLII sub Daciano imperatore', 113), which makes her a more universal figure. The third is in the marble inscription, where the ponderous and scholarly tone of the original is made more straightforward:

Erat autem in praedicta tabula scriptum: 'Mentem sanctam, spontaneam, honorem Deo et patriae liberationem.' Quod sic intelligitur: 'Mentem sanctam habuit, spontaneam se obtulit, honorem Deo dedit et patriae liberationem fecit.' (118-20)	E fallaron escripto en aquella tabla: '¡Aquésta ovo alma santa e rescibió de grado martirio por amor de Dios, e diole honrra que le franqueó su tierra!' (114-16)

The *Passión* simplifies the wording of the tablet to make it instantly recognizable as a celebration of the faith and resilience of a Christian martyr. It could, of course, have retained the compressed wording of its original by reworking it into Castilian with a gloss. The fact that this is not so, however, should be taken not merely as an indication of its sophisticated interpretative ability, but the possibility that it was designed for a lay audience, interested more in the spirit of the martyr's death than the disentanglement of complex passages of scholarly prose.

The account of Quintianus's death is also simplified. In the *Vida* the interpolation of 'E un día' (125) establishes a more robust impression of chronological development, while in the *Vida de la virgen* the replacement of 'fue' (125) by 'cavalgó' (114) introduces equine imagery, in this way bringing to mind notions of wealth, power, and nobility. The texts thereafter tend towards compression, but other than the omission of the report that Quintianus's body is never found ('ita quod corpus ejus nusquam potuit inveniri', 126-27), there is little agreement between them.[13]

In the concluding section, which focuses on the power of the miraculous, there is greater coherence, as the texts omit the erudite paraphrase of Ambrose's *De virginibus* in order to deal more plainly with saint's posthu-

---

13   Compare, for instance, 'el uno resinchando el el otro lançando las coçes. E con muessos echáronlo en el río e murió' (*Passión*, 119-20), 'E los cavallos reninchando, alçáronse en coces e echarónle en el río. E el uno a coces e el otro a muesos, matáronlo' (*Vida*, 131-33), and 'E aquellos cavallos tornaron muy bravos para Quinciano, e el uno a coces e el otro a muessos, echáronlo en el río. E afogáronlo en el río' (*Vida de la virgen*, 115-17).

mous significance. In place of metaphorical expression ('Revoluto anno circa diem natalis ejus', 128), the anniversary of her death is discussed from a purely literal perspective ('a cabo de un año que que ella finó', 126), while Voragine's flowery prolixity ('unde coopertum erat sepulchrum, arripuit et ipsum statuit contra ignem statimque in die natalis ipsius virginis ignis stetit et ultra ullatenus non processit', 132-34) is made more direct: 'E tomaron un velo que estava sobre el altar e pusiéronlo contra el fuego. E estovo quedo e non fue más adelante' (125-26).

This paves the way in the *Vida* for the inclusion of fresh material, with a miracle in which a palfrey wanders accidentally into a hellmouth, setting in motion a series of events that climax in the destruction of pagans led astray by avarice:

> En Acatania era un obispo de santa vida e avía un palafrén a maravilla muy noble. E una vegada escapósele e fuésele áquel que le guardava. E fuxó e metióse por la boca del infierrno. E él yva dando grandes bozes e entró en pos dél. E los diablos mostráronle muchos cavallos e palafrenes e muchos manjares muy nobles. E en cabo de todo aquesto, diéronle su palafrén e una capa de oro bien cerrada e de dentro llena de fuego inferrnal. E dixiéronle que la presentase a su señor, el obispo. E el obispo entendiólo por Spíritu Santo. E mandó a dos moros que tomasen la capa, e que la fuesen echar en el mar e que se viniesen. E ellos, con cobdicia del oro, ronpieron la capa e salió el fuego. E quemó a ellos e el agua e las piedras e las peñas e la tierra. E non quedó fasta que sacaron el velo de Santa Águeda. E luego estudo quedo, que non fue más adelante. (136-48)

The origin of this material is uncertain, but the decision to include it is telling, for in contrast to the lofty and erudite tone of Voragine's conclusion, the hellmouth provides a vivid image of the dangers of evil and a reminder that virtuous souls must always be on their guard. The appeal of this material, particularly to a lay audience accustomed to tales of wonder and awe, should not be underestimated.

Lucy

As is the case with Agatha, the Compilation B versions of Lucy's legend begin not with reworkings of Voragine's prefatory etymologies, but a series of concrete details—in this instance an introduction to Lucy and her concern for her mother's illness. The rejection of Voragine's material points once again to the demands of popular reception, and the unstated assumption that the learned and scientific discussion of the properties of light would have provided too complex or theoretical an introduction to a narrative founded on basic issues such as love, suffering, sacrifice, and faith. Readers are in this way invited to establish an emotional as well as intellectual rapport, appraising relationships between characters in everyday terms and endorsing their decisions accordingly.

Agatha and Lucy, for instance, although raised by interpolations specifically to the level of saints, remain united by a bond of sisterly devotion. Euthicia, on the other hand, moves silently to the background, becoming less significant as a character in her own right, but more important as a representation of the dual archetypes of mother and confidante. This can be seen most clearly in the fact that she is referred to in both texts simply as 'madre' (4), as the narrative in this way eliminates the specificity of her identity in the interests of universality. Her illness, correspondingly, is made more acute, first as we learn that she has been suffering from a haemorrhage for fourteen (rather than four) years, and then as we are provided with a more evocative impression of the difficulties involved in curing her ailment, with 'incurabiliter patiente' (13) reworked in the *Vida de Santa Lucía* (from FLG 419) as 'non podía sanar dello' (5), but more sensationally in the *Vida e passión de Santa Lucía* (from Escorial h-1-14) as 'non podía sanar por ninguna melezina que le fazían' (5). In this way she becomes a symbolic representation of female suffering, and thus, a perfect foil for Lucy.[14]

Further evidence of popularization can be seen in relation to Agatha, as Voragine's matter-of-fact wording ('pro cujus nomine sustinuit

---

14   It is difficult to see how even the most inattentive scribe could translate 'quatour' (13) as 'catorze' (4, 5), a reading preserved by all manuscripts. The Compilation A text ('avía quatro años que tenía fluxo de sangre', 15-16) is closer to the Latin.

passionem', 17) is modified initially in the *Vida* to incorporate references to her love of Christ ('por cuyo amor sufrió muerte e passión', 9-10) and then in the *Vida e passión* to the corporeal nature of her suffering: 'por cuyo amor ella rescibió pasión en el su cuerpo' (10). In this instance an interpolated physical phrase succeeds in presenting her demise as a quasi-sexual experience—a conception of martyrdom that would have had most effect on a lay audience, where a tendency towards sensationalism could be excused in the interests of affirming a sense of collective consciousness.[15] It is perhaps for this reason that a reworking of 'solemnia' (14) is omitted from the description of Mass, while additional emphasis ('que avía luengo tienpo', 7) is interpolated by the *Vida e passión* into the tale of the woman with a haemorrhage. It could also be used to explain the presence of an enthusiastic amplification in Lucy's address to her mother, as 'santitate gaudebis' (18-19) is reworked first 'serás a la sazón sana e alegre' (10-11), and then, more emphatically, as 'luego serás sana e alegre de tu dolencia' (11-12).

The relationship between the two characters is further modified by the description of the dream vision, for while the Latin discusses the actions of 'matre et filia' (20), the Castilian texts dismiss suggestions of parity by speaking of 'Santa Lucía e su madre' (12, 13). This transformation, which marks a radical distinction in status, is followed by a section in which the *Vida* follows the Latin ('Luciam somnus arripuit', 21) by stating that Lucy falls asleep ('adormescióse Lucía', 13) while the *Vida e passión* affirms that the action is collective: 'dormiéronse amas a dos' (14). The expectation raised by this development, however, is soon defeated, for although Euthicia sleeps peacefully, it is only Lucy who is rewarded by a visitation.

In contrast to the vagueness of Voragine's original, Agatha's words ('quid a me petis, quod ipsa poteris praestare continuo matri tuae?', 23-24) are made more precise by means of the inclusion of a specific reference to Euthicia's health: '¿por qué me demandas que sane a tu madre,

---

[15] For the sexualization of religious terminology in Castilian hagiography, see Beresford 2007a, and for a more general survey, Robertson 1990. For an engaging analysis of the juxtaposition of contraries (with particular reference to sexual and sacred), see Burke 1998.

lo que tú puedes bien fazer?' (15-16). This is developed in turn by the *Vida e passión*, where the request for assistance becomes a demand for intervention: '¿por qué me mandas que dé sanidat a tu madre, lo que tú puedes luego fazer?' (16-17). A parallel development can be seen slightly later, as 'por las oraciones de Santa Ágada eres sana' (17-18) is rendered more plainly as 'sabe que eres sana' (19). The result is a shift in the balance of power, as Lucy rather than Agatha is presented (even before her martyrdom) as a conduit to the divine.

In the conclusion to the dream-vision, the popularizing quality of the Compilation B texts leads them to break a generic rule by failing to mark the end of the visitation. The Latin, as one might expect, adheres to the norms of scholarly construction by commenting on the fact that Lucy wakes from her dream: 'Evigilans autem Lucia' (25). The *Vida* and the *Vida e passión*, however, are less concerned with erudite notions of generic conformity, and instead proceed to a revelation of the fact that Euthicia has been cured. Significantly, the miracle is attributed to Christ rather than Agatha:[16]

| per ipsam ergo te deprecor, quae suis orationibus te sanavit, ne mihi de caetero nomines sponsum, sed quidquid mihi datura eras pro dote, pauperibus elargire. (26-28) | Ruégote, por amor de aquél que te sanó, que nunca de oy más me digas de fechos de casamiento, mas todo lo que me dieres en logar de arras, dalo a los pobres. (*Vida*, 18-20) |

---

16 The Compilation A text follows the Latin with 'E despertando Santa Lucía' (30). Harriet Goldberg notes that 'Perhaps the most frequently remembered moment in the act of dreaming is the awakening. The verb *espertar/despertar* is the most usual, but we also find *recordar/acordarse* and even *entrar en su memoria* to describe the return to waking' (1983: 25). She also finds that awakenings can be fearful or joyful, and that 'Authors situated a dream experience in space and often informed the reader about the dreamer's condition, both physical and emotional. [...] The contents of the enigmatic dream is anticipated by the dreamer's inability to stop thinking about the events of the day or of his problems, a clearly human phenomenon recognizable to the audience' (1983: 25). For studies of dreams and dream-theory, see Kelchner 1935, Hieatt 1967, Spearing 1976, Kruger 1992, Lynch 1992, and in relation to Castilian, Thompson 1976, Palley 1983, and Beresford 2007b: 104-06 and 117-20 (on Thaïs and Pelagia). A point made by Andrew Galloway, however, is also worth bearing in mind: 'dream-theory is less known to the early (and indeed the later) Middle Ages than has often been assumed' (1994: 475).

Lucy's words are remarkable not only for their warmth and directness, but the way in which they transform the hierarchical emphasis of Voragine's original, making Agatha less of an authority in her own right. A related feature is a transition from prayer ('orationibus') to love ('amor'), as the virgin martyr's desire is expressed not in dry theological terms, but an emotional bond centred on the celestial spouse. These transformations, which seem tailored to the demands of a lay audience, lead to a related aspect of reworking, as the discussion of Lucy's husband-to-be is replaced by a sweeping reference to all that pertains to marriage. This paves the way for a subsequent modification, as an erudite Latin construction ('Quod moriens das, ideo das', 29-30) is replaced by a more accessible statement, rich in homely realism: 'Lo que después que mueres das, por esso lo das, porque non lo puedes levar contigo' (22-23).[17]

As Lucy and Euthicia return from church, a series of modifications prepares readers for the reaction of Lucy's husband-to-be—a section that takes advantage of the various thematic and intellectual possibilities that can be exploited in relation to a character of particular ignorance.[18] The process begins with the precise rendering of Voragine's original ('requirit sponsus a nutrice de his', 34), initially in the *Vida* as 'demandó a su ama que qué era aquello' (26-27), and then, more expansively, in the *Vida e passión* as 'demandó a su ama que la criara que qué era esto, que ansí vendía todo lo que avía' (28-29). This statement, which establishes an impression of his child-like state of ingenu-

---

17   In the *Vida e passión* there is a shift in verbal structure in the form of the future subjunctive: 'Lo que después que tú murieres dieres, por esso lo darás, porque lo non podrás levar contigo' (23-25).

18   In his analysis of the fool as social type, Orrin E. Klapp offers comments on the fact that the 'fool is distinguished from the normal group member by a deviation in person or conduct which is regarded as ludicrous and improper. He is usually defined as a person lacking in judgement, who behaves absurdly or stupidly [...]. The fool is the antithesis of decorum, beauty, grace, intelligence, strength, and other virtues; and, therefore, as a type is antiheroic' (1949: 157). He also draws a distinction between fool and villain, noting that despite his shortcomings, the fool 'is distinguished from the villain by the fact that his pranks involve no evil intent or are too stupid to be taken seriously. The fool is thus tolerated and is regarded with amusement rather than being punished' (1949: 158).

ousness, takes readers through a learning experience in which complex theological notions are expressed in everyday terms.[19]

Further evidence can be seen in his reaction to the machinations of Lucy's wet-nurse, as 'Credidit stultus carnale commercium et coepit auctor esse vendentium' (37) is glossed and expanded to create an impression of frenzied materialism, first with 'E el loco pensando que era alguna heredat deste mundo, así mesmo començó a vender' (29-30), and then with a more extensive formulation: 'E el loco creyólo, cuydando que alguna heredat era deste mundo. E otrosí començó él de vender de lo suyo e dárgelo para que conprase más' (31-33). The result is the establishment of a more tangible distinction between temporal and celestial, with the latent connotations of the Latin expanded and reinterpreted in a popularizing passage aimed at a partisan audience that would have relished the humiliation of a greedy pagan fool.[20]

The start of the trial is marked by the interpolation of 'a juyzio' (31, 34-35), while the demotion of Paschasius from 'consulari' (39) to

---

19   The words of Lucy's wet-nurse are presented as indirect speech in the Latin ('Respondit illa caute, quod utiliorem possessionem sponsa sua invenisset, quam suo volebat nomine comparare, et ideo videbatur aliquanta distrahere', 34-36), but as direct speech in the *Vida*: 'E respondióle como sabia diziendo: "Tu esposa falló otra heredat más provechosa que quiere conprar en tu nonbre e por ende paresce que vende algunas cosas"' (*Vida*, 27-29). Curiously, the *Vida e passión* returns to indirect speech: 'E respondióle ella e díxole como su esposa fallara otra heredat más provechosa e quería conprarla, e por ende vende algunas cosas de las que ha' (*Vida e passión*, 29-31).

20   The formulation of the episode is comparable to the Cid's duping of the moneylenders, Rachel and Vidas, in the *Cantar de Mio Cid*. Although, as Seymour Resnick has shown, the characters are 'not specifically designated as Jews' (1956: 302), the critical debate is ongoing (see, for instance, Salomonski 1957, Cantera 1958, Smith 1965, Salvador Miguel 1977, and Montaner 1993: 406-08). In a study of solidarity, Thomas Montgomery argues that the episode 'is based squarely on a "we-they" opposition', the function of which is 'to reaffirm the sense of community by setting the inside group against the others' (1987: 198). It is likely in this respect that it was derived from a comic folktale (see also Deyermond 1973: 60-61) and it could be—in view of the development of a similar frame of reference in the Compilation B versions of Lucy's legend—that the scribes were influenced by secular materials. In this respect we should perhaps read the duping of Lucy's husband-to-be as a version *a lo divino* of a traditional act of comic hoodwinking, celebrating (as Montgomery affirms) the prioritization of one set of values over another.

'alcalde' (32, 35) establishes a partial process of medievalization, with a historically distant and potentially unfamiliar term replaced by one with a more immediate frame of reference. In so doing it also, perhaps, establishes an impression of petty vindictiveness, as Paschasius effectively falls from a position of genuine political power and influence to assume the level of a mere functionary. A more significant distinction can be seen in the structuring of the dialogue that ensues, for in place of the formulaic *verba dicendi* adopted by the *Pasión* (which, as we have seen, lend themselves perfectly to the demands of oral delivery), the *Vida* opts for greater flexibility. This is followed, with some variation, by the *Vida e passión*, which adopts a series of more extensive formulations.[21]

In the debate itself, the tendency is towards simplification. Lucy's understanding of Christian service, for instance, leads her to concretize the abstract emphasis of the Latin ('visitare pauperes et eis in necessitatibus subvenire', 42-43) with the introduction of a more everyday turn of phrase: 'vesitar a los pobres e fazerles limosnas' (34-35).[22] Voragine's erudite prolixity ('Ista verba tibi simili stulto narrare poteris, mihi autem, qui principum decreta custodio, ista frustra persequeris', 44-46), in contrast, is simplified and made more direct: 'A los christianos locos deves e puedes dezir estas palabras, e non a mí, que guardo la ley de los enperadores' (36-38). A third transformation can be seen in the modification of the frame of reference, as the virgin martyr affixes her attention not on God ('Tu principum tuorum decreta custodis

---

21 The following phrases are adopted: 'respondióle ella' (33-34), 'respondió Lucía' (52), 'dixo(le) Lucía' (38, 51, 56, 59, 74, and 81), 'respondióle Pascual' (43-44, 46), and 'dixo(le) Pascual' (36, 42, 50, 55, 57, and 72). The Latin original, on the other hand, has: 'respondit' (41), 'Ad quem Lucia' (46), 'Cui Lucia' (52, 62, and 65), 'Lucia dixit' (55 and 79), 'Cui Lucia dixit' (59), 'Respondit Lucia' (60), 'Dixitque Lucia' (85), 'Cui Paschasius' (44, 51, 59-60, and 63), 'Respondit Paschasius' (54) 'Paschasius dixit' (57 and 62), and 'Tunc dixit Paschasius' (77-78). Variation in the *Vida e passión* can be seen in the following: 'respondió ella e dixo esta razón' (38), 'dixo Santa Lucía esta razón' (89-90), 'le dixo Pascual' (75-76), and 'preguntó Pascual' (50).

22 In the *Vida e passión* Lucy's response develops the *Vida*'s frame of reference ('porque yo non he otra cosa que le ofrezca, dóte a mí mesma, que me le ofrezcas', 35-36) by emphasizing the sacrificial nature of her predicament: 'porque ya non tengo otra cosa de que le faga sacrificio, quiero fazerle sacrificio de mí misma' (39-40).

et ego Dei mei legem custodiam', 46-47) but Christ: 'Tú guardas los decretos de los príncipes e yo guardo la ley de Jhesu Christo' (38-39). This is paralleled by a related development in the *Vida e passión*, which amplifies its source text with the introduction of tautology: 'Tú guardas los decretos de los tus príncipes e enperadores e yo guardaré la ley de Jhesu Christo' (42-44).

With the accusation of harlotry, the *Vida* opts for popular turns of phrase, as 'corruptoribus' and 'meretrix' (52-53) are reworked as 'garçones' and 'mala muger' (43). A related transformation can be seen in the discussion of corruption, as the distinction between fleshly pleasure and eternal joy ('qui corporalem delectationem praeponunt epulis sempiternis', 56-57) is refocused as an antithesis between temporal and celestial: 'los [corronpedores] del cuerpo son los que aman más las cosas tenporales que las celestiales' (48-49). While at this point Voragine offers an erudite play on words ('Cessabunt verba, cum perventum fuerit ad verbera', 58-59), the *Vida* emphasizes the extent of Paschasius's cruelty by recasting his observation in the form of a question: '¿Qué darán las palabras quando rescibieres las feridas?' (50-51). The *Vida e passión*, on the other hand, takes the process a step further with a technique based on restatement and tautology: '¿Qué darán las tus razones quando sufrieres penas e las feridas?' (55-56).

This leads in both texts to an expanded response in which Lucy offers a series of scriptural citations:

Ancilla Dei sum, qui dixit: 'Cum steteritis ante reges et praesides, etc. Non enim vos estis etc.' (60-62)	Yo só vassalla de Dios que dixo: 'Quando estovieredes ante los reyes o príncipes non pensaredes como devedes fablar, ca yo fablaré por vos'. E Sant Paulo dixo: 'Vos sodes casa de Spíritu Santo'. (52-55)

While the Latin takes its biblical citations for granted, the *Vida* leaves nothing to chance, taking the opportunity instead to place words of spiritual wisdom in Lucy's mouth. As is the case with Compilation A, this may, of course, reflect more on Graesse's editorial technique (1846: 29-32) than Voragine's approach to narrative. One suspects in this instance, however, that the initial citation (from Matthew 10:18-20) was expanded in Latin and that at a subsequent point the reference to Paul was appended in the vernacular in the interests of clarity.[23]

With the threat of imprisonment, the *Vida* maintains a preference for popular turns of phrase, rendering 'lupanar' (64) as 'logar de las malas mugeres' (57-58). This leads to a modified statement of resistance, as Lucy draws strength from a variation of the widely-held assumption that the body cannot be defiled if the mind is not willing:

| Non inquinatur corpus nisi de consensu mentis, nam si me invitam violari feceris, castitas mihi duplicabitur ad coronam. Nunquam autem voluntatem meam ad consensum poteris provocare. Ecce corpus meum ad omne supplicium est paratum. Quid moraris? Incipe fili dyaboli desideria poenarum tuarum exercere. (65-69) | Nunca se ensuzia el alma si la voluntad non consiente, ca si me fizieres corronper e yo non consiento, yo avré la corona de la castidat doblada. E la voluntad nunca la podrás adozir que consienta en pecado. Evaste aquí el mi cuerpo presto para rescebir tormento. ¿Para qué estás tardando? ¡Comiença ya, fijo del diablo, e cunple la pena que se ha de tornar sobre ty! (59-65) |

---

23   The modification suggests familiarity with I Corinthians 3:16-18, and perhaps also, Romans 8:1-7 and II Corinthians 5:1-10. For studies of the diffusion of the *Legenda aurea*, see Seybolt 1946a and 1946b, Reames 1985, Thompson 1990, and Vitz 1991. Lucy's statement is revised in the *Vida e passión*: 'Non só yo Dios, mas só sierva de Dios, que dixo estas palabras: "Quando estudieres ante los reyes e príncipes non pensedes qué digades ca yo fablaré por vos". E Sant Pablo dixo: "Vos sodes e sabedes casa de Spíritu Santo"' (57-61). In the online version of the Latin in the Biblioteca Augustana, in contrast, the citation is expanded: 'Respondit Lucia: "Ancilla Dei sum, qui dixit: Cum steteritis ante reges et praesides, nolite praecogitare, quid loquamini... Non enim vos estis loquentes, sed Spiritus sanctus"' (see http://www.fh-augsburg.de/~harsch/Chronologia/Lspost13/Voragine/jav_lluc.html). However, as the editors do not list their sources, questions remain as to its validity.

While the Latin focuses on the physical body as a corporeal gateway (as is the case in the body-and-soul tradition), the *Vida* affirms that the soul will remain inviolate if its will is not compromised. The theological and intellectual validity of this observation is questionable, but it is noticeable that it leads into a modified corollary, not with the doubling of chastity in pursuit of the crown of martyrdom, but the doubling of the crown of virginity.[24]

With the attempt to have Lucy defiled, the *Vida* follows the Latin by opting for the terseness of direct speech, while the *Vida e passión* reworks the section into reported speech, underlining the extent of Paschasius's cruelty with the introduction of a more direct turn of phrase: 'estonce Pascual fizo venir los garçones e mandólos que conbidasen todo el pueblo e que la escarnesciesen fasta que muriese' (69-70).[25] His humiliation, on the other hand, is expanded in both versions, first as the interpolation of 'non pudieron' (67) emphasizes the nature of his difficulty, and then as 'movere' (75) is expanded through tautology to become 'levar nin mover' (68). Equally noticeable is that while the *Vida* replaces a flowery epithet ('tunc et cum viris mille paria boum adhibuit, sed tamen virgo domini immobilis permansit', 74-76) with

---

24   The Compilation B text (most likely, Escorial K-II-12, which has 'Non se ensuziará el mi cuerpo si la voluntad non consiente', fol. 14vb) is the source of a similar observation in Fray Martín de Córdoba's *Jardín de nobles donzellas*: 'Digo, pues, quel dicho de Sant Agostín se puede entender en dos maneras: la vna, que enla concepción & el parto fuese abertura, ya por eso no se perdía la virginidad. Esto es, porque la virginidad más está enel ánima que enel cuerpo. Como dixo Santa Luzía, no se ensuzia el cuerpo si la voluntad no consiente. Donde si alguna virgen, ni avn por esso no pierde el aureola que es doctada alas virgines enel cielo, antes les es doblada. Así es agora la corrupción de la virginidad' (Goldberg 1974: 184-85). For a discussion of the body-and-soul tradition, see Franchini 2001. The *Vida e passión* alters the emotional pitch of the ultimatum, attributing Paschasius's cruelty not to malevolence, but the pain in his heart: 'Nunca se ensuzia el ánima si la voluntad non lo consiente, e si me fizieres corronper sin consentimiento, averé la corona de la virginidat doblada e la voluntat non corronpida. Nin me podrás adozir que consienta en peccado. E evas mi cuerpo presto para sofrir tormentos. ¿Para qué estás tardando? ¡Comiença ya, fijo del diablo, e cunple las penas que tienes en el coraçón!' (63-68).

25   Compare with 'Invitate ad eam omnem populum et tamdiu illudatur, donec mortua nuntietur' (70-71) and 'Conbidat todo el pueblo e tanto la escarnesced fasta que la matedes' (65-66).

a pronoun ('E mandó venir Pascual mill yuntas de bueyes mas non la pudieron mover', 70-71), the *Vida e passión* eliminates the reference in its entirety.

The judge's frustration is expressed more effectively by the *Vida* as it expands on the content of the Latin ('Quae sunt illa maleficia, quod una puella a mille viris non moveretur?', 78-79) by offering a fuller enumeration of the strategies that he has been forced to employ: '¿Qué son estos encantamientos, que tantos millares de bueyes e de omnes non han podido mover una niña?' (72-74). This leads to a modified version of Lucy's response, as the musicality of the Latin ('Non sunt ista maleficia, sed beneficia Christi', 79) is reworked in a semantically legitimate although less polished manner: 'Non son encantamentos, mas beneficios de Jhesu Christo' (74-75). A further, although more puzzling, distinction is a tenfold diminution in the scale of Lucy's threat, for while the Latin discusses the actions of ten thousand men ('Porro si adhuc decem millia adhibueris, aeque ut primum immobilem me videbis', 80-81), the *Vida* mentions a mere thousand: 'Enpero si me aduxieres otros mill omnes, non me podrán mover más que ante' (75-76). Reasons for this transformation are unclear, but as the text elsewhere tends towards sensationalism and overstatement, one suspects scribal error.

As is the case in Compilation A, Paschasius resolves to have Lucy doused not with urine ('lotio', 82) but water ('agua', 78).[26] This parallels the reworking of 'resinam' (84) as 'pez e resina' (80), which is also attested by Compilation A, but a series of more notable modifications appear in relation to the death blow. The *Vida* follows the Latin ('Videntes autem amici Paschasii eum angustiari', 87) by focusing on Paschasius's despondency ('E veyendo los amigos de Pascual que él tomava por esto grand pesar', 83), while the *Vida e passión* explores the collapse of power from a different perspective by describing the anguish of his friends: 'Viéndolo esto los amigos de Pascual, que avían por ello grant pesar' (86).

---

26   The *Vida e passión* has 'lavamiento' (83). This reading, which is preserved also by BMP 9, is probably closer to that of the archetype. The problematic position of Escorial K-II-12, on the other hand, can be seen in that it replaces 'lavadura' by 'levadura'.

This lays the foundation for a modified version of Lucy's final words, which introduces an unusual subdivision:[27]

'Annuntio vobis pacem ecclesiae redditam Maximiano hodie mortuo et de regno suo Dyocletiano expulso, et sicut civitati Catanensi soror mea Agatha data est protectrix, sic et ego civitati Syracusanae concessa sum interventrix.' (89-92)	'Dígovos buenas nuevas: que avedes paz, ca el enperador Maximiano es muerto e Diocleciano desterrado.' E dixo Santa Lucía esta razón: 'Bien ansí como Santa Águeda defiende e guarda la cibdat de Quinorancia, bien ansí he yo de defender la cibdat de Siracusana.' (88-91)

The structuring of the text in this way is without precedent. A possible explanation could be found in the delaying tactics of popular storytelling, but in view of the absence of a reference to the Church, it could have been designed to produce a shift from official to individual experience. This could to some extent be used to explain the interpolation of a tautologous reference to Agatha's personal custodianship ('defiende e guarda') and the forging of inviolable links between saints and their cities. We should also perhaps think of female recipients, with the suggestion of emulation confirming not that they should bear the weight of the Church on their shoulders, but that they should aspire merely to become the guardians of their immediate communities.[28]

The narrative concludes with Paschasius's trial and execution—a section that succeeds in systematically undermining his status. The process begins as soon as he is apprehended, for in place of the of-

---

27 The *Vida* is closer to the Latin: 'Dígovos buenas nuevas: que avredes paz, ca el enperador Maximiano es muerto e el enperador Diocleciano es desterrado. E bien como Santa Águeda defiende la cibdat de Quitanea, bien asý he yo de rogar por la cibdat de Siracusana' (86-88).

28 The role of female saint as communal exemplar is explored by Gonzalo de Berceo's *Vida de Santa Oria*, with Oria regarded as 'luz […] e confuerto de la su vezindad' (Uría 1992: 505, st.25d). Likewise, in death, her tomb becomes a focal point for the community.

ficial 'ministri Romanorum' (93), the Castilian versions speak only of 'los sayones de los romanos' (89-90, 92-93). The trial before Caesar, on the other hand, becomes a trial before the Emperor, but in place of a journey in chains, he is held prisoner before being condemned by the Senate. His death, in contrast, is rendered in more visually evocative terms, for in place of the dryness of the Latin ('capitali sentencia est punitus', 96-97), he is condemned to decapitation: 'dieron sentencia que lo descabeçasen' (93). Equally noticeable is the establishment of a dual (and to some extent inconsistent) rationale, for having noted already that he was tried for having 'robado toda la provincia' (91), the *Vida e passión* maintains that he is to be beheaded on account of his treatment of Lucy: 'dieron sentencia que le cortasen la cabeça por los males que fiziera a la virgen' (94-96).

This second accusation, although implausible, draws a powerful distinction between the saint and her executioner, underlining the extent to which she has risen in status. It also paves the way for a final modification, with the text concluding not with the dating of her martyrdom ('Passa autem est tempore Constantini et Maxentii circa annos domini CCCX', 101-02), but a description of her final moments. The significance of this development should not be underestimated, for in a narrative predicated on the human and everyday aspects of her predicament, the unfixing of the date of her death turns her into a more universal figure—one who is capable of inspiring the devout (particularly women) in the never-ending struggle to retain their virtue.

Her representation is in this respect broadly consistent with that of Agatha, for although there are differences between recensions, the texts of the Compilation exude an ethos that is fundamentally as popular as it is accessible. In those preserved in FLG 419 and related manuscripts (the *Passión de Santa Águeda* and the *Vida de Santa Lucía*), the impression of sanctity is clearly constructed and influenced not by erudite or abstract concerns, but a process of simplification driven by a tendency towards the prioritization of the needs of storytelling over theological reflection. This produces a richness of homely detail and a certain degree of familiarity, matched in parallel recensions by a marked tendency towards sensationalization. This, to some extent, can be seen in Escorial M-II-6 in the *Vida de la virgen señora Santa Águeda*, which offers a precise and conceptually distinctive portrait of Agatha which must be taken seriously and read not simply in its own right, but in conjunction with parallel treatments. Most notable, however, are the texts of Escorial h-I-14 (the *Vida de Santa Águeda* and the *Vida e passión de Santa Lucía*), which continue the process of sensationalization whilst attempting at the same time to introduce a series of clarifying adjustments in styling, tone, and emphasis. This produces a sequence of texts, popular in orientation, although rich in diversity, that offer a series of subtly differing explorations of the function and meaning of female sanctity.

5
Agatha and Lucy in Context

The Critical Legacy

Despite their elevated status, Agatha and Lucy have not always fared well with the critics. Some elements of their cultural and intellectual legacy have been considered in monographic treatments of female sanctity and chapters of books, often in the form of fleeting references to their representation and significance. This work has been invaluable, and has done much to rescue their legends from the void into which they had once fallen. It is noticeable, however, that discrete conceptual discussions, with the emphasis on specific rather than generic, have been few. The result is that with the exception of a handful of scholarly contributions, little of substance has been written.[1]

A pioneering discussion, focusing on the representation of Saint Lucy, was published by Ángel González Palencia in 1932 and reprinted a decade later in a volume of collected essays. His argument, which is applicable not simply to Lucy, but the way in which she is paired with her earlier hagiographic counterpart, falls on the distinction between the majority of artistic and literary representations, which present her as a figure either whose eyes have been gouged out or who gouges them

---

[1] For background and brief references, see Capdevila 1949, Lewison 1950, Garana 1955, Costanza 1957, Brusa 1957, Cracco Ruggini 1984, D'Arrigo 1985, Stuart 1996, Cazelles 1991, Gravdal 1991, Winstead 1997: 29-33, Nast & Pile 1998: 293, Ferrer 2000, Caviness 2001, Hernández Amez 2004-05, Lligadas 2006, Lombardo 2007, Raudino 2007, and Zaniboni 2007.

out in order to make herself unattractive, and the various medieval literary treatments derived from Jacobus de Voragine, which are structured and expressed in an entirely different way. His analysis, which offers a broad survey of materials drawn from a variety of languages and periods, cautions against the danger of generalization, showing that Lucy's cult was by no means static, and was in certain instances conflated with materials derived from alternative textual sources. This produces a certain degree of incongruity, with the saint's status as patron of eyesight and diseases of the eye effectively challenged elsewhere by contradictory modes of representation.[2]

A more ambitious analysis is that of Magdalena Elizabeth Carrasco (1985), whose discussion of an early illustrated manuscript cycle of the passion of Saint Agatha for the first time offered readers an intellectual framework in which to place the legend. Carrasco's work shows that although there are common elements, the emphasis of the narrative is often subject to variation. In some versions, as is the case with Voragine, Agatha is suspended above the ground so that she can be tortured more effectively. In some the focus falls on a single breast, which is implacably severed, while in others the remit of the narrative is developed and expanded in order to refer to both (1985: 25). Similar divergences can be seen in the instruments of torture, which are sometimes depicted as pincers or long poles, but on other occasions specifically as knives, rakes, shears, or even ropes. Saint Peter, in contrast, is in one illustration identified by a key, while in another he places his curative hand on the saint's chest as she stares back in wonderment. In one illustration Agatha 'appears at the threshold of an architectural structure whose towered forms suggest her nobility and wealth and

---

2   'Y como todos hemos visto representada a Santa Lucía con los ojos en un plato, lo primero que ocurre es ir al santoral y leer su vida. La confusion nace en seguida; en la vida de Santa Lucía, tal como aparece en los textos más comunes, no hay nada relacionado con los ojos' (1942: 12). As proof, he offers a transcription of BNM 12688 (1942: 13-17). For a corroborating analysis, see Capdevila 1949, but perhaps more important are the later poems by Alonso de Ledesma ('Entre las vírgines juega / la belíssima Lucía' and 'Un ciervo voraz os sigue, / tanto, que os sacais los ojos / por estorbar sus antojos'), which focus specifically on the saint's eyes (see Sancha 1855: 173 no.421 & 317 no.914).

the sheltered life she so abruptly leaves behind' (1985: 21). Perhaps the most striking innovation, however, is the introduction of 'lapidatores', who, in a gruesome development, stand ready to stone her to death if she refuses to submit to Quintianus's demands.

Carrasco's study, which offers a finely nuanced reading of the relationship between text and paratext in a sample illuminated manuscript, was accompanied in the same year by Santo D'Arrigo's historical and legal analysis (1985), and shortly afterwards, by Liana de Girolami Cheney's examination of later artistic representations (1986). This work expanded on earlier studies by focusing on the question of Agatha's intelligence and eloquence, which, as she rightly affirms, 'attest to her intellectual and cultural training as a *nobil donna*' (1986: 3). The most significant discussion of the visual dimension, however, is that of Martha Easton (1995), whose analysis of the sanctification of sexual violence is underpinned by an application of reader-response theory in which the location of meaning is shifted from object to audience. Easton's approach shows not only that there are a broad range of possible responses to a work of art, but that the dichotomy between message and response is fluid and often blurred. This, as one might expect, impacts on the perception of meaning and the production of interpretative responses, which are both varied and gradational.

Easton argues, in view of this, that the severing of Agatha's breast, which is the most commonly depicted aspect of her legend, can be appraised from simultaneously erotic and theological perspectives. The tension between the two, which is in part responsible for her popularity, is subject to finite variation, and perhaps the most notable distinction in this respect can be seen in the relationship between art and literature, for while the former generally depicts the severing of two breasts, the latter usually only mentions one (1995: 88). The overwhelming majority of extant medieval images of the saint, particularly those in manuscripts, would of course have been employed in liturgical contexts (1995: 92), and so in this light it also becomes important to measure the sadistic and voyeuristic potential embedded in the torture scene against the timeless image of the breast as a source of life-giving sustenance, notably in the context of traditional Christian exegesis.

Agatha, in this respect, becomes a conflation of sacrificial victim and sexual woman, and although critics, eager to detect gendered patterns of sympathy, have read such scenes as products of fetishistic scopophilia, it becomes simplistic, Easton argues, 'to assume that male viewers identify only with Agatha's male torturers or view Agatha's displayed body with the same sexualized voyeurism as does Quintianus' (1995: 99). Agatha, in fact, experiences a form of sexualized rejection in which desire manifests itself as coercion and violence. Her torture and martyrdom may be underpinned by elements of sadomasochistic eroticism focused on the most visible outward sign of her sexuality, but in sacrificing herself she becomes a Christological surrogate, and is in this respect likely to evoke empathy rather than desire. The way in which she is occasionally depicted—suspended above the ground, arms outstretched, while those below poke at her with long-handled implements—enhances the extent of the similarity. A further visual correspondence, of course, is with Lucy, whose traditionally gouged out eyes function as a physical correlative of Agatha's severed breasts.

In an application of psychosexual criticism, Easton reads Agatha's forced double mastectomy as a parallel of castration, in this way relating breasts to testicles not merely in shape and form, but in their function as visible signs of sexuality and the ensuing production or nurturing of offspring. Agatha's severed breast could in this light be read 'as a visual signifier for the threat of castration' (1995: 101). She also argues that by dispensing with her breasts, Agatha enters into 'a process of masculinization that connotes a state of spiritual grace attainable by women only if they suppress physical and social indicators that are understood to be manifestations of the female' (1995: 103). This, she affirms, establishes an empathetic response on the part of male viewers, who would in this way identify with her, understand her rational behaviour and androgynous looks as male-gendered, and no longer feel sexually threatened. Further evidence of transformation can be seen in the fact that by idealizing the female virgin and contemplating her wounds, the male viewer would experience a secondary process of gendered inversion, as he effectively 'becomes infantilized and sees the object of his mythical devotion as a mother figure' (1995: 105).

The fluidity of these relationships is paralleled by not only by female viewers, who would have regarded the severing of Agatha's breast as an image of sanctity rather than of sexualized violence, but by Agatha, who submits herself provocatively to torture so as to separate the wheat from the chaff and thereby enter heaven. The result, Easton claims, is that it becomes difficult to understand the relationship between sadism and masochism in isolation from the question of power, either in relation to Agatha, who exploits violence for personal gain, or the female viewer, who could be regarded as empowered by experiencing, and in this way, sharing, the spiritual witness of a surrogate female Christ. This leads her to conclude by focusing on the question of ambivalence, noting that 'the mutilation and public display of the saint's private body creates a simultaneously empathetic and voyeuristic response. [Agatha] becomes a conflation of heroic and anti-heroic body, epitomizing physicality yet denying it, glorifying femininity yet reworking it' (1995: 109).

The first discrete literary examination of Agatha's legend—an article by Kirsten Wolf on the topos of the severed breast (1997b)—reiterates some of Easton's conclusions but is predicated on different branches of theory. Wolf's point of departure is the excessive and spectacular nature of Agatha's physical suffering, which, as she maintains, is sexually orientated. As a counterpoint, she discusses the legends of various male saints, but her most illuminating example is James the Dismembered, who is subjected to twenty-nine forced amputations, beginning with his fingers and toes, followed by his hands, feet, arms, and eventually, his head. Most noteworthy is that 'in comparison with those of female virgin martyrs, so many of which have their breasts, the most visible sign of their female gender, severed, is not so much what is cut off, but what is not cut off: the insignia of his maleness. In fact, not a single male martyr is described as being castrated' (1997b: 100).[3]

---

3   For discussions of the body, torture, and dismemberment in the *Legenda aurea*, see Pouchelle 1976 and Bynum 1990: 82-84, and for broader theoretical

In the light of the distinction between the sexes, Wolf offers an analysis of the relationship between sexuality, sadism, and eroticism, citing Thomas J. Heffernan's view that the 'dominant image of the female invariably turned sacred biography into something akin to a sexual melodrama, replete with anguish and physical cruelty depicted in an unashamedly erotic manner' (1988: 281-82).[4] The central portion of her discussion, however, is centred on the theology of womanhood and patristic views of the female body, and whilst accepting that the legends of female saints could be regarded as 'a by-product of some libidinal restraint that generates vivid sexual fantasizing under the guise of anti-sensual polemics' (1997b: 101-02), Wolf cites the example of Catherine of Alexandria, who served in the Middle Ages as a model of piety and courage. This, she notes, is the result of Catherine's exceptional intellectual superiority and eloquence, factors that can be seen in the debate between her and the pagan philosophers (which, of course, she wins) and that led to an explosion in her popularity, particularly as patroness and advisor to holy women.[5]

Although all of the tortures that are inflicted on saints can be viewed as ritualized re-enactments of Christ's suffering on the Cross (a process known as *imitatio Christi*), Wolf argues that the focus on the breast, which is commonly 'battered, burned, pierced, cut or severed entirely' occurs so frequently that 'it is nearly formulaic' (1997b: 103). To explain this obsession she draws on the work of John Anson, who,

---

considerations, Scarry 1985, Brown 1988, Boureau & Semple 1994, Naguib 1994, Semple 1994, and Stuart 1996.

4   Wolf draws on the work of Gad (1971: 58) and Carlé (1980), but most thought provoking is the incorporation of Clarissa W. Atkinson's (1983: 189) working distinction between erotic ('designed to arouse sexual feelings') and pornographic ('arouse such feelings through suggestion of violence, abuse, or degradation of the sexual object'). The distinction, Wolf argues, is often overlooked, particularly in relation the question of reception by audiences not necessarily comprised exclusively of men (1997b: 101n15).

5   Catherine's fate differs from that of the queen, whom she converts, and who is later subjected to the severing of her breasts—a point considered later in this discussion. For recent approaches to Catherine, see Lewis 2000, Jenkins & Lewis 2003, and Walsh 2007, and with reference to Spain, Knust 1890 and Francomano 2003.

in a seminal treatment of the female transvestite, offers a comparison with the legends of the virgin martyrs, affirming that in addition to bringing to mind connotations of 'latent sexual sadism of great psychological interest' (1974: 27), the severed breast could potentially be read as a euphemism 'for the pre-execution defloration of virgins practised to meet the Roman law that forbade their execution' (1974: 27n69). This ensures that although we cannot discount the possibility that the sufferings of female saints provide an echo of ancient Roman legislature, we cannot, by the same token, take the severed breast purely as an example of male aggression, but 'a synecdoche that has nearly become a hagiographic cliché [in which] sexually humiliating tortures should not be summarily dismissed as mere fantasy or exaggeration, but be viewed as allegorical' (1997b: 104).

This point leads to a consideration of the legend of Agnes, where virginity is presented as a prerequisite for salvation, and that of Cecilia, where the saint admonishes her husband on their wedding night about the value of corporeal integrity. These texts show that while sexual activity erodes consciousness and rational control, virginity draws the individual away from the corporeal and relocates a core of being within the spiritual that promotes an intensified form of divine love that approximates a recovery of the purer prelapsarian state (1997b: 105). This, of course, is a telling factor in the representation of male and female saints alike, although its influence is disproportionate. The reason is that the soul-flesh dualism that grows out of the traditional male-female bipolarity in patristic theology is predicated on a fundamental imbalance, with the conflict of body versus soul becoming important only to women. The result is that although the souls of male and female were considered equal (Galatians 3:28), their bodies were not, and as the flesh was inferior to the soul, women were subordinate to men. This ensures that transcendence of the flesh is presented as a severing of ties with Eve, and that the preservation of virginity allows women to achieve parity with men, even to the point of adopting male attributes. In this light, salvation is a repudiation of sexuality and a negation of nature—it is a process of approximating the male (1997b: 106).

As examples of the struggle for sexless perfection, Wolf discusses Perpetua, who imagines a confrontation in the amphitheatre in which she is stripped naked and becomes a man (Shewring 1931: 10), along with Pelagia and Marina, who 'shed all affinity with the female sex by literally donning a male disguise' (1997b: 107). In relation to the latter, she expands with reference to the work of Vern L. Bullough (1974), noting that despite the traditional hostility to transvestism (see Deuteronomy 22:5), the division in practice between the sexes was not uniform. The reason is that while the female transvestite would be imitating the superior sex and attempting to become rational, the male transvestite would merely experience a loss in status (1997b: 108). For Bullough, the duality is such that while there are no male transvestite saints, 'the Christian Church to a certain extent encouraged women to adopt the guise of men and live like men in order to attain the higher level of spirituality normally reserved for males' (1974: 1383). This female-to-male metamorphosis, however, can never wholly be completed, for despite assuming masculine traits, female saints are unable to escape their inherent weakness—unless, of course, they do so by drawing strength from Christ, the celestial bridegroom. The result is that in this way they revert to their gendered stereotype, tempering suggestions of autonomy by confirming their Christological dependence.[6]

In Wolf's eyes, the fact that hagiography is able to extol matters of the soul and negate those of the body whilst dwelling simultaneously on female saintly corporeality, is paradoxical. However, paradox stands at the centre of the virgin martyr tradition, as the saint 'navigates the movement from the corporeal to the spiritual' and in so doing finds herself 'stripped of the outward mark of gender identity' (1997b: 109). Furthermore, in suffering a violent and sexual mutilation of the body with specific emphasis on torments that negate the perceived function of the virgin martyr as sexual and procreative, she effectively 'redefines herself as *sponsa Christi* within the celestial state' (1997b: 109). The process begins 'with [the] self-denial of her own sex-

---

6   See also Delcourt 1958 and 1961, Anson 1974, McLaughlin 1974, Meeks 1974, Bullough 1977, Salisbury 1991: 97-110, Jantzen 1995: 43-58, Hotchkiss 1996, Stuart 1996: 60-61, and to a lesser extent, French 1998.

uality, [and] moves through the mutilation of the outward signs of the sexual presence to achieve, paradoxically, authentication of the sexual self realized in spiritual union with God' (1997b: 109). This ensures that that physicality is not only a woman's problem but her solution (see Robertson 1991), and for this reason issues relating to the body are of primary importance in the description of the trials to which female saints are subjected.

The breast is the most visual aspect of the saint's womanliness, and in view of this Wolf argues that its amputation 'presents in a dramatic and concrete manner the defeminization which, according to medieval theologians, is essential for her salvation' (1997b: 110). In this light it becomes clear that Agatha can almost become a spiritual equal to the male, but she can only do so by transcending the weakness and limitations of her female nature to become a sexless being. This point is sustained in relation to the work of Thomas J. Heffernan, who maintains that the virgin 'becomes the bride of God, and finally the mother of God, while retaining her virginity. Her breasts as the symbol of her maternity are mutilated and finally severed, to underscore the miraculous metamorphosis of the virgin into a nurturing mother and deity in her own right' (1988: 283). Needless to say, the incorporation of elements of eroticism and pornography in scenes of physical mutilation tempers the power of this relationship, and it is an awareness of this that leads Wolf to conclude by affirming that 'the final transformation of the virgin—the ungendering of the body that paradoxically reengenders it as bride and nurturing mother—refocuses the narrative away from male discourse and appropriation, reclaiming it within a specifically female locus distinct from male experience' (1997b: 110).

Torture, the Breast, and the Castilian Context
Critical studies of the legend of Saint Agatha, particularly the contributions by Carrasco (1985), Easton (1995), and Wolf (1997b), have done much to shed light not merely on its content and orientation, but a number of deeper questions. These include the gendering and sexualization of the female religious experience, the relationship between torturer and tortured subject, and the symbolic connotations of

the breast. This research, which can be read alongside González Palencia's examination of traditions associated with Saint Lucy (1942), has enriched our critical understanding and provided a solid platform for detailed theoretical and conceptual analysis. Despite these advances, however, the bond between Agatha and Lucy—the only virgin martyrs to be explicitly linked in Voragine's canon at the level of plot and narrative development—has not yet been subjected to detailed critical scrutiny. A cognate issue concerns the application of existing branches of theory and the extent to which ideas developed in relation to parallel representations composed at different times, in different languages, or in different media should necessarily inform our understanding of the medieval Castilian recensions or the frameworks in which they appear.

As the analysis of source and translation context in Chapters 1-4 has shown, the legends of Agatha and Lucy can be found in Castilian in Compilations A and B, which were reworked independently (and in differing ways) during the late fourteenth century from the Latin text composed by Jacobus de Voragine in the 1260s. The process of adaptation and development is not one that is complicated by questions of grammatical, cultural, or spiritual incompatibility, and so it becomes logical to assume that distinctions between the two versions are the result of specific strategies of reworking. In Compilation A, as we have seen, the formal organization of the texts, with their polished lexical formulation and incorporation of oral formulas, suggests that they were written specifically with the requirements of oral delivery in mind—perhaps to monks as they ate in the refectory or in the context of the liturgy. In Compilation B, in contrast, the transition from Latin to Castilian is more complex, and in addition to a certain intricacy of syntax, the texts are marked by a tendency towards sensationalism and a corresponding rejection of many of Voragine's more abstract or overly theological turns of phrase. This produces streamlined narratives, which are further modified by a secondary stage of development that took place exclusively in the vernacular.

The result of this complex process of textual dissemination is that the representation of Agatha and Lucy, and of sanctity in general, becomes subject to a finite process of variation, with the identity of the saints and the circumstances of their martyrdoms honed to suit the requirements of a series of differing contexts. The distinction between versions is by no means as great as that which can be seen in relation to other female saints, notably Thecla, who begins life as an evangelizing apostle but is eventually transformed into a virgin martyr, or Apollonia, who suffers a corresponding diminution in status from elderly and venerable virgin to vulnerable teenage princess. It is, however, important to bear González Palencia's (1942) work in mind, and to recognize that it is difficult to see either that there is a single Lucy or a single Agatha, or indeed, a definitive version of their legends. In fact, both can be found in a variety of subtly differing incarnations.[7]

A parallel consideration concerns the formation of the Castilian Compilations and the establishment of a frame of reference in which individual aspects of the two legends can be understood in relation to analogous or dissimilar representations. A commonly cited analogue is the legend of Saint Perpetua (7 March), which offers a description of a scene in which the saint imagines that she has been stripped of her clothes and becomes a man (Wolf 1997b: 107). The episode, which counterpoints various aspects of the way in which Agatha is represented in the early Castilian narratives, can be read as the embodiment of a broad tradition of gender transformation in which female saints are granted the status of honorary males. However, as the legend does not appear in either of the medieval Castilian Compilations (or, indeed, elsewhere in the early Castilian canon), we should be wary of assuming that it should necessarily be regarded as an influence on medieval Castilian hagiography.[8]

---

7   For Thecla, see Rordorf 1986, Hayne 1994, and Davis 1998 and 2001, and for Apollonia, Beresford 2001. For further information on art and its influence, see amongst others, Capdevila 1949, Carrasco 1985, Winstead 1997: 25-32, Burke 2006, Lucca 2007, and Malesani 2007.

8   In a much later and highly stylized composition, 'No es la felicidad el gran linaje' (Sancha 1855: 304-05 no.724), Cairasco de Figueroa pairs Perpetua with Felicity, but does not mention the episode in the amphitheatre. Earlier references to the saint are not recorded.

Similar problems affect the representation of the severed breast and the extent to which we can regard Agatha's suffering as part of a tradition of sadistic torture. Theodosia of Tyre (2 April), for instance, is reputed to have had her breasts torn with hooks and then severed, while Encratia (16 April) was subjected to a forced mastectomy as one of the Eighteen Martyrs of Saragossa. The fortunes of the latter are recorded by none other than Prudentius in Carmen IV of his *Peristephanon liber* (lines 109-44), but despite her status as a Spanish national saint, her legend (as is the case with the more obscure Theodosia) was not incorporated into either of the medieval Castilian Compilations.[9] The same is true of Victoria (23 December), who is reputed to have been stabbed in the breast (Butler 1903: IV, 756), Reparata (8 October), who had hers mutilated by branding irons (Yalom 1997: 36), and Julia Falconieri (19 June), whose breasts were found in death with the mark of the host upon them (Butler 1903: II, 604-05).

A more notable omission is Dorothy (6 February), who although occasionally cited as an analogue, was not included in Voragine's original. A copy of her legend was subsequently appended to a number of later manuscript versions of the *Legenda aurea*, but as is the case elsewhere, it was not reworked into Castilian in the Middle Ages, either within the two Compilations or as a fleeting reference embedded into a larger work. In this respect, despite the fact that she is subjected to a variety of savage tortures, including the searing of her breast with burning torches, her relationship to the various Castilian incarnations of Agatha is more tenuous than it might at first appear.[10]

---

9   For Theodosia, see Butler 1903: II, 17-18, and for Encratia, Butler 1903: II, 93-95 and Petruccione 1991 and 1995. Jane Frances de Chantal (21 August), who falls outside the chronological remit of this discussion, is reputed to have inscribed the name of Christ onto her breast (Butler 1903: III, 427-35).

10   'Ipsa autem Dorothea equuleo est suspensa pedibus elevatis, uncis laceratur corpus ejus, virgis castigatur, flagellis flagellatur, deinde ad mammillas virginis faculae ardentes applicate sunt et ipsa semimortua usque ad crastinum reclusa est' (Graesse 1846: 911). See also Wolf 1997a, and for an important critique, Cormack 2000. A counterpoint to Dorothy's representation is Francisco de Zurbarán's painting (of around 1640) in which she is presented in elegant period dress.

Other potential analogues prove to be equally elusive. The legend of Saint Sophia and her Daughters, for instance, offers a series of graphic descriptions of torture, the most significant of which appear in relation to the eldest daughter, Faith. In Voragine's version she is beaten by thirty-six soldiers before having her breasts torn off. Miraculously, milk rather than blood flows from her wounds, but although many of those in attendance object to the torture, her tormentor, the emperor, remains unimpressed. As a result, he has her thrown onto a red-hot grid-iron, basted in a frying pan full of oil and wax, and eventually beheaded.[11] As is the case with Dorothy, the episode offers a number of significant points of contact in relation to the severing of Agatha's breast. The fact, however, that it was not subsequently reworked into Castilian suggests once again that we should be wary of classifying it as anything other than an illustration of a broad tradition.

Some analogues are shaped in such a way as to deflect attention away from the breast. A notable example is Margaret of Antioch, whose legend was incorporated into the *Legenda aurea* and reworked thereafter into both of the medieval Castilian Compilations. In all of the extant accounts Margaret is subjected to a variety of gruesome tortures. She is imprisoned, hung on a rack, beaten with rods, lacerated with rakes, stripped, and burned. The last of the tortures would almost certainly, as is the case with Dorothy, have affected her breasts, but it is noticeable that the Castilian texts comment only on the extent of the damage to her body as a whole:[12]

> E otro día ayuntóse el pueblo e fue trayda Santa Margarita delante el adelantado, e non queriendo sacrificar, fue desnudada; e fue quemado todo el cuerpo con fachas ardiendo fasta los huesos

---

11   'Fides primo a XXXVI militibus caeditur, secundo mamillae praecisae coram cunctis evelluntur, lac de vulneribus, sed de mamillis sanguis profluit' (Graesse 1846: 203).

12   BNM 780 fol. 246[vb], but see also BMP 8 fol. 46[ra] and FLG 419 fol. 81rb, which deal with the episode in a similar way. Significantly, the episode is omitted in its entirety from the other manuscripts of Compilation B: Escorial K-II-12 fol. 113va, Escorial M-II-6 fol. 101[r], and Escorial h-I-14 fol. 167rb.

en man*er*a q*ue* todos se maravillava*n* como moça tan tierna podía sofrir tan grandes penas.

Elsewhere in the early Castilian canon, notably in the *Poema de Fernán González*, the *Libro de buen amor*, and Juan de Padilla's *Doze triumfos*, Margaret is identified with the most thought-provoking episode in her martyrdom, her victory over the dragon.[13]

In other legends emphasis falls on the breast but is either expressed differently or integrated into a different type of narrative structure. Perhaps the most telling example is Barbara, whose legend was appended to the *Legenda aurea* and reworked thereafter into both of the Castilian Compilations. In Compilation A the emphasis of the narrative falls on the act of severing, with the prefect's anger boiling over into a rage that unbalances him: 'E oyendo aq*ue*sto, el adelantado fue muy yrado e mandóle cortar las tetas' (BNM 780 fol. 143rb, but see also Escorial h-III-22 fol. 412vb). The episode, however, is not otherwise developed, and in contrast to Agatha, who remarks on the severing of the organ from which her inquisitor drew life, Barbara merely prays for a solution to her nakedness. A further distinction becomes apparent during the act of restoration, which focuses not on Barbara's breast, but the wounds she has received and the dress that covers her modesty: 'E vino luego un ángell del Señor e sanóla de todas sus llagas, e no*n* quedó en *e*lla una sola señal, e vistióla de una vestidura de grand claridat' (BNM 780 fol. 143rb, but see also Escorial h-III-22 fol. 413ra). This approach is all but duplicated in Compilation B, which, despite a tendency to gloss and expand, presents her reaction much as it is in the Latin, with the emphasis of the narrative falling on the bizarre and protracted succession of tortures to which she is subjected.[14]

---

13 Compare respectively 'e del dragon libreste a la virgen Maryna' (Zamora Vicente 1946: 32, st. 106c), 'a la santa Marina librest' del vientre del dragón / libra a mí, Dios mío, d'esta presión do yaga' (Joset 1974: 3; st. 3cd), and 'Aqui resplandece la virgen Margarita, / con el triunfo del vasto dragon' (Foulché-Delbosc 1912-15: I, 349, st. 9ab). For a study of iconographic representations, see Rodado Ruiz 1990. For Zurbarán's pictorial tribute, see Brown 1991: 84-85.

14 See Escorial K-II-12 fol. 8rb, FLG 419 fol. 206ra, and Escorial h-I-14 fol. 7rb. Ancillary references to Barbara do not appear elsewhere in Castilian before Diego

The legend of Saint Christina, which appears in Voragine and both of the Castilian Compilations, is broadly comparable. In all of the extant versions Christina is subjected to a variety of torments, including the breaking of her limbs and the tearing of her flesh with hooks. She is even stretched on a flaming wheel and thrown into the sea with a large stone tied around her neck. The most significant torture, however, comes towards the end of the narrative, as Julianus, the last of her tormentors, orders the severing of her breasts. In common with the treatment of Faith, the eldest of Sophia's daughters, the action is undertaken as planned, but it is milk rather than blood that flows from the wounds: 'E el adelantado Juliano, veyendo aquesto, mandóle cortar las tetas. E en lugar de sangre salió leche dellas' (BNM 780 fol. 258ra). The episode, which is phrased all but identically in Compilation B, is not otherwise developed, and moments later, having seen his latest attempt at torture come to nothing, Julianus moves onto a different part of the body—in this instance severing her tongue. The result is that the relationship between her and Agatha is in this way much diminished, with the breast seen not as the central and most significant torture, but one of many.[15]

Sánchez de Badajoz (see Wiltrout 1971), while the two most significant versions in Catalan say nothing about the saint's breasts. Compare, for instance, *De Santa Barbara* in the *Vides de sants rosselloneses* (Maneikis Kniazzeh & Neugarrd 1977: III, 474) and the *Cobles fetes en laor de la gloriosa senta Barbera* in the *Cançoner sagrat de vides de sants* (Foulché-Delbosc & Massó y Torrents 1912: II, 162-67).

15   See Escorial K-II-12 fol. 122va and Escorial h-I-14 fol. 183rb. A related aspect of symbolism, covered in the *Espéculo de los legos*, focuses on the life-giving and maternal qualities of the breast: 'Leese en la vida de Santa Christina, que commo ella estouiese delante el juez por la fe de Ihesu Christo, vino su madre con las vestiduras rasgadas e el cabello despedaçado e el pecho decubierto e demostrandole las tetas con que fuera criada porque la apartase del proposito de la fe, mas ella teniendo mientes más a Dios que a los parientes, perseueró en la fé, queriendo más morir por Dios que beuir a los parientes. Esta pudo dezir aquello del Apostol en el otauo capitulo a los Romanos: ¿Quién nos apartará de la caridat de Ihesu Christo? ¿La angustia o la fanbre o la desnuedat o la persecuçión o el peligro o el cuchillo? Onde el bienauenturado San Jeronimo dize a Heliodoro en la Epistola triçesima terçia: Aunque la madre te demuestre las tetas con que te crió, con cabello messado e con uestiduras rasgadas, e aunque yaga el padre en el unbral, pasa pisando al padre e buela con ojos secos a la sennal de la cruz de Ihesu Christo, ca piedat es ser en esta cosa

A more noticeable diminution in emphasis can be seen in the legend of Catherine of Alexandria in the fate of the queen who upbraids the emperor for his cruelty and is sentenced to be tortured and killed. The Compilation B version follows Voragine relatively closely, while Compilation A offers an account that is much embellished:[16]

> 'Yo te juro [...] que si non te arrepentieres luego [...] e non adorares a los nuestros dioses, que te faré arrancar con grandes tormentos las tetas de los pechos e cortar la tu cabeça e echar las tus carnes a las aves e a las bestias.' [...] E tomándola entonces los carniceros, lleváronla fuera de la cibdad e arrancáronle las tetas de los pechos con garanatos de fierro. E después cortáronle la cabeça e acabó esta vida por martirio bienaventurado. (Escorial h-II-18, fol. 256^{ra-rb}, but see also BNM 12689 fol. 207va)

A common denominator in both Compilations is that the amputation functions not as a self-contained or structurally important episode in its own right, but as the first stage of martyrdom. In contrast to other legends, therefore, where female subjects are subjected to a progression of tortures, each one generally more severe that the last, the fate of the queen is sealed by the emperor's first pronouncement. In this respect, despite the presence of an obvious thematic and conceptual point of contact, the relationship between her and Agatha is more tenuous than it might at first appear.

Other analogues recorded in the Compilations deal not with severing, but acts of mutilation directed specifically against the breast. In a miracle included in the reading for Peter Martyr, for instance, a woman plagued by demons approaches the saint's tomb in the hope of finding a solution to her predicament. Initially, the demons resist, but before long they abandon her body—in the process tearing the skin vengefully from her neck and breast. The woman falls half dead in a

---

crúel' (Mohedano Hernández 1951: 31, ch. VII, no.46). This parallels the reaction of the mother of Marcellian and Marcus, who in Voragine's treatment of Saint Sebastian, bares her breast when her sons are martyred.

16 See BMP 9, fol. 57ra, FLG 419 fol. 153^{ra-rb}, and Escorial h-I-14 fol. 312^{ra-rb}.

swoon, but as a result of the saint's posthumous power, she soon finds that her wounds have been healed.[17]

A related incident appears in the legend of Mary of Egypt, as the saint offers a symbolic display of contrition by weeping profusely and tearing savagely at her breasts—the most tangibly feminine symbol of her sexual allure: 'començé a llorar e a aver grand contrición además, e a ferir mis pechos, e ha suspirar de todo coraçón además' (Thompson & Walsh: 1977: 19). As is the case in the previous example, Mary's breasts remain intact. The attempt at self-mutilation, however, provides more than a passing reminiscence not simply of the ordeal to which Agatha is subjected, but the way in which the destruction of the most anatomically visible sign of her gender impacts on the representation of gendered identity.[18]

A final example, unique to the Castilian Compilations, can be seen in the legend of the virgin martyr, Eulalia of Merida, who, at the age of thirteen is tortured by her oppressor, Calpurnian, for refusing to submit to his desires. The Compilation B version, preserved in Escorial K-II-12 (fols 13[ra]-14[ra]), offers a relatively compressed version of events and makes no specific reference to the breast. In Compilation A, in contrast, Eulalia is subjected to a dazzling and implausible series of torments. These include burning, beating, whipping, roasting, crucifixion, and most importantly, the searing of her breasts with oil:[19]

> E oyendo aquesto Calpurniano dixo a sus servidores: 'Traed azeyte e escalentaldo fasta que fierva e echádgelo sobre las tetas.' E traxieron luego el azeyte e escalentáronlo, e tendiéronla en tierra e

---

17   For Compilation A, see BNM 780 fol. 94vb and Escorial h-III-22 fols 405vb-06ra, and for Compilation B, Escorial K-II-12 fol. 84rb, FLG 419 fol. 164va, Escorial h-I-14 fol. 105va, and Escorial M-II-6 fol. 71[v].

18   For Compilation B, see Thompson & Walsh 1977: 35-46, Scarborough 1994, and Baños Vallejo & Uría Maqua 2000: 121-23.

19   For the legend of Eulalia of Barcelona, which borrows a number of key elements, see BNM 780 fols 149rb-51vb, BNM 12688 fols 277vb-79vb, and Escorial h-III-22 fols 526rb-28va, and for discussions, Butler 1903: IV, 694-97, Fábrega Grau 1957, Petruccione 1990, Farmer 1997: 174, and Haliczer 2002: 236.

echárongelo firviendo sobre las tetas. (BNM 780 fol. 386^{ra-rb}, but see also BNM 12688 fol. 50va and Escorial h-III-22 fol. 432va)

SEX, TORTURE, AND GENDER

A survey of the Castilian Compilations shows that various legends focus on the power and potential of the breast. In some the breast is severed, while in others it is severed and subsequently restored. In some the emphasis falls on the pain of torture, while in one instance torture is self-inflicted. Some breasts are burned, some are mutilated, and some bleed milk. Narrative strategies, and the position of the breast within them, are as complex as they are varied; and while in some examples the breast is central to the intellectual and conceptual development of a legend, on other occasions it appears purely in the context of a sequence of barbaric acts and is not otherwise singled out as being worthy of comment. The result, as far as the Castilian Compilations are concerned, is that the focus on the breast, although common, cannot by any means be regarded as formulaic. In fact, Agatha, who has her breast severed and restored in the context of a narrative dealing specifically with the act of restoration, is the exception rather than the norm.

In the absence of a common denominator, the depiction of the breast raises a series of further questions. One of the most significant concerns the sexualization of torture and the extent to which the experiences of saints such as Agatha can be regarded as representative of a genuinely rigid distinction between the sexes. A partial answer to this question can be found in the legend of Vitus, where in contrast to the traditionally binary representation of male aggression pitted against innocent female vulnerability, the young saint refuses to acquiesce to his father's demands and is subjected to a form of sexualized coercion in which he is locked in a room and surrounded by music, dancing, and women of easy virtue. The incident, which functions as one of a number of attempts to undermine his commitment to Christianity, is modified in Compilation A, which conflates the roles of musician and prostitute ('fizo traer muchos joglares por mudar el coraçón del moço', BNM fol. 194vb), and presented in a series of differing ways in Compilation B. Its retention in both, however, suggests that we should be wary of assuming that the sexualization of torture is necessarily gender specific, or that the legends of female saints can be read in isolation from those of their male counterparts.[20]

A brief survey of comparable readings confirms this impression. Thomas Aquinas, for instance, whose legend was overlooked by Voragine but incorporated thereafter into Compilation A, attempts to enter holy orders but is subjected to an all but identical ordeal:

> E veyendo aquesto los hermanos carnales, tomáronlo por fuerça e pusiéronlo en una torre, asý como en cárcel. E como el varón santo non pudiese ser apartado de su entinción por amenzas nin por afálagos e palabras blandas, quisieron quebrantar la fortaleza de la su bondat por la cobdicia de la delectación carnal, e fizieron que entrase una muger a dormir con él. E veyéndola el santo mancebo, arrebató un tizón del fuego e echó con él fuera de la cámara a aquella mala muger que entrara a tentar la su castidat. E fizo la señal de la cruz e derribóse en tierra a orar con toda humildat, e rogó al Señor con muchas lágrimas que le pluguiese de le dar perseverança de castidat. (BNM 780 fol. 147rb, but see also BNM 12688 fol. 292$^{rb\text{-}va}$, and Escorial h-III-22 fols 530vb-31ra)

While Vitus is tortured by his father, Thomas is set upon by his brothers, who, in an attempt to undermine his commitment to chastity, imprison him in a tower with a woman of easy virtue. His actions, which ensure the preservation of his corporeal integrity, are predicated on an assumption that sexual contact is a polluting force and that its imposition in the form of torture must be resisted. This leads him,

---

20 'Tunc eum in domum ducens diversis musicorum generibus et puellarum insibus aliarumque deliciarum generibus immutare animam pueri satagebat' (350). Escorial h-I-14 has 'e troxo allí muchos joglares e trabajávanse mucho de le mudar de coraçón' (fol. 127va), and it is perhaps worth noting in this respect that the harlot saint, Pelagia, is referred to as 'huna juglara muy fremosa' (Beresford 2007b: 141). However, the adoption of 'instrumentos de cantares' in Escorial K-II-12 (fol. 99va) and the elimination of the episode in Escorial M-II-6 (fol. 81^{v}) shows that the emphasis of the narrative is variable.

rather pointedly, to counter the all-consuming fire of passion by drawing a carbonized ember from the fire in order to drive the woman away. Thereafter, it provides him with a means with which to draw a crucifix on the wall, and in so doing identify his lifelong commitment to chastity with that of Christ. The text in this way manipulates a clearly sexualized frame of reference, which, taken in conjunction with potentially phallic quality of the tower in which the action unfolds, can be read as powerful comment on the dangers to which male saints can be subjected.[21]

A counterpoint to both episodes can be seen in the reading for Saint Benedict, where the evil priest, Florentius, first attempts to poison the saint, but eventually resorts to a more elaborate form of coercion. This sees him contract the services of seven girls who dance naked in the orchard of the monastery in an attempt to undermine Benedict's virtue:

> E veyendo el preste Florencio que non lo pudiera matar con aquel pan ervolado, tornóse a buscar otro consejo e a querer matar las almas de los discípulos de Sant Benito. E fizo entrar a cantar e dançar e baylar a siete moças desnudas en una huerta del monesterio del santo abad por que pudiese mover sus monjes a las cobdiciar. E veyendo aquello el varón santo, e temiendo el daño de los discípulos, dio logar a la enbidia e tomó consigo algunos monjes e fuése de allí a otro logar. (Escorial h-III-22 fol. 205rb, but see also BNM 12688 fol. 314^{ra-rb})

In this instance the threat of temptation is multiplied, as Benedict and his fellows are surrounded not by one girl but seven, who, as is the case in the legend of Saint Vitus, manifest their sexual allure and availability in the time-honoured form of dancing. The location of the

---

21 The temptation of Thomas Aquinas is a popular subject in painting, and perhaps most worthy of note are the works of Pedro Berruguete (Brown 1998: 21) and Velázquez (Brown & Garrido 1998: 62-69 and Carr et al 2006: 158-61), which opt for slightly differing interpretations, with the former emphasizing resilience and determination, and the latter, human weakness and frailty.

episode in an orchard brings to mind the traditional pleasures of the *locus amoenus*, but a more convincing parallel is with Eve, the fruit of temptation, and the Expulsion from Paradise. It is perhaps an awareness of this that leads the saint to rescue his fellow monks and flee, for with the sacred space of the monastery now tainted and violated by lust, it becomes clear that the prelapsarian calm of the cloister has effectively been destroyed from within.

A common denominator in the readings for Vitus, Thomas, and Benedict is that in each instance a source of temptation is introduced by an external force into an enclosed space that functions almost as a type of prison. The saints, drawing on their commitment to virtue, find it relatively easy to resist, and are not in any way corporeally violated by the experience. The extent of the similarity between the three accounts suggests that the imposition of sexualized torture, although evident, is by no means as significant a factor as it is in the legends of female saints. There are, however, a number of exceptions, and a striking example is Christopher, whose legend was included by Voragine in the *Legenda aurea* but appears only in Compilation B:

> E fizo encerrar en la cárcel dos niñas muy fermosas, e a la una dizién Nicea, e a la otra Aquilina, e prometiéndoles muchas cosas syl pudiesen adozir a que peccase con ellas. E entendiólo Christóval, e echóse luego en oración, mas las niñas, faziéndolo fuerça, feriéndol de las palmas e abraçándol, levantóse él. E díxoles: 'Fijas, ¿qué demandades, o por qué entrastes acá?' (Buxton 2006: 112, but see also Baños Vallejo & Uría Maqua 2000: 225-32)

In contrast to other saints, Christopher is imprisoned with two prostitutes, who, in a brief sadomasochistic interlude, cover his body with slaps and caresses in an attempt to seduce him and thereby ensure that he falls from grace. Their endeavours, of course, are unsuccessful, but the eroticism of the episode, with its suggestion of a threesome predicated on the pleasure and pain of sexual experience, provides a more convincing counterpoint to the way in which female saints are treated.

An equally tantalizing encounter is integrated into the reading for Bernard of Clairvaux, where the saint is sexually humiliated at the hands of a naked girl who enters his bed and proceeds thereafter to touch and caress his body:[22]

> Cerca aun de ese mesmo tienpo, seyendo aun bien mancebo, vino a él una moça por amonestación del diablo, estando él durmiendo, e echóse desnuda con él en el lecho. E él, sintiéndola, con toda paz e silencio le dexó la parte de la cama ado se acostara e tornóse a dormir del otro costado con seguridat. E la mesquina, esperando algunt espacio e veyendo que non se movió a la tentar, començóle ella a palpar e tractar, mas veyendo que non se movía más que si fuera una piedra, ovo grant vergüeña, e espantándose además, levantóse e fuése e non le tornó a tentar más. (BNM 12689 fol. 35[rb-va])

As is the case with Christopher, Bernard's flesh comes into direct contact with female hands. A difference in this instance, of course, is that the action is set in motion by the devil rather than a human force eager to ensure that the saint is overcome by temptation. The eroticism of the encounter, however, is undeniable, and in the deliberate tautology of 'palpar e tractar', the text clearly lingers—perhaps in prurient delight, or perhaps in stern admonition—not simply on the proximity of naked female flesh, but the lightness and softness of its touch. The result is the establishment of a superbly constructed distinction between the sexes, with an implicit and circular contrast formed between the premeditated silence of the female protagonist's tiptoeing footfall and the fact that Bernard lies as still and rigid as stone.

In a second encounter, presented more noticeably as an *exemplum*, Bernard offers a bolder and more elaborate display of his commitment to corporeal integrity by accusing an assailant of attempting to steal the treasure of his chastity. In so doing, he shows not only that he regards the attempt at seduction as a form of unwarranted sexualized

---

22 For Compilation B, see Escorial h-I-14 fol. 224[va-vb], Escorial K-II-12 fol. 165ra, and FLG 419 fol. 188ra, and for a brief discussion, Beresford 2003.

torture, but that the preservation of virginity—a gift that can never be regained—is central to his personal conception of sanctity:[23]

> Como otra vez posase en casa de una dueña, veyéndole ella ser mancebo fermoso, fue encendida en el su amor e fízole fazer cama aparte de los otros. E levantóse de noche quando los otros dormían e fuése a él sin vergüeña. E sintiéndolo el varón santo, llamó a grandes bozes, diziendo: '¡Ladrones, ladrones!' E ella, oyendo esto, dio a fuyr, e levantóse la compaña de casa e encendió candela e fue a buscar el ladrón. Mas non le falló e tornóse cada uno a dormir a su casa. E ella, non cesando de lo que avía començado, fuése otra vez a la cama ado estava Sant Bernaldo. Mas sintiéndola él, començó a llamar otra vez: '¡Ladrones, ladrones!' E levantáronse otra vez los que estavan en la posada, e fue el ladrón buscado, mas non fue fallado nin quería él publicar quién era el ladrón que le venía a robar la castidat. E tornáronse todos a acostar. E levantóse la muger la tercera vez e fuése a la cama ado estava Sant Bernardo, mas fue desechada segunt que primero, e ella, oyendo aquesto, cesó vencida por themor o por desesperación. E otro día, yendo en el camino, preguntáronle los compañeros, reprehendiéndole que qué ladrones eran aquellos que soñara tantas vezes aquella noche. E respondióles diziendo: 'Verdaderamente ladrón era, ca la huéspeda vino a mí por tress vezes por me robar el thesoro de la castidat, el qual después de perdido en alguna manera se puede cobrar.'

In the legend of Paul of Thebes the description of sexualized torture is taken a stage further as we are offered a description of a young martyr tied down in a flowering garden (or *locus amoenus*) so that he can be forcibly seduced by a prostitute:[24]

---

23 BNM 12689 fol. 35[va-vb], but see also Escorial h-I-14 fol. 224[vb], Escorial K-II-12 fol. 165[ra-rb], and FLG 419 fol. 188[ra-rb].

24 The Compilation A version, derived from Jerome's *Vita Pauli*, can be found in BNM 12688 fols 190va-97rb and Escorial h-III-22 fols 95vb-103vb, but there is no corresponding version in Compilation B. For further information, see Beresford in preparation.

E otro mancebo, que aún florescía en la hedat de la mancebía, fue levado a un huerto muy deleĉtable. E fue puesto en una cama mucho mollida e blanda entre la blancura de los lilios e la bermejura de las rosas, a la orilla de un río que corría con muy suave sonido, e ado avía muchos árboles e fazía muy manso ayre que movía las fojas de los árboles. E fue atado de pies e de manos con vergas verdes e floridas e blandas. E como se partiesen de allí los que lo ataran, vino a él una muger pública muy fermosa e començólo a abraçar muy dulcemente e a lo traĉtar con las manos los mienbros varoniles turpemente, por que despertados los mienbros al deseo de la deleĉtación carnal, se echase sobre él aquella muger, obradora de maldat. E veyéndose atado el cavallero de Jhesu Christo, e non se poder ayudar e ser vencido de la deleĉtación, amonestado divynalmente en el coraçón, cortóse la lengua con los dientes e escupióla en la cara de aquella muger mala. E atajó el deseo e sentimiento de la deleĉtación con la grandeza del dolor, por que non venciese la torpedat de la luxuria al que non vencieran las penas crueles e duras.

In contrast to the treatment of other saints, whose bodies are touched but not otherwise violated, in this instance the harlot succeeds in initiating a process of genital stimulation, using both hands in order to prepare the young man's member for coitus. The explicit and graphic way in which the action is reported—following on, as it does, from the lilting poetic rhythms established by the description of the garden in which the event takes place—establishes an element of incongruity. The most striking development, however, can be seen shortly afterwards, as the young man severs his tongue with his teeth and spits it in the prostitute's face. The text in this way pits an act of sexualized torture against one of self-inflicted mutilation, as the tongue of the martyr effectively comes to stand for the phallus that cannot otherwise be defended. The result is the establishment of a symbolic representation of the act of self-castration, which could effectively be read in conjunction with the severing of Agatha's breast as a process of corporeal ungendering. A further implication is that, as is the case with various female saints, physicality is represented in this instance not merely as a problem to be overcome, but, paradoxically, a solution that facilitates the young man's progression from corporeal to spiritual.

The relationship between sexual temptation and self-mutilation is explored in various other legends. Jerome, for instance, retires to the desert but is tormented by visions of pretty girls. To drive them away, we are told, he starves himself, and like Mary of Egypt, beats furiously at his breast:[25]

> E seyendo solamente conpañero de los escorpiones e de las animalias bravas, muchas vezes me parescía q*ue* estaba en los corros de las moças de Roma. E teniendo el cuerpo e la carne más muerta q*ue* biva, bivía*n* en mí los encendimientos de luxuria. E llorava continuamente e domava la carne, pasando sin comer toda la semana. E muchas vezes ayunava el día co*n* la noche, estando en oración, e no*n* cesava de ferir en los pechos fasta q*ue* se ama*n*sava aq*ue*l ardor por mandamie*n*to del Señor. (BNM 12689 fol. 111rb, but see also Escorial h-II-18 fol. 167[ra-rb])

In contrast to the martyr in the garden in the legend of Paul of Thebes, Jerome is confronted not by a figure of flesh and blood, but a vision in his mind. His response, although by no means as shocking, is to impose a series of corporeal tortures upon himself, pitting lustful desires against self-inflicted torments in an attempt to rid himself of the past and thereby rise to a higher state of being. His actions in this way function as a counterpoint to the legends of various female saints, for in addition to establishing a relationship between sex and torture, the emphasis of the incident falls once again on the progression from corporeal to spiritual, as the saint's physicality is effectively presented both as problem and solution.

---

25   For Compilation B, see Escorial h-1-14 fol. 269[rb], but note that the accounts offered by BMP 9 fols 60[vb]-62[ra] and FLG 419 fols 128[va]-30[rb] are more condensed. For a treatment of the translation of Jerome's relics, see BNM 780 fols 144[ra]-45[rb], and for a study of ascetic imagery, Taylor 1997. Bynum, in contrast, explores the relationship between food, sex, and the satisfaction of appetite (1987: 214).

A similar series of relationships can be seen in an episode included in the reading for Bernard of Clairvaux, where the saint is tempted by the sight of a beautiful woman, but instead jumps into a stagnant pool of ice-cold water where he remains until almost frozen to death:[26]

> Veyendo otrosí el diablo la entención loable de Sant Bernado, ovo enbidia de la su castidat e armóle muchos lazos de tentación carnal. Onde como una vez tudiese fincados los ojos por algunt espacio en una muger, tornando en sí mesmo e parando mientes a lo que avía fecho, e aviendo vergüeña dello, ensañóse contra sí mesmo así como juez riguroso e estrecho, e menóse en un estanco de agua elada. E estovo en ella fasta que poco menos salió medio muerto. E por la gracia divinal por aquel tormento se esfrió en él la cobdicia carnal.

The rise in Bernard's libido is presented as the work of the devil, but as is the case elsewhere, eroticism and sexual desire are once again thwarted by a process of self-inflicted corporeal torture. In this instance the heat of passion finds its natural antithesis in frozen water, which succeeds in dampening Bernard's ardour and saving him from the sin of temptation. The text in this way focuses not on a single part of the body, but as is the case with Jerome, on male corporeality as a whole. The suggestion, by implication, is that the path to salvation is related either to the temporary ungendering of the male body or the attempted destruction of masculinity itself.

A series of more potent suggestions can be seen in the reading for Benedict, where the saint also finds himself tempted by the sight of a beautiful woman. A difference in this instance, however, is that in place of frozen water, he opts to strip himself of his garments and roll naked amongst the hawthorns and brambles:

> E tráxole luego el diablo a la memoria una muger que viera alguna vez, e representava su ymajen delante los ojos del su coraçón, e en-

---

26 BNM 12689 fol. 35rb. For Compilation B, see Escorial h-I-14 fol. 224va, Escorial K-II-12 fols 167vb-68ra, and FLG 419 fol. 188ra.

cendíalo con grant ardor a la cobdiciar. E atanto fue encendido en deseo de la su fermosura que poco menos fue vencida la su voluntad e pensava de dexar aquella soledad. Mas vino sobre él adesora la gracia divinal e tornó en sí mesmo, e desnudóse en cuero e bolcóse en las espinas e çarças que ende estavan. E así fue llagado de las espinas y de las çarças, que por el dolor de las llagas sacó el venino de la mala cobdicia que quemava la su alma. E dende adelante asý fue libre de las tenptaciones carnales, que nunca fue más tenptado de tenptación semejable. (Escorial h-III-22 fol. 203^{rbva}, but see also BNM 12688 fol. 313ra)

As is the case with Bernard, Benedict subjects his entire body to a process of self-inflicted torture, purging himself of the corruption of sexual desire in order to ascend to a higher state of being. His actions in this respect impact on representations of gender, for having fallen foul of the sin of sexual temptation, it is striking not only that he should divest himself of his outer garments, but that he should thereafter submit his body to a series of multiple penetrations, as the spikes of hawthorns and brambles tear savagely into his naked flesh. The text in this way pits the imagined phallic penetration of the female body against the tangible violations that Benedict chooses to endure, suggesting in so doing that sin must be atoned for in the most direct and literal of ways. The result is a suggestion not of ungendering, but of cross- or inverse-gendering, as in this instance male physicality is transformed from ardent desire to passive subservience in an attempt to quell or potentially even destroy sexual identity itself.[27]

The significance of this episode should not be underestimated, as it sheds light not simply on the legends of male saints, but the representation of Agatha and the series of commonplaces that underpin and condition the severing of her breast. There are, of course, a num-

---

[27] Other correspondences are typological, for while the conjunction of sexual shame and nakedness recalls the Expulsion from Paradise, the hawthorn is linked most commonly to the Passion. The text in this respect plays on the distinction between Adam and Christ, suggesting a duality in Benedict's behaviour that is resolved as he rejects the former in order to identify himself with the latter.

ber of significant and insuperable distinctions, for while the source of male sexual torment is generally blamed on the devil, it is noticeable at the same time that references to comparable levels of sexual desire and temptation do not appear in the legends of female saints—other than in those of the holy harlots, where the presence of such material serves an entirely different purpose. Torture, however, whether inflicted by the self or by external forces, is clearly sexualized in the legends of male and female saints alike. On certain occasions the context is moralizing, but in other instances the relationship between torture and sex is explored in frameworks redolent with erotic connotations. A common denominator, as we have seen, is a denial either of physicality or of selfhood, which leads on some occasions to a blurring of the boundaries of gender. This produces a paradoxical situation in which physicality is seen not simply as a cause of suffering, but a means with which to engineer a progression from corporeal to spiritual, and in so doing, ensure the salvation of the soul.

Dichotomies of Gender and Transformation

A brief survey of the legends of male saints shows that although there are a number of important differences, the relationship between sanctity, corporeality, and the sexualization of torture cannot by any means be reduced to a simplistic binary distinction between male and female. More fundamentally, it behoves readers to think again about female saints and to appreciate that a nuanced understanding of gender paradigms cannot be developed in isolation from a consideration of comparable patterns in the depiction of male sanctity. The corollary, of course, is that it becomes necessary, in view of this, to reconsider the significance of the severed breast as a gendered construct, asking in so doing, how exactly it equates to male sanctity, and how gendered identity is manifested anatomically, particularly in relation to the question of transformation and the extent to which Agatha inverts, transcends, and retains gendered characteristics.

A traditional and obvious opposition between male and female is suggested by the distinction between the breast on the one hand, and the phallus on the other. The organs, which serve as the most visible external manifestations of gendered identity, function in some respects as synecdochic representations of the distinction between the sexes. In purely anatomical terms, however, the breast and the phallus cannot be regarded as absolute equivalents. The phallus, unlike the breast, is a procreative organ, and so, if we are to consider patterns of direct correspondence, it should be compared most appropriately to the vagina. It is here, however, that Castilian hagiography offers one of its most curious twists, for although sexualized tortures appear more frequently in (and are more fundamental to the narrative development of) the legends of female saints, a comparison between male and female unearths a series of significant dichotomies.

One of the most notable can be seen in relation to the question of corporeal violation in the form of rape, which is as significant a potential peril for Bernard or Christopher as it is for any number of female saints. An important factor to recognize, of course, is that while rape is often threatened, it is never realized: female saints may be stripped and taken to brothels, but those who attempt to touch them are prevented from so doing; some are even killed. A good example is Agnes, who, in both of the medieval Castilian Compilations, is protected from those who attempt to take her virginity by a combination of celestial defences. These include the gift of a dress, hair that grows so long that it shields her nakedness, and a blinding light that confounds lustful intentions. The result is that those who attempt to claim her virginity emerge from her chamber merely in a state of religious stupefaction. The exception is the son of the Roman prefect, who ignores the warning signs, falls in a swoon, and is strangled by the devil:[28]

> E el fijo del adelantado [...] vino al logar de aquella suziedat con otros mancebos, sus conpañeros, por aver ayuntamiento con Santa Ynés e la escarnescer. E veyendo que algunos de sus servidores que

---

28   Compilation B is more concise, and it is perhaps as a result that it introduces a vulgar play on words, with *entrar* referring to the saint and the room in which she is trapped: 'E vino allý el fijo del adelantado con los otros conpañeros, e mandóles que entrasen a ella. E ellos entrando, vieron el ángel e torrnáronse con grant dolor' (2007a: 86, but see also 56).

entraran delante él encendidos en deseo de torpedat, salían maravillados dando onrra a la claridat, començólos él a reprehender, además encendido en ardor de suziedat, e a los llamar vanos e mesquinos e menguados de coraçón. E faziendo escarnio dellos, entró con atrevimiento al logar ado orava la virgen santa. E veyendo la grandeza de la claridat que aderredor della estava, non dio onrra a Dios, mas arremetióse a ella. E primero que llegase a ella, cayó en tierra e afogólo el diablo. (Beresford 2007a: 75)

Bernard, in contrast, is twice physically accosted while in bed, and, as is the case with Christopher, who is tainted by lustful kisses, his body comes into sexualized physical contact with the hands of a licentious woman. Castration, as is the case with vaginal mutilation, is a topic avoided in the early Castilian Compilations, but while the legend of Paul of Thebes, as we have seen, offers readers a vivid and lurid description of an act of phallic violation (with a prostitute attempting to produce an unwanted erection), it is striking that the vagina remains untouched. The episode, of course, is by no means statistically representative, and it is important to bear in mind that the threat of forced seduction or rape is a far more common element in the legends of female saints than in those of their male equivalents. This caveat aside, however, the episode shows that the distinction between male and female is not as clear as it first appears. In fact, in some respects the traditional polarity makes better sense if inverted, with the divinely protected female body standing in opposition to its vulnerable male equivalent.

The opposition between breast and phallus questions the extent to which the torture inflicted on Agatha can be understood as an act of defeminization, ungendering, or an approximation of male status. The problem, of course, is that the early Castilian narratives explore the ambiguity of her transformation in such a way as to confound simplistic attempts at classification or categorization. If Agatha, for instance, is ungendered by the severing of her breast, it follows that she must, by implication, be regendered by the act of restoration that takes place at around midnight on the same day. Yet even if we are to think of ungendering as a temporary phenomenon, it is noticeable that when the supposedly defeminized Agatha is visited by Saint Peter in prison, she remains quintessentially female, speaking not as an ungendered entity, but a dutiful and obedient daughter of the Church.

The most noticeable textual evidence of gender retention can be seen in the adoption of a mode of address marked for gender, with *padre* and *fija* playing on the traditionally deferential bond between the vulnerable female saint and her authoritative male guardian. The conversation with Saint Peter alights on a number of topics, but Agatha's concern is not that she has been defeminized or made male, but that having relied throughout her life on Christ's curative ability, the use of medicine could potentially interfere with divine will. Her admission, which is expressed all but identically in the medieval Castilian Compilations, focuses the audience's attention not on gender inversion, but questions of daughterly obedience:[29]

> Yo nunca puse en mi cuerpo melezina carnal, e mucho sería a mí grant torpedat quebrantar agora lo que he guardado fasta aquí por la gracia divinal. [...] Yo he por físico al mi señor Jhesu Christo, e quando a él plaze, él sana todas las enfermedades e llagas por sola su palabra. E si quisiere, él me puede sanar.

More importantly, Agatha's words are accompanied by a starkly feminine acknowledgment—the fact that as her body has been so badly mutilated, she has become undesirable in the eyes of men:[30]

> Yo non he por qué aver vergueña, como tú seas viejo e de grant hedat, e yo esté llagada de tan grant crueldat, que non avría onbre que me pudiese en este estado cobdiciar. Mas fágote muchas gracias, señor padre, porque te plogo de aver de mí cuydado e me venir a vesitar.

---

29   *Istoria*, 105-06. See also: *Passión* (70-79), *Vida* (72-82), and *Vida de la virgen* (67-75).

30   *Istoria*, 108-12. See also: *Passión* (74-77), *Vida* (76-79), and *Vida de la virgen* (70-72).

These words, which smack of a highly developed sense of female self-awareness, would make little sense if Agatha's gendered identity were truly in question. It is perhaps for this reason that when she touches her body and realizes that the breast has been restored, she expresses her gratitude by kneeling in prayer and (in an act of ritualized feudal deference) thanking Christ and Saint Peter for their assistance and protection: 'E catándose Santa Ágata, fallóse toda sana e tornada la teta a los pechos. E derribóse en tierra, faziendo gracias al señor Jhesu Christo e al apóstol Sant Pedro'.[31]

The restoration of the breast allows the final stage of Agatha's legend to complete a frame of reference in which she is presented as an anatomically intact *sponsa Christi*. Although, as we have seen, the representation of female sanctity is often conditioned by paradox, the content of this section is saturated by a tone of sublimated courtly love, with Agatha destined for celestial union with her male suitor. The process begins as she emerges from prison and is quizzed by Quintianus about the restoration of the breast. Agatha's response is that it has been healed by Christ, and on hearing this, her antagonist becomes enraged, characterizing himself as a spurned and wounded lover: '¿Aún te atreves a nonbrar a Jhesu Christo, non queriendo yo oýr el su nonbre?'[32]

An explicit opposition between imperfect terrestrial suitor and perfect celestial spouse becomes more noticeable as the altercation continues, first as Agatha gives voice to an outburst in which she pledges unswerving devotion to Christ ('Llamaré a Jhesu Christo con el coraçón e con la boca demientra biviere', 142), and then as Quintianus, acting partly out of jilted spite, has her subjected to a final sexualized torture, rolling her naked flesh over broken potsherds in a symbolic representation of the multiple phallic violations that she has managed so diligently to avoid. The symbolic connotations of this torture would make little or no symbolic sense if Agatha's gendered identity were truly in question, but what is remarkable is that it leads

---

31 *Istoria*, 119-21. See also: *Passión* (82-84), *Vida* (85-87), and *Vida de la virgen* (76-78).

32 *Istoria*, 133-34. See also: *Passión* (92-93), *Vida* (98-99), and *Vida de la virgen* (90).

into a prayer in which she thanks Christ for patience, strength, and protection from physical corruption before ardently entreating him to receive her soul. The Compilation B versions differ relatively little from one another (or, indeed, Voragine) at this point, but in Compilation A there is a subtle but significant development in phrasing:[33]

> Señor Jhesu Christo, que me criaste e me guardaste desde la mi niñez, e me feziste trabajar varonilmente en la mi mancebía, e quitaste de mí el amor del siglo, e apartaste el mi cuerpo de todo ensuziamiento, e me feziste vencer los tormentos de los carniceros (el fierro e las prisiones e el fuego), e me diste virtud de paciencia entre los tormentos, ruégote que rescibas agora el mi espíritu, ca tienpo es, Señor, que me mandes dexar aqueste siglo e yr a la tu misericordia. (154-61)

The interpolation of the adverb 'varonilmente' impacts on the representation of gendered identity, showing not simply that Agatha's legend is conditioned by paradox, but that the boundaries of gender are blurred and constantly shifting. By robustly defending her corporeal integrity, Agatha has mastered the weakness and limitations of the flesh. In so doing, she has matched the achievements of male saints by displaying degrees of heroism and resistance that would not ordinarily have been expected of members of her sex. This marks her out as a figure of manly status, but although this succeeds in some respects in suggesting a process of ungendering or defeminization, it is noticeable that the remaining portion of the narrative offers a protracted description of the solemnization of her relationship with Christ. This can be seen most clearly in Compilation B, which follows the emphasis of Voragine's original by presenting the description of the handsome youth, bedecked from head to foot in finest silk, most obviously as an image of union with her celestial suitor.[34]

---

33   For a discussion of 'varonilmente' in the Compilation A treatment of Agnes, see Beresford 2007a: 79, and for a study of the problem of literal versus figurative interpretation, Jantzen 1995: 43-58.
34   See *Passión* (109-17), *Vida* (115-24), and *Vida de la virgen* (105-13).

The dichotomous representation of Agatha as *muger varonil* and demure celestial bride relates her transformation to those of saints such as Pelagia and Marina, whose legends are underpinned by explorations of the function and meaning of transvestism. Pelagia, although more effectively characterized as a penitent prostitute (in view of the fact that transvestism is a mere element in her legend rather than its principal focus), flees to the Holy Land dressed as a hermit, and in this way gains a limited degree of autonomy that could in some respects be regarded as an approximation of male status. The Compilation A version offers a matter-of-fact description of her transformation and comments specifically on the assumption of male identity: 'E tomó hábito de hermitaño e encerróse en una cela pequeña. E sirvió allí a Dios en mucha abstinencia e era avido de todos en grand reverencia. E llamávase Pelagio' (Beresford 2007b: 138). This is all but duplicated by Compilation B: 'E tomó ý ábito de hermitaño e moró ý en una celda muy pequeña. E sirvió ý a Dios e estudo ý en grant abstinencia. E avía grant fama entre los omnes. E llamávanla fray Pelayo' (140).

As the two versions make clear, however, Pelagia's transformation lasts years rather than hours, and in contrast to the severing of Agatha's breast, is entirely self-imposed, coming not as the result of an act of physical violence or external coercion, but a pragmatic desire to conceal her gender so as to avoid being seen and coveted by the eyes of overcurious and lustful men. The episode in this way follows on organically from the decision to travel at night (which emphasizes the importance of disguise and concealment) whilst simultaneously establishing a broader structural contrast with the opening section of the legend, where she is presented in the context of a brazen public spectacle as the most luxurious and visually desirable woman in Antioch. In this respect the assumption of male attire also functions as a symbol of reversal, shame, and self-conscious corporeal modesty, comparable not merely to the sentiments uttered by Agatha in prison, but broader trends in the representation of female sanctity.

A more significant distinction can be seen in the fact that the gendering of Pelagia's transformation is manifested in her outer garments, which are described as being those of a hermit. The most extensive of the early Castilian texts, the *Vida e conversión de Santa Pelagia*, is more specific, and comments on the roughness of her hairshirt and the fact that it obscures her gender to the point where it becomes uncertain whether she is a man or a woman: 'vestió huna saya de hun sellicio mucho áspero, e esto de guisa que non lo sopo nin honbre nin mogier' (Beresford 2007b: 146). However, as this version belongs to a different manuscript tradition, we should be wary either of conflating it with texts derived from the *Legenda aurea*, or of assuming that it necessarily espouses an identical ethos.

Pelagia, of course, is transformed physically, but the emphasis of her legend falls not on a process of anatomical defeminization, but the traditionally withering rigours of asceticism, which, of course, are gender-neutral. A variant of the standard ascetic pattern is present in the legends of Voragine's other prostitute saints, as the once beautiful harlots become ugly and haggard as the sins of their soul bubble to the surface, leaving them purged and of saintly status. This can be seen in Compilation A in the discussion of Pelagia's 'grand magreza' (138), and in Compilation B in the fact that she is characterized in later life as being 'mucho desfecha de las carnes' (140). During this process, her anatomical gender is not in question, and as is the case in other legends, the representation of femininity becomes in some ways more intense. The most obvious parallel is with Mary of Egypt, who, at the end of her period of isolation, coyly entreats Zosimus to lend her a garment to conceal her shame and nakedness—an action that forms a contrast with her earlier life where she is characterized as a figure immersed in the joys of wanton lechery. Thaïs, in contrast, is rewarded in a vision with the gift of nuptial bed fit for a revirginalized celestial bride, but a perhaps more thought-provoking parallel can be seen in the relationship between Nonnus and Pelagia, which is governed by a sublimated undercurrent of courtly love, with Nonnus, her clerical guardian, as infatuated with her spiritual accomplishments as he was, prior to her conversion, with her corporeal magnificence.

A perhaps more telling point of contact can be seen in the fact that Pelagia, despite dying in male hermit's garb, is celebrated in death not as a man but as a woman, a factor that underlines the extent to which her transformation (like that of Agatha) is as superficial as it is temporary. This, of course, also relates her legend to that of Marina, as in each instance the concluding portion of the narrative focuses on the discovery of female identities in those who had concealed them for a portion of their adult lives. With Pelagia, as we have seen, the decision to opt for concealment comes partly as a result of pragmatic necessity, and partly as a product of the symbolism of shame and reversal. However, with Marina the situation is more complex, as her fate is imposed upon her by her father as he takes her to a monastery. This, of course, makes her situation more akin to that of Agatha, whose transformation comes as a result of external control, than it does to Pelagia, who exercises autonomy.

The parallel between Agatha and Marina, however, is weakened by the fact that while the former is subjected to a process of sexualized or coercive violence that forcibly defeminizes her in anatomical terms, the latter is presented throughout the narrative as a willing and complicit party, who embraces transformation almost without question. Obviously, the fact that Marina is subsequently accused of fathering a child, a crime of which she would have been biologically incapable, succeeds in blurring the traditional boundaries of gender, and in this way recalls the status not simply of Agatha, but various other saints—male and female alike. It is important to note, however, that the transformation affects only Marina's outer garments, and in this sense serves as a timely reminder of the fact that she has participated in a form of deceit from which she cannot now extricate herself without in the process revealing the secret of her sex. This leads her, despite being innocent, to confess to the crime and undertake the punishment and penance that are deemed appropriate.

Marina's disguise serves in this respect as a useful protective measure, and one that as John Anson rightly claims, could be regarded either as an indication of 'a violent rupture with a former mode of existence' (1974: 5) or an assimilation of Christological values 'by an act of mimetic magic' (1974: 11). The pattern, however, is by no means gender-neutral, and can be applied to the legends of a significant number of male saints, many of whom define or redefine their identities in relation to the assumption of alternative modes of attire. A perhaps more convincing interpretation is anchored on the notion of *imitatio Christi*, as Marina follows in Christ's footsteps by accepting punishment for a crime that redeems the community in which she lives. An added complication, of course, is that as she has sinned in order to elevate herself to such a lofty position, she stands in this way as a type of surrogate Eve, righting the wrongs not simply of her community, but her sex (1974: 30).

The trajectory of Marina's transformation, which espouses an ethos different from that which is embedded into Agatha's legend, is illustrated to varying degrees elsewhere in the medieval Castilian Compilations by the legends of Theodora, Eugenia, and Margaret. A thorough examination of the significance of these texts is long overdue. Even on a cursory reading, however, it becomes possible to see that although there are a number of significant overlaps—particularly in the blurring of the traditional lines of demarcation between the genders and the concealment and restoration of gendered identity—the assumption of male attire cannot in itself be regarded as a functional equivalent of Agatha's severed breast. In this sense, therefore, her position is unique, and as such, merits further and more detailed scrutiny.[35]

---

35   For Compilation A, see BNM 780 fols 233rb-35vb (Theodora), BNM 12689 fols 76vb-78va and Escorial h-ii-18 fols 132vb-34va (Eugenia—in the chapter on Protus and Hyacinthus), and BNM 12689 fol. 124^{a-d} and Escorial h-ii-18 fols 178va-79rb (Margaret), and for Compilation B, Appendix III.

6
Rereading Agatha and Lucy

Corporeality and Rhetoric

The depiction of Agatha in the medieval Castilian Compilations shows not simply that she is unique, but that as far as the severed breast is concerned, we may not yet have developed a critical framework flexible enough to deal with legends individually, or sophisticated enough to allow readers to posit questions capable of helping them understand the complexity of its literary representation. The result has been detrimental not merely to the process of textual classification and the exploration of relationships to other saints—male and female alike—but to comprehension, particularly with regard to our understanding of questions such as the sexualization of torture, the gendering of identity, and the representation of corporeal experience.

This, to a large extent, could be regarded merely as an issue of asking different questions; or less radically, of reformulating the order in which such questions have traditionally been asked so that they can elicit more specific and beneficial responses. It may be, for instance, that instead of taking the severed breast as the starting point of an analysis and searching for analogues elsewhere, we could arrive at a more coherent understanding of its significance by looking at it not as a discrete issue, but as one of the most extreme, degrading, and sexualized manifestations of a series of innate and inexorable factors that are present throughout the corpus as a whole. We could, therefore, look not at the breast *per se*, but at the wider process that conditions its severing, asking first why saints are tortured, and then why torture is sometimes sexualized.

To provide a solid platform for analysis, it becomes necessary in the first instance to gauge the importance of corporeality in context, and to frame the issue within appropriate limits by considering its significance in relation to themes that arise naturally from a reading of the early Castilian redactions. In this way it should become possible to generate a more nuanced and context sensitive theory rather than focusing arbitrarily on a single issue in isolation.

A natural starting point is in the prefatory discussions of etymology, which can be found exclusively in Compilation A. These serve as framing devices, prompting readers to evaluate the significance of the saints in a number of specific and predetermined ways. 'Ágata', for instance, can be interpreted as 'santa de Dios' (2), a quality that requires little or no explanation. A subsequent meaning, 'servidunbre mayor' (9), underlines the extent to which she regards service as the highest form of expression, while 'deesa sin tierra' (6) refers not to geographical isolation, but an abhorrence of earthly things. An alternative derivation, 'acabada solepnemente' (12), anticipates her posthumous fate and the act of celestial solemnization in the form of the subsequent visitation.

The most significant assertion, however, draws attention to an aspect of characterization that has not yet received adequate critical attention— the fact that identity can also be defined in relation to verbal dexterity: 'E aun Ágata quiere dezir "fabladora conplida e acabada". E aquesto paresce asaz claramente en sus respuestas' (7-8). This definition, which is presented structurally as the third in a series of five (and thus, potentially, as Agatha's most fundamental characteristic), places the emphasis of the introductory frame not on corporeality (a topic not considered important enough to be mentioned at this stage), but the cognitive and rational functions of Agatha's intellect as manifested by verbal articulation.

The narrator's remarks, of course, are not included in Compilation B, and so we should be wary of allowing them to colour or potentially distort an interpretation of the legend as a whole. The problem, however, is that allusions to Agatha's rhetorical eloquence appear too frequently to be ignored, and are more often than not presented in conjunction with references to corporeality, notably in relation to the sexualization of the female anatomy.

The correlation between the two is clearly in evidence as Agatha is summoned before the prefect. Quintianus, we are told, is determined to possess her, but at this stage his motivation for so doing is only partly sexual. During an initial encounter, the content of which is not reported, the characters meet for the first time, and the fact that Agatha is immediately sent away suggests that the professional Roman consul, skilled in debate and litigious rhetoric, is instantly bested in discussion (if not roundly humiliated) by a teenage female adversary. As a result, he places her in the care of the brothel-keeper, Aphrodisia, who is charged not with the responsibility of converting her to paganism or confiscating her wealth (topics mentioned only slightly earlier), but shattering her sexual resolve.

The Compilation B versions follow Voragine closely and report on Quintianus's decision in a matter-of-fact way. In Compilation A, in contrast, the account is much embellished and the emphasis on coitus made more explicit:[1]

> diola a guardar a una mala muger que avía nonbre Afrodisan, que tenía nueve fijas que eran todas malas mugeres, por que mudase el su coraçón de la entinción de la christiandat e la ynclinase a aver ayuntamiento con él.

The configuration of the narrative at this point suggests that the relationship between corporeality and rhetoric is one that should be ignored only at great peril. The prefect, hoping to possess Agatha, attempts initially to gain various elements of prestige and personal satisfaction, but now, having been subjected to her rhetoric, his complex motivation is distilled into a single objective. It is as if Agatha's verbal dexterity, which he has been unable to counter, has enraged and unbalanced him, forcing him to abandon an appeal to her intellect in favour of an attack directed specifically against her corporeal integrity. In this respect, control of Agatha's body becomes a means with which to control her behaviour, if not her identity, and so sex becomes a weapon of conquest that seeks to shatter Christian resistance and assert pagan control.

---

[1] *Istoria*, 24-27. See also: *Passión* (12-14), *Vida* (11-13), and *Vida de la virgen* (13-15).

The problem, however, is that by placing Agatha in a uniquely female environment, where she is to be indoctrinated by Aphrodisia and her nine harlot daughters, Quintianus effectively replaces the threat of the phallus as coercive weapon by that of the word—a weapon that has already been deployed unsuccessfully and that seems even less likely to succeed when placed in the mouth of a mere brothel-keeper. The result is predictable: Aphrodisia combines stern threats with tempting promises and is roundly rebuffed. In response, Agatha deploys a rhetorical arsenal designed to belittle the weak and ineffectual nature of her assailant's verbal ability:[2]

> El mi coraçón está asentado sobre piedra muy firme, e está fundado sobre Jhesu Christo, fijo de Dios bivo. E las vuestras palabras son asý como viento, e los vuestros prometimientos son así como lluvias que fallescen de ligero, e los vuestros espantos son así como ríos que pasan arrebatados. E non podrán derribar los cimientos de mi casa porque están asentados sobre piedra de grant firmeza.

The juxtaposition of verbal and corporeal is striking. Agatha receives threats designed to overwhelm her corporeal integrity, but instead mocks Aphrodisia's rhetoric with a tirade drenched in the language of biblical allusion (Matthew 7:24-27). Her heart, and by implication, the fleshly body in which it is housed, are impervious to assault, and, as she argues, they are founded in physicality on none other than Christ. In this way she succeeds in presenting herself as a fixed and immobile entity, characterized by physicality, yet able nonetheless to flourish without being affected by the standard laws of transformation.

Unable to compete with such lofty erudition, Aphrodisia admits defeat, and in a spectacular inversion, returns her ward to Quintianus with an affirmation not of corporeal acceptance, but unwavering cognitive resistance: 'Más aýna podrían ser molidos los guijarros e tornado el fierro así como plomo blando, que ser apartada esta donzella de la su

---

2 *Istoria*, 31-37. See also: *Passión* (17-21), *Vida* (16-19), and *Vida de la virgen* (18-22).

creencia'.³ Her words, which assume the form of an extended metaphor that expands Agatha's earlier line of rhetoric, show not merely that she has been influenced by the encounter, notably at a linguistic level, but that she has found it impossible to function in her primary social role as brothel-keeper. The parallel with Quintianus is thus only partial, for while both characters fail in their respective professions, Aphrodisia learns and understands something of the nature of Agatha's faith. In so doing, she reveals a cognitive (if not prophetic) appreciation, which paves the way for the concluding section, with the eruption of Mount Etna pulverizing rocks into dust before the eyes of the assembled masses. This, of course, provides a convenient and timely reminder of the fact that the rock of Agatha's faith, just as she claims, will remain forever unshaken.⁴

As the narrative develops, the relationship between corporeality and rhetoric becomes more noticeable. In a second encounter, Quintianus asks three questions, and in each instance Agatha undermines his frame of reference by providing him with figurative responses that he is too stupid to understand:⁵

> E asentóse en su silla e díxole: '¿De qué condición eres tú?' E respondióle Santa Ágata e dixo: 'Non solamente só libre, mas aun de muy noble linaje, segunt lo demuestra todo el parentesco que yo tengo.' E díxole Quinciano: 'Si eres libre e noble, ¿por qué te de-

---

3   Istoria, 40-42. See also: Passión (23-25), Vida (22-24), and Vida de la virgen (24-26).

4   'E fue fecho luego un grant movimiento de la tierra e movió toda la cibdat. E cayó parte de la casa ado estava Quinciano asentado a judgar e mató a dos consejeros e amigos de Quinciano. E allegóse todo el pueblo e dezía a grandes bozes a Quinciano que por los agravios e tormentos syn justicia que dava a Santa Ágata viniera aquel movimiento de la tierra. E Quinciano, aviendo grant temor de la una parte del movimiento de la tierra, e de la otra parte de la discordia del pueblo, mandó tornar a la cárcel a Santa Ágata' (Istoria, 138-45). See also Passión (98-103), Vida (103-09), and Vida de la virgen (95-100). A further irony, although not one that specifically recieves comment within the texts, is that the etymology of Peter's name ('Petrus') relates him specifically to the rock of faith.

5   Istoria, 43-53. See also Passión (26-33), Vida (25-32), and Vida de la virgen (27-34).

muestras en las costunbres aver persona de sierva?' E respondióle Santa Ágata e dixo: 'Muéstrome tener persona de sierva porque só sierva de Jhesu Christo, fijo de Dios bivo.' E díxole Quinciano: 'Si libre eres e noble como dizes, ¿en qué manera te afirmas ser sierva?' E respondióle Santa Ágata e dixo: 'La clarydat de la nobleza se demuestra en la servidunbre de Jhesu Christo, criador del syglo.'

The shaping of this passage presents the interrogative not as a measure of intellectual inquiry, but of cerebral inadequacy. Quintianus struggles to comprehend a series of ideas that are beyond him, and despite sitting on his throne of office—a tangible symbol of worldly authority—he remains in a position of childish and brutish ignorance. This produces a striking inversion of status, which becomes more pronounced as the dialogue continues and the interrogative is replaced by an imperative outlining the threat of torture: '¡Conviene escoger de dos cosas la una: o ofrescer sacreficio a los dioses non mortales o sofrir muchos tormentos e grandes!'[6]

The transition from interrogative to imperative brings the relationship between corporeality and rhetoric into sharper focus, as Quintianus effectively turns from soul to body, venting his befuddled spleen in the threat of corporeal torture. In so doing, he reveals the inconsistency of his motivation, which now turns to issues of theological conformity. Exploiting the change of tack, Agatha impresses the notion of *imitatio Christi* upon him, arguing that as imitation is the most appropriate form of homage, he should attempt to imitate Jupiter: '¡Tales seades tú e tu muger qual fue el tu dios Júpiter!'[7] Unable to fathom the logic of the recommendation, Quintianus instead resorts to physical punishment and has her slapped: 'E oyendo esto, Quinciano mandóla ferir a palmadas e díxole: "¡Non te deves atrever a ynjuriar locamente al juez!"'[8] The result is the establishment of an engaging and appropriate juxtaposition, for faced by a wise child or *puella senex*, his actions

---

6 *Istoria*, 53-55. See also: *Passión* (33-34), *Vida* (32-33), and *Vida de la virgen* (34-35).
7 *Istoria*, 56. See also *Passión* (34-35), *Vida* (34-35), and *Vida de la virgen* (36-37).
8 *Istoria*, 56-58. See also *Passión* (35-37), *Vida* (35-37), and *Vida de la virgen* (37-38).

and discourse become increasingly childish as he mistakenly assumes that he has been insulted.

In response to the imposition of corporeal violence, Agatha offers a more detailed exploration of the question of imitation, focusing specifically on the bond between Quintianus and Jupiter:[9]

> Mucho me maravillo de ty, que te tienes por onbre sabio e te crees ser ynjuriado porque te digo que agora fueses tal como aquél a quien te ynclinas a adorar. E si tú e tu muger non deseades remedar la vida de aquél que adorades por dios, ¿en qué manera te ynclinas a le sacreficar e onrrar? Ca si Júpiter es tu dios, non te desee mal mas bien, conviene saber que fueses semejable a él. E si aborresces de le semejar, ¿por qué me costriñes a lo adorar? Ca sy aborresces la su conpañía, eso mesmo sientes que yo siento, e non deves querer que yo le ofresca encienso.

In this, one of the longest of her speeches, Agatha offers an eloquent and authoritative response, upbraiding Quintianus for his ignorance and stupidity while imparting complex theological notions with relative rhetorical ease. Her words in this respect establish an element of irony, for despite a clear distinction in age and status, she speaks as the voice of maternal orthodoxy, dealing with Quintianus as if he were an unruly child in need of instruction. The episode in this way plays not only on the traditional balance of power between the genders, but the paradox of transformation, with the unflappable and unchanging Agatha predicating her identity on sexual resistance yet oscillating at the same time between the roles of virgin and mother. Quintianus, in contrast, as is the case with Aphrodisia, suffers a corresponding transformation, first as his will is challenged and he is forced, correspondingly, to replace rhetoric by violence, and then as his actions effectively lower his status from powerful ruler to petulant little boy.

It is at this point that we are offered a telling reminder of the dialectic upon which the legend is founded, as Quintianus rejects the

---

9 *Istoria*, 59-67. See also: *Passión* (37-42), *Vida* (37-42), and *Vida de la virgen* (39-41).

power of the word and replaces it with the threat of pain and murder: '¿Para qué me detienes en palabras demasiadas? ¡O sacrefica a los dioses o te faré morir a tormentos de grandes dolores!'[10] The transition here from 'palabras' to 'dolores' reinforces the power of the complex and symbiotic relationship between rhetorical and corporeal, demonstrating that a nuanced interpretation of the narrative must at all times be grounded on an appreciation of the interaction between the two. The corporeal is threatened by the pagan aggressor, while the Christian martyr defends herself and her religion with rhetorical eloquence and sophisticated intellectual disputation. This produces a gradual degradation in behaviour, as Quintianus, unable to match (or indeed fathom) Agatha's cognitive ability, resorts to the threat of ever more severe and spectacular forms of corporeal violence.

Agatha, however, remains undaunted, and instead offers an eloquent and detailed commentary on the futility of corporeal torture:[11]

> Si me amenazas que me echarás a las vestias bravas, oyendo el nonbre de Jhesu Christo serán amansadas. E sy me amenazas que me quemarás en el fuego, los ángeles me enbiarán rocío saludable del cielo. E si me amenazas con otros tormentos, yo he comigo el Spíritu Santo, que me da esfuerço e me librará dellos.

As is the case elsewhere, Agatha's words establish a contrast between corporeality and rhetoric, as she makes it clear that any potential threat to her corporeal body—verbal or otherwise—will be protected by the hand of the divine. Her words in this way pick up on the theme of transformation, reminding readers not only of Aphrodisia's prophetic understanding, but the paradoxical way in which Agatha herself is characterized as a static yet constantly evolving creature who forces all those with whom she comes into contact to change their attitudes or identities.

---

10 *Istoria*, 68-69. See also: *Passión* (42-43), *Vida* (42-44), and *Vida de la virgen* (41-42).

11 *Istoria*, 69-74. See also: *Passión* (44-48), *Vida* (44-48), and *Vida de la virgen* (43-46).

In response to Agatha's determination, Quintianus resolves to have her returned to prison. The phrasing of the text at this point, with the emphasis of the narrative falling once again on the question of transformation, undermines his frame of reference by presenting the experience in an antithetical light: 'E Santa Ágata fuése muy alegre e gloriándose a la cárcel como sy fuera conbidada a manjares muy delectables.'[12] The same technique is used when Agatha emerges from prison and is subjected to a series of further tortures, initially in the form of racking, and then in the severing of her breast:[13]

> Así me deleyto yo en aquestas penas en que estó, como el que oye algunt buen mensaje, o vee al que mucho desea veer, o falla thesoros muy presciosos. Ca non puede ser metido el trigo en el alfolí si non fuere primero la paja trillada e alinpiada. E así la mi alma non podrá entrar en el Paraýso del mi Dios con el vencimiento de martirio si non fuere atormentado con toda diligiencia el mi cuerpo de los tus carniceros.

Agatha's words convert pleasure into pain and torture into deliverance, as she effectively challenges Quintianus by affirming that assaults on her corporeal integrity will ensure the liberation of the soul rather than the destruction of the flesh. The violence of her imagery, with the separation of soul from body compared to the separation of wheat from chaff, is shocking, but it succeeds in undermining Quintianus's credibility, showing that while Agatha is an intellectual creature, able to reach beyond the immediacy of an action and understand its implications, his lack of intellect is such that he cannot see beyond purely literalistic interpretation. In this way Quintianus and Rome become identified with corporeality, while Agatha and Christianity stand in opposition, championing the immortal quality of the soul with the voice of intellectual reason.

---

12   *Istoria*, 76-78. See also: *Passión* (48-50), *Vida* (48-49), and *Vida de la virgen* (46-47).

13   *Istoria*, 83-89. See also: *Passión* (53-58), *Vida* (55-60), and *Vida de la virgen* (50-55).

The futility of the decision to sever Agatha's breast is in this respect axiomatic. Unable to cope with constant intellectual humiliation, Quintianus orders his henchmen to perform a forced mastectomy. Agatha's reaction produces her only question, and in it—presenting herself in the process as a sexualized damsel and nursing mother—she strikes at the heart of his understanding of humanity by reminding him of the fact that he has severed the organ from which he once drew life:[14]

> Tirano cruel e malo, ¿cómo non as vergueña de cortar en la fenbra lo que mamaste en tu madre mesma? Yo he otras tetas entregas en la mi alma que consagré al Señor desde la mi niñez, e con ellas dó yo a los mis sesos fartura de leche.

Agatha's words abruptly underline the extent to which she and Quintianus differ in their understanding and appreciation of the encounter. Quintianus, unable to impose his will on Agatha's intellect, instead assaults her corporeal integrity, assuming no doubt that as he cannot affect a transformation in her mental resolve, he can do so by striking at the lability of the flesh. Agatha, in contrast, fights corporeal violence with intellectual dexterity, and while remaining constant in the definition of her identity in relation to her commitment to faith and chastity, she paradoxically effects a transformation of her own, with the severing of the breast allowing her to present herself as a paradoxical amalgam of untarnished virgin, sexualized damsel, and nursing mother.

Shortly afterwards, as Agatha is thrown once again into prison, the power of her statement receives comment, as Saint Peter affirms that she has inflicted greater damage on her assailant than he has inflicted on her:[15]

> Aqueste cónsul loco, Quinciano, te ha mucho atormentado, mas más atormentaste tú a él con tus respuestas sabias e enseñadas. E

---

14   *Istoria*, 91-94. See also: *Passión* (59-62), *Vida* (62-64), and *Vida de la virgen* (56-59).

15   *Istoria*, 99-102. See also: *Passión* (66-69), *Vida* (69-71), and *Vida de la virgen* (63-66).

aunque él te fizo cortar la teta, la su alegría se le tornará en amargura e tristeza.

Suffering, in this respect, is presented as a two-way process: Quintianus is tortured by Agatha's rhetoric and so he inflicts a variety of torments on her physical body; Agatha, in contrast, rises above corporeal limitations and focuses on the power of rhetoric, which in many ways is a more powerful and destructive weapon. In so doing she is able to draw on the strength of Christ, who, as she rather pointedly affirms, is able to cure wounds and ailments purely with his word: 'sana todas las enfermedades e llagas por sola su palabra'.[16]

This observation, of course, places the emphasis of the narrative on the resurrection of the flesh, and it is perhaps for this reason that in her final encounter she comments not simply on the futile and vacuous nature of Quintianus's words (as opposed to the constructive power of those of Christ as *logos*), but his spectacular lack of intellect: 'Tus palabras son locas e vanas e desiguales e ensuzian el ayre, ca ¿cómo quieres tú, mezquino syn seso e sin entendimiento, que adore las piedras e dexe de adorar al Criador que me fizo?'[17] Her words in this way provide the narrative with a degree of structural and intellectual unity, curtly underlining the extent to which rhetoric should be understood as a measure of intelligence.

Lucy's legend is predicated on similar relationships. The preface to the Compilation A version is a more abstract and theoretical piece of writing, but in it we are invited to evaluate her significance in a number of interrelated ways. Her name, we are told, means 'light' and light has various properties: it is beautiful to behold, it cannot be sullied, and it cannot be twisted. These observations are glossed by the narrator as he comments specifically on the beauty of Lucy's virginity and her unswerving commitment to the divine:

---

16 *Istoria*, 115-16. See also: *Passión* (78-79), *Vida* (80-82), and *Vida de la virgen* (73-75).

17 *Istoria*, 128-31. See also: *Passión* (89-92), *Vida* (93-96), and *Vida de la virgen* (87-89).

> E por aquesto es demostrado que Santa Lucía ovo fermosura de virginidat syn corrupción, e derramamiento de la su claridat sin suziedad de amor, e enderesçamiento a Dios de la su entinción sin algunt torcimiento. E aun ovo luengo rayo de obra continua e buena sin tardança de nigligiencia. (*Pasión*, 7-11)

His most telling observation, however, appears in relation to the pouring out or dissemination of light, which affirms by implication that her example, whether it be verbal or otherwise, provides a source of enlightenment. This is confirmed by the second possible interpretation, which is given as 'carrera de luz' (12), a phrase rooted in the rhetoric of scriptural allusion (John 14:6) and that suggests that she will be presented as a mouthpiece of orthodoxy, capable not merely of illuminating the path to salvation by action and gesture, but with divinely inspired words.

As is the case with Agatha, the narrator's comments are not included in Compilation B. The configuration of the narrative, however, is such that it presents a series of encounters between Lucy and figures who are in need of enlightenment. This produces a contrast between those who are prepared to listen and reap the rewards, and those who remain in a state of sullied ignorance, countering the dissemination of words of wise counsel with futile attacks directed against the physical body.

The first encounter is with Euthicia, a character named in Compilation A, but presented merely according to her status as mother in Compilation B. Euthicia, we are told, has been suffering from a vaginal haemorrhage for several years, but despite the best efforts of doctors and physicians, they have been unable to stop the bleeding. The corporeal emphasis of the narrative falls initially, therefore, not on Lucy, but her mother, and in the first of a number of juxtapositions, the threat to the physical body is countered not by corporeal solutions, but with reference to the power of the word:[18]

---

18   *Pasión*, 17-23. See also: *Vida* (5-11) and *Vida e passión* (5-12). A further reference to the power of the word can be seen in the fact that in all three texts Lucy makes explicit reference to Agatha's fame and posthumous reputation in popular tradition.

E como a la misa se leyese el evangelio que dize de cómo sanó el Señor a la muger que tenía fluxo de sangre doze años avía, díxole Santa Lucía: 'Madre mía, sy creyes a estas cosas que agora son leýdas, creet que Santa Ágata está sienpre presente delante aquél por cuyo amor rescibió muerte; e llega al su sepulcro creyendo firmemente e rescebirás luego sanidat conplidamente.'

As is the case with Agatha, who builds consciously on imagery derived from Matthew 7:24-27, Lucy takes the power of the written word (in this instance orally disseminated in the context of the liturgy) as her starting point, and formulates wise counsel in the form of a clearly articulated and eloquently expressed outpouring of interpretive logic. Written and verbal are in this way bound together, and collectively they emphasize the value of faith, with Lucy encouraging her mother to forsake worldly solutions and instead rely on the power of the divine doctor, as expressed through Agatha as proxy.

The shaping of the episode in this way reveals a suspicion of worldly medicine, but its most significant function (as far as the pairing of the two saints is concerned) is to relate Lucy's words to those that Agatha directs to Saint Peter while she is in prison. Most notable in this respect is the way in which she is able to place herself exclusively in the hands of the divine doctor, who, as she claims, is able to heal worldly wounds and ailments with nothing more than his word: 'Yo he por físico al mi señor Jhesu Christo, e quando a él plaze, él sana todas las enfermedades e llagas por sola su palabra.'[19] In this way the texts juxtapose the two most intimate and distinctive parts of the female anatomy, affirming that solutions to the pain of corporeal suffering, whether in the form of a severed breast or an incurable vaginal haemorrhage, will be found not in the world but the word of Christ.

The progression from corporeal to rhetorical relates Euthicia not simply to Agatha, but to Lucy, as her experience at the hands of Paschasius will involve a series of corporeal threats that will be countered through the power of rhetoric. In this sense she functions to some ex-

---

19   *Istoria*, 114-16. See also: *Passión* (78-79), *Vida* (80-82), and *Vida de la virgen* (73-75).

tent as a prefiguration of her daughter's suffering. A deeper and more complex parallel, however, is with Aphrodisia, as in each narrative an initial confrontation between female characters with opposing views and perspectives on matters corporeal reaches its resolution in the form of an affirmation not simply of the value of rhetorical expression, but rhetoric derived from the Bible. With Aphrodisia, of course, this leads to an admission of defeat and a prophetic understanding of Agatha's resistance, although not to a conversion. With Euthicia, on the other hand, the conversion is immediate, but when Lucy raises the thorny problem of her inheritance, she displays resistance, affirming that it would be better to act only when life has left her corporeal body: 'Fija, cubre primero mis ojos e después faz lo que quisieres de todo lo que quedare después de mi muerte.'[20]

The admixture of motives and attitudes in Aphrodisia and Euthicia is not expressed identically, although in both instances there is a certain degree of reluctance to shed responsibilities or perceived social functions that have taken years to establish and perfect. With Aphrodisia, whose primary function is that of brothel-keeper, the challenge to her status is such that when confronted by Agatha, she is able to admit defeat but not change her vocation. It is doubtful, therefore, that she can be saved. Euthicia, on the other hand, is able to accept her daughter's counsel and seek a cure to her predicament, but despite an improvement in her circumstances, she finds herself unable, when it comes to the subject of wealth, to relinquish her function as nurturing and protecting mother.

The clash between Lucy and Euthicia can be appraised on many levels. Structurally, it functions as the first of a sequence of debates, and in contrast to those that Lucy has with Paschasius and her husband-to-be, it has a positive outcome. In this way it serves as a point of contrast and comparison, pitting a learning experience or vertical debate against encounters in which characters either refuse to learn or are unable to do so. The contrast is further underpinned by a distinction between male and female, and between life and death: Euthicia, effectively moribund within life, finds a solution to her ailment as a result of her daughter's

---

20 *Pasión*, 34-36. See also: *Vida* (20-22) and *Vida e passión* (22-23).

advice; subsequently, she unburdens herself of a heavy financial burden, and in so doing guarantees that she will inherit eternal life.

In this respect it becomes possible to argue that the dissemination of Christian rhetoric is a life-giving exercise, and that a parallel relationship is established between the obstacles that she overcomes. The haemorrhage, which reflects on Euthicia's life-giving function as mother, and her wealth, which is symbolic of basic maternal protection, are physical burdens that impede spiritual development. More noticeable, however, is that in each instance the power of rhetoric provides a solution, first as Lucy fashions a conscious typology and encourages her mother to place her faith in Christ, and then as she attacks the vanity of human possession:[21]

> Madre mía, lo que dieres después de la muerte, non lo darás si non porque non lo podrás contigo levar. E por ende dalo mientra bives e has sanidat por que ayas gualardón en el regno celestial.

The result is that in this way Lucy associates wealth with spiritual death, and poverty with life, counterbalancing a reference to corporeal resurrection within life by an allusion to the salvation of the soul and the resurrection of the flesh at the Last Judgement.

The shaping of Euthicia's conversion brings to mind a number of ideas relating to nurturing and motherhood, but it is Lucy's wet-nurse who is most active in the disbursal of her inheritance. The text in this respect establishes something of a female micro-society, with the three characters presenting a unified and coherent understanding of their religious vocation by embarking on a course of action that will lead inexorably to confrontation. The specificity of the narrative, however, is such that it raises a number of deeper questions, for while Euthicia is associated with vaginal bleeding, and Lucy, the defence of her maidenhead, the primary function of the wet-nurse reminds readers once again of the nurturing quality of the breast—a characteristic pointedly discussed by Agatha in her confrontation with Quintianus. The relationship between the three characters presents them in this way as a type of

---

21   *Pasión*, 36-39. See also: *Vida* (22-24) and *Vida e passión* (23-25).

female Trinity with individually specified roles and functions, but what is most noticeable is a striking juxtaposition between corporeal and rhetorical, with the hoodwinking of Lucy's husband-to-be predicated on a distinction between literal and figurative interpretation:[22]

> E oyendo dezir el esposo que su esposa vendía todo lo que su madre avía, vínolo a preguntar a una ama que criara a su esposa. E ella respondióle sabiamente e díxole: 'Tu esposa ha fallado otra heredat mucho mejor e querríala conprar para sí e en su nonbre, e vende algunas cosas de las de su madre para la poder aver.' E el esposo, creyendo esto, començó a la ayudar a vender, creyendo ser verdat lo que le dixiera la ama que criara a su esposa, e que quería conprar alguna heredat tenporal.

As with Quintianus, Lucy's fiancé is too stupid to understand the sophistication of such rhetoric, and too literal minded to focus on anything other than the physical. As a result, he unwittingly helps to disburse the inheritance that he had greedily hoped to gain for himself. When he realizes what has happened, his anger is such that he delivers Lucy directly into the hands of Paschasius, without in the process either engaging in debate with her or offering a single word of direct speech. His silence is telling, for it points not only to a sense of powerlessness (a spectacular inversion of the traditional distinction between the genders), but a polarization between corporeal and rhetorical, with the verbal dexterity of the female characters counterbalanced by the threat of male judicial punishment.

The debate between Lucy and Paschasius exploits similar distinctions. Paschasius orders Lucy to offer sacrifice but she confounds his understanding by modifying his frame of reference in order to redefine the subject in terms of Christian ministry:[23]

> E oyendo esto, el juez don Pasqual mandó que ofresciese sacreficios a los dioses. E respondió Santa Lucía e dixo: 'El sacreficio aplazible a

---

22   *Pasión*, 41-48. See also: *Vida* (26-30) and *Vida e passión* (27-33).
23   *Pasión*, 52-55. See also: *Vida* (33-36) and *Vida e passión* (37-40).

Dios es vesitar a los pobres e acorrerlos en sus nescesidades, e porque ya non he otra cosa que le pueda ofrescer, ofresco a mi mesma a él.'

Unable or unwilling to engage with this ploy, Paschasius advises Lucy to save such words for her fellow Christians ('Estas palabras puedes tú dezir a otro christiano que es tan loco como tú') and instead affirms that he is loyal to the laws of Empire.[24] When Lucy undermines this observation, however, he attacks her rhetoric again, on this occasion associating her words with those of a shameless harlot: 'fablas así como muger pública que non ha vergueña nin temor'.[25]

This observation establishes a further link between Agatha and Lucy, as in each instance rhetorical disobedience becomes associated explicitly with prostitution. Agatha, as we recall, spurned Quintianus and was imprisoned in a brothel in an attempt to shatter her resolve. Lucy, in contrast, undermines Paschasius's rhetoric, and in so doing, is characterized as a shameless public whore. The result is that questions of loyalty and obedience become sexualized, with the control and domination of female rhetoric becoming identified with the regulation and commodification of female sexuality. The texts in this way adopt the traditional language of androcentric domination, with the obedient and monogamous wife (subjugated by acts of verbal and corporeal submission) pitted against the harlot, whose scurrilous words function as a correlative of unrestrained sexual activity.

As one might expect, Lucy rejects Paschasius's terminology and opts once again for figurative expression, claiming that she has located her patrimony 'en logar seguro'—a reference to the parable of the talents.[26] This phrase, which brings to mind the words used by the wet-nurse in the duping of Lucy's husband-to-be, leads to an exchange in which references to corporeal corruption are replaced by allusions to the corruption of the soul. The shaping of this statement confounds Paschasius's limited intellectual ability, and as is the case with Quin-

---

24 *Pasión*, 56-58. See also: *Vida* (35-38) and *Vida e passión* (41-42).
25 *Pasión*, 65-66. See also: *Vida* (43) and *Vida e passión* (47-48).
26 *Pasión*, 67. See also: *Vida* (44) and *Vida e passión* (48-49). For the parable of the talents, see: Matthew 25:14-30 and Luke 19:12-28.

tianus, his subsequent interrogative stands not as a measure of intellectual enquiry, but of his limitations.

The most spectacular evidence of inadequacy, however, is offered shortly afterwards, as Paschasius grows weary of the confrontation and attempts to silence Lucy's words with the threat of torture: '¡Cesarán las palabras quando viniéramos a los açotes e a las llagas!'[27] With this statement, the parallel between Paschasius and Quintianus becomes more noticeable, as in each instance the Roman inquisitor uses the threat of corporeal punishment in an attempt to stifle the power of Christian rhetoric. The principal difference is that Lucy responds with a twofold statement, arguing first that the word of God cannot be silenced, and then, that the Holy Spirit speaks through those who defend themselves before judges and kings:[28]

> Non só yo Dios, mas só sierva de Dios. E él dixo que quando estoviésemos delante los reyes e de los juezes, non oviésemos cuydado de pensar lo que avíamos de fablar, que él nos diría lo que oviésemos a dezir, e que non seríamos nós los que fablávamos, mas el Spíritu Santo que fablaría en nós.

With the power of the Holy Spirit within her, Lucy cannot be silenced, and so Paschasius threatens her with violation in a brothel. His motivation in so doing is to force the Holy Spirit to leave her, assuming erroneously that a ritualized process of corporeal corruption will allow him to gain power not simply over her person, but the rhetorical ability with which she has been able to torture his limited intellect.

The way in which this relationship is explored within the narrative is significant, for while the presence of the Holy Spirit is presented in gender-neutral terms, the decision to silence Lucy's rhetoric by subjecting her to a form of sexualized coercion relates her to Agatha and various other saints—male and female alike. Needless to say, Pascha-

---

27 *Pasión*, 74-75. See also: *Vida* (50-51) and *Vida e passión* (55-56).
28 *Pasión*, 77-82. See also: *Vida* (52-55) and *Vida e passión* (57-61).

sius's efforts are unsuccessful, and despite employing a variety of different stratagems, he is unable to have Lucy moved:[29]

> E queriéndola levar los rufianes al burdel, asieron della, e de tan grant peso la fizo ser el Spíritu Santo que non la pudieron mover. E mandó don Pasqual que le atasen los pies e las manos con sogas e tirasen dellas mill onbres, mas non la pudieron mover. E fizo traer muchos pares de bueyes e fízolos atar a las sogas e tyrar, mas non la pudieron mover punto nin más. E fizo llamar a unos encantadores para que la fiziesen mover con sus encantamentos, mas non pudieron. [...] E pensando don Pasqual que con azeyte podría fazer fuyr al diablo e desatar aquellos encantamentos, mandó echar azeyte encima della. E como non la pudiesen mover con todo esto, començó a se ensangustiar mucho más, e fizo encender grant fuego enderredor della, e mandó echar sobre ella pez e resina e azeyte.

As is the case with Agatha, whose will is characterized throughout the text as being stronger than rock, Lucy is presented in this passage as a figure impervious to transformation or external coercion. Her resistance, which is bolstered by the power of the Holy Spirit, ensures that others are forced to change around her, and it is for this reason that Paschasius resorts to an ever more frenzied series of stratagems, attempting to have her dragged away by thugs, tied by hands and feet, pulled by men and oxen, charmed by spells, and then basted and burned.

When these efforts come to nothing, he eventually has her stabbed in the throat. This action can be appraised on a number of levels, notably as an act of vengeance and petulant frustration, but also in phallic terms, as a sublimated representation of the physical violation that Lucy has so far managed to avoid. Its most significant function, however, is to shed further light on the relationship between rhetorical and corporeal, with the executioner's blade directed specifically against the part of the body responsible for speech. It is perhaps for this reason that Lucy miraculously continues to speak until Paschasius is summoned to execution, even taking the opportunity to compare herself to Agatha,

---

29   *Pasión*, 96-113. See also: *Vida* (66-80) and *Vida e passión* (70-83).

claiming that she will protect Syracuse as her counterpart protects Catania: 'E asý como por mi hermana Santa Ágata es anparada la cibdat de Catania, asý será anparada por mí aquesta cibdat Ciracusana.'[30] In so doing she shows clearly while her assailant has achieved a partial and token victory over the flesh, the word—as manifested in the power and eloquence of her rhetoric—will forever remain inviolate.

Torture, Sexualization, and the Breast

A consideration of the relationship between corporeality and rhetoric makes it possible to return to the question posed at the start of this discussion, and to ask not only why saints are tortured, but why torture is sometimes sexualized. The work of early Church historians has done much to enhance our understanding of some aspects of this problem, notably with regard to their focus on the clash between the nascent monotheistic Christian religion, and polytheistic Rome, with its religion of Empire effectively compelling subjects to make a choice between loyalty and treason. This entrenched polarity, ended only by the conversion to Christianity promulgated by the Edict of Milan in 313, ensured that devotion to a deity not yet officially incorporated into the existing structures of Empire became, in legal terms, a crime punishable by death. A cognate argument, expressed succinctly by G. W. Bowersock (1995), is centred on salvation as a reenactment of Christ's suffering (*imitatio Christi*) and the triumph of the martyr as voluntary *mors mortis*. In this light, submission to torture is both a gesture of defiance and a form of Christological homage, ensuring that those who suffer as Christ suffered will be rewarded as he was rewarded. For this reason Gregory of Tours argues that sanctity de-individualizes to such an extent that we should talk not of the lives of the saints ('vitae sanctorum'), but the life of the saint ('vita sanctorum')—all saints surrendering their individuality and becoming mere refractions of Christ.[31]

---

30 *Pasión*, 121-22. See also: *Vida* (86-88) and *Vida e passión* (90-91).

31 See Elliott 1987: 5-6 and Winstead 1997: 3, and for historical studies of Roman persecution, Guterman 1951, Frend 1959 and 1965, and Lane Fox 1986. The characteristics of the *passio* and its impact on the relationship between Christianity and Rome have been discussed by Altman 1975.

These approaches are illuminating, but in their application to literature they run the risk of focusing on the tortured subject at the exclusion of the torturer, who is effectively reduced to a collective and unthinking determination merely to uphold the norms of orthodoxy. To generate a less partial interpretation it behoves the reader to consider the impact of overarching sociological factors such as the display and degradation of matrices of power and their effect on the individual. In his groundbreaking but now largely superseded theoretical analysis, Stephen Lukes (1975) proposes a three-dimensional view of the conflict of preferences, affirming that while successful control of one subject over another can ensure the latter's compliance, in a more nuanced and multi-tiered model we must also bear in mind that 'the domination of defenders of the status quo may be so secure and pervasive that they are unaware of any potential challengers to their position and thus of any alternative to the existing political process, whose bias they work to maintain' (1975: 21).

This interpretation sheds a good deal of light on the behaviour not only of Quintianus, who is responsible for severing Agatha's breast, but Paschasius, whose deeply (but differently) sexualized treatment of Lucy could otherwise, from a purely partisan perspective, be dismissed as nothing more than a pathological product of traditional Roman savagery. It also dovetails with the conclusions of early feminist scholarship, a well-known example being Hannah Arendt's pioneering study of violence (1970), in which she maintains that political institutions are manifestations and materializations of consensual power that petrify and decay as soon as the living power of the people ceases to uphold them. This, she argues, can result in revolution; but if power is threatened, it is often replaced by violence. In this respect we have little option but to regard power and violence not as interrelated aspects of a continuum of coercion, but rather more simplistically, as antitheses.

Read in this light, the actions of Quintianus and Paschasius make greater psychological sense, as their descent into depravity can be seen not simply as a product of ignorance or of individual or collective psychopathology, but failing political control and domination, and a dawning awareness of the potential for revolutionary upheaval. This, to some extent, could be dismissed as an anachronistic reading, as a Christian audience in the Middle Ages would almost certainly have taken an opposing view, regarding polytheistic Rome and its ministers in more black-and-white terms as a veritable fount of iniquity. Yet anachronism is relative, and while we may on the one hand feel it legitimate to apply modern theories to the literary depiction of ancient Rome in a series of fourteenth-century texts (reworked, it must be said, in an act of partial ventriloquism from Latin originals composed more than a century earlier), we need also to bear in mind that Voragine's narratives are in themselves anachronistic reworkings of confrontations, historical or imaginary, that either happened or were thought to have happened in the third and fourth centuries.

In this respect, the most beneficial approach is to focus not on medieval or modern readers, but the characterization of the Roman inquisitors and the way in which their culturally sophisticated and radically advanced society is challenged by a seemingly primitive and fanatical sect that refuses to accept its most basic assumptions. The severity of the treatment meted out to Agatha and Lucy, therefore, is partly a product of frustration, and partly one of disbelief, with Quintianus and Paschasius incapable of envisioning an alternative to Roman authority or even of understanding why it should be challenged.

Rereading the texts in this way goes a good way towards accounting for the violence and severity of the interaction between martyr and inquisitor, but it does not explain the gendering or sexualization of torture. To do so, it becomes vital to return to an issue of critical importance: the fact that far from being defeminized, or even denying her sexuality, the virgin martyr reaffirms her position in the patriarchy by sexualizing her relationship to Christ, her celestial bridegroom, at the expense of all earthly rivals.

This, as we have seen, is an opposition that dominates the concluding stages of Agatha's legend, where the narrative is saturated by a tone of courtly love. It is equally noticeable in that of Lucy, initially in relation to the duping of her husband-to-be, which smacks of a traditional act of wifely infidelity, and then in the debate between her and Paschasius, where he equates disloyalty to Empire with the actions of a prostitute, condemning her to be gang-raped in a brothel. The logic of his sentence is that as Lucy has become a prostitute in mind and action, forsaking Roman authority in the form of her husband and judge, she will be forced to become one in the flesh.[32]

The treatment of the two virgin martyrs is in this way different, but it is noticeable in both instances that it is the choice of a different, unacceptable, and to a large extent, unfathomable 'other' that confounds and infuriates the Roman authorities, leading them not simply to the imposition of violence, but a form of coercive violence manifested specifically in sexualized terms. In this light, there are clear parallels between the situation presented within the texts and the conclusions of early lesbian theory, particularly in its understanding of sexualized violence inflicted on women by men stemming from the choice of an incomprehensible 'other' and the resultant perceived threat to universal patriarchal dominance (see Rich 1983).

With Lucy, the process of sexualized torture is directed specifically against her reproductive organ, and as is the case elsewhere, the attempt at genital violation is categorically rebuffed. Her sexual integrity in this way remains intact, but the most appreciable effect is the establishment of an awkward—if not pornographic—fusion of ideas, in which notions of rape, coercion, and sexual degradation are subsumed within the context of an overarching sexualized framework redolent with erotic connotations.

Agatha, in contrast, suffers a fate that partly relates her to other female saints but that is unique in the specificity of its formulation, with the emphasis of the encounter with Saint Peter falling on mammary restoration, and the moment of torture on the unique and distinctive function of the breast as a provider of milk. It is for this reason that she alludes not only to Quintianus's lack of shame in severing the organ from which he once drew life, but the auxiliary breasts that have for many years existed in her soul. From this point onwards the Castilian versions offer slightly differing readings, but while in one she claims that Christ has always been the focus of her desire, in others she comments on the

---

32   For studies on the correlation between disloyalty and prostitution, see Karras 1996: 115, and in relation to the early Castilian canon, Beresford 2007a: 53-54.

consecration of her breasts, boldly affirming that they have been reserved since she was a little girl exclusively for the celestial bridegroom.[33]

It is here that the significance of Agatha's torture becomes most apparent, for although her legend appears in early Castilian in the context of devotional anthologies designed to enhance Christian piety, it is noticeable that it draws at the same time on the cumulative value of centuries of popular assumptions focused on the uniquely female, life-giving, and yet simultaneously erotic qualities that have traditionally been associated with the breast.

Some, such as the prehistoric belief in the powers of the mammary shrine, the *dea nutrix* or nursing goddess, and the primeval veneration of the womanly mysteries of procreation and lactation fall outside a realistic chronological frame of reference, but are part, nonetheless, of an ancient underlying consciousness that influenced later conceptions as a result of a process of syncretism.[34] The same is true of the multi-breasted figure of the goddess Artemis of Ephesus, whose rows of supernumerary breasts or nipples, arranged along an extended mammary ridge, establish a conceptual link between human and animal fecundity, in this way relating breasts to the multiple teats and udders found in other mammals. It is for this reason that artistic representations have often shown a child suckling at one of the goddess's breasts or milk streams flowing from several breasts into the mouths of hungry children. In this way Artemis came to represent the miraculous notion of a never-ending supply of milk—a response, no doubt, to a

---

33   Compare: 'Yo he otras tetas entregas en la mi alma que consagré al Señor desde la mi niñez, e con ellas dó yo a los mis sesos fartura de leche' (*Istoria*, 93-94), 'Enpero yo tengo otras tetas enteras de dentro en mi alma de que se crian todos los mis sesos. E los ofrescí a Dios de pequeña' (*Passión*, 61-62), 'Enpero yo tengo otras tetas de dentro en la mi alma. E las ofresçí de pequeña a Dios' (*Vida*, 63-64), and 'Pero yo tengo otras tetas entregas en la mi alma do se crian todos los mis deseos. E los ofrecí de pequeña a Dios' (*Vida de la virgen*, 58-59).

34   For discussions of the *Dea nutrix*, the mammary shrine, and other primeval forms of veneration, see amongst others: Avigad 1977, Yalom 1997: 9-15, Lutzky 1998, Byrne 2004, and Burleigh, Fitzpatrick-Matthews, & Aldhouse-Green 2006.

universal maternal neurosis that ended only in the nineteenth century with the advent of pasteurization.[35]

Other associations, in contrast, are by no means as historically remote, and in the confrontation between Agatha and Quintianus, there may well be a submerged echo of the myth of the foundation of Rome, with the infants Romulus and Remus rescued from the Tiber by a she-wolf and raised thereafter by suckling her milk. This, according to Roman tradition, accounted for their invincible courage and daring, as the process of nursing ensured that in addition to gaining a life-preserving form of sustenance, they managed simultaneously to imbibe the she-wolf's fierce martial qualities. The breast in this respect is not simply a source of nourishment, but a means with which to transmit and absorb inherited characteristics.

An equally plausible analogue can be seen in the goddess of love, Venus (or in Greek, Aphrodite), who from around the time of the fourth century, has commonly been depicted in artistic representation in a state of semi- or complete undress, with her breasts either outlined or fully exposed. Furthermore, as a result of a perceived relationship with Helen of Troy, who, on her return from the Trojan wars is reported to have bared the apples of her bosom to her husband, her breasts (in addition to being firm and muscular) are commonly represented as apple-like, in this way bringing together notions of worship and desire (or piety and eroticism) in the form of a single female image.[36]

The most significant mythological relationship, however, is between Agatha and the Amazons, a race of female warriors descended from Ares, god of war, who were accustomed to severing their breasts so that they could carry quivers and shoot arrows more effectively at their enemies. Legend has it that the right breast was removed by cauterization in infancy so that physical strength could be transferred to the corresponding shoulder and arm. The race was renewed through sexual contact with foreigners, and

---

35   Yalom 1997: 9, 16. See also Buck 1889, Astor 1989, LiDonnici 1992, and Schiebinger 1993.

36   See Yalom 1997: 18-19 and 24-25, and Schiebinger 1993. A similar analogy appears in the poetic *Vida de Santa María Egipciaca*: 'De sus tetiellas bien es sana, / tales son como maçana' (Alvar 1970-72: II, 56, lines 223-24).

while male sons were crippled and turned into slaves, female offspring were held in high regard. The result was that the Amazons came in this way to represent a reversal of all they were expected to be.

In her groundbreaking discussion of the history of the breast, Marilyn Yalom interprets the Amazon myth as a deep-seated expression of gynophobia manifested specifically as a fear of vengeance slumbering in the psyche of those in positions of gendered dominance (1997: 21-24). This, she argues, assumes the form of a fear not only of the breast denied, but the possibility that absence could denote aggression. The result is a spectacular shift in the characterization of woman from mother to virago and self to shadow self. The myth in this respect is predicated on a terrifying asymmetry, for as Yalom later explains, 'one breast is retained to nurture female offspring [while] the other is removed so as to facilitate violence against men' (1997: 23).[37]

More relevant than the residue of pagan mythology, however, is the process of syncretism that can be seen in the absorption and adaptation of ancient ideas in Christianity, notably in the form of its most celebrated female figure, the Virgin Mary. As a mother saved by an angel from the corruption of sexual impregnation on the part of her husband, Mary assumes special status, functioning as the antithesis of Eve—a figure punished after the expulsion from Paradise with the infliction of the pains of childbirth. She also, in the timeless and homely image of the infant Christ suckling (often greedily) at her breast, provides a powerful maternal image and a metaphor for the spiritual nourishment of Christian souls.

A potent reworking of these ideas can be seen in artistic and literary representations of Bernard of Clairvaux, where, in order to offer the benefit of divine wisdom, the Virgin appears within the context of a vision and either sprinkles milk onto his lips or inserts her breast into his mouth.[38] Similar tales can be found in the visions of Henry de Suso

---

37 For further information on the Amazons, see amongst others, Bisset 1971 and Schiebinger 1993. The theme is best known in early Castilian literature in the *Planto de Pantasilea*, a poem commonly attributed to Juan Rodríguez del Padrón (see Wardropper 1967: 37-43).

38 See Yalom 1997: 46-48, and for analogues in Castilian, Beresford 2003. The wider background has been studied by Bynum 1982: 115-20 and 1987: 270-72. For

and in relation to various medieval nuns, some of whom claimed that their breasts would fill with milk at the sight of Christ. Likewise, mystics such as Margery Kempe and Ida of Louvain identified themselves with Mary as she suckled the infant Christ, while lactation legends were attached to hagiographic treatments of figures such as Dominic of Guzmán, founder of the Dominicans, and Peter Nolasco, founder of the Mercedarians.[39] The underlying assumption, as Marilyn Yalom points out, is that milk is seen as a spiritual as well as material form of nourishment, and so 'to give the breast to one's baby was decidedly more than a simple matter of alimentation: the mother transmitted with her milk a whole religio-ethical belief system' (1997: 38).

The deeper implications of this relationship are explored in the Compilation A account of the Ascension, where a parallel is established between the nurturing quality of Mary's breast and the redemptive power of Christ's blood:[40]

> Seguramente puedes llegar, omne, a Dios, ado has a la Madre por abogada delante el Fijo, e al Fijo delante del Padre, e ado la Madre amuestra al Fijo los pechos e las tetas, e el Fijo demuestra al Padre el costado e las llagas.

The origin of this image can be traced to medieval physiological theory and the assumption that breast milk is a form of transmuted blood that becomes available to the suckling infant not only as the food of life, but a form of nourishment of benefit to the soul.[41]

---

discussions of the role and function of the nursing Virgin, see Bétérous 1975, Miles 1986, and Boss 2000: 37-39. The lactation was a popular theme in Spanish art, and perhaps most worthy of note are the works of Alonso Cano (Bray et al 2009: 102-03) and Juan de las Roelas (Brown 1998: 106). A variation on the image of the lactating Virgin can be seen in Pedro Machuca's *Virgin of Souls in Purgatory* (Brown 1998: 32), where streams of milk pour from Mary's breasts and are gathered at the foot of the composition by desperate souls hoping for a release from their torment in Purgatory.

39   See Bynum 1987: 123, 126, 211, and 270-72.

40   See BNM 780 fol. 162[vb]. The Compilation B accounts are significantly abbreviated. See BMP 8 fols 26[ra]-27[vb], BMP 9 fol. 16[r], FLG 419 fols 58[ra]-60[ra], Escorial k-II-12 fol. 93[rb-va], Escorial h-I-14 fol. 119[ra-va], and Escorial M-II-6 fol. 77[r].

41   See Bynum 1987: 65 and 270-72, and for a discussion of the physiological background, Atkinson 1991: 23-63.

The emphasis, of course, is on transferability, and just as milk and blood become symbolically fused, so too do the roles of Christ and Mary. Indeed, as Caroline Walker Bynum notes, in some instances this leads to symbolic reversal, with Christ sometimes represented as mother and Mary as nursing child (1982). In fact, in one (now lost) painting 'Mary drinks from the breast of Christ while holding him in her arms' (1987: 272). In other accounts, such as those that deal with Gertrude of Helfta, the image of Christ as nursemaid becomes subject to further evolution as he allows her to receive his heart through the wound in his side (1987: 151). A related inversion is discussed in the *Libro de las virtuosas e claras mugeres* in accounts (II.17 & 18) dealing with daughters who nurse their parents to prevent them from starving to death.

The transferability of the relationship between blood and milk is explored in the legend of Saint Blaise in a section dealing with the martyrdom of seven women arrested for collecting the saint's blood. A reason for their action is not offered explicitly, although the subsequent shaping of the episode establishes links between notions of protection, redemption, and the transmission of divine knowledge in the form of liquid nourishment. The process begins when one of the women provokes the prefect's anger by mocking his attempt to force her to worship pagan icons. Her children, realizing that her words will lead to martyrdom, implore her to take them with her, and in so doing establish an analogy between breast milk and the joy of heaven:

> Non nos dexes acá, madre muy dulce, mas así como nos fenchiste de la dulcedunbre de la leche, así nos finche de la dulcedunbre del regno celestial.

In response, the prefect has them carded with iron combs, but in place of blood, it is milk that flows from their wounds:[42]

---

42   BNM 12688 fol. 271vb, but see also Escorial h-III-22 fol. 170ra. For accounts in Compilation B, see: BMP 9 fol. 14^{r}, FLG 419 fol. 26ra, Escorial K-II-12 fol. 48rb, Escorial h-I-14 fols 60rb-61va, and Escorial M-II-6 fol. 22$^{a\text{-}b}$. For an edition of BNM 10252 fols 100va-103va, which belongs to a different textual tradition, see Schiff 1905: 252-58.

E oyendo esto el adelantado, mandólas colgar e rasgar sus carnes con peyndes de fierro. E desque sus carnes fueron rasgadas con los peyndes, parescían blancas como la nieve, e corría, en logar de sangre, leche.

The episode in this way offers a symbolic exploration not simply of the bond between mother and child (focusing on the nurturing quality of the breast), but the relationship between milk, blood, and martyrdom, suggesting that an analogue to the redemptive power of sacrifice can be found in the nurturing properties of milk.

A different aspect of transferability can be seen in the legend of Saint Paul, as the saint suffers death by decapitation, spouting forth a stream of milk followed by one of blood: 'E desque fue ferido con el cuchillo, salió luego dél leche, e mojó la vestidura del caballero que lo degolló, e después salió sangre'.[43] In contrast to other accounts, which focus on the maternal function of the breast, the relationship between blood and milk is so powerful in this respect that its logic transcends anatomical function and becomes applicable to a man. Authority for this relationship can be found in Revelation 7:14 in the description of the properties of the Lamb, whose blood renders the robes of martyrs white, and so in this respect Paul functions as Christ's surrogate, with the sacrificial and Eucharistic quality of his blood preceded by an outpouring of nourishing milk. The relationship is further strengthened by the inclusion of symbolic references to clothing, which in each instance function as visual indicators of status.[44]

---

43   BNM 780 fol. 222va. For Compilation B, see: BMP 8 fol. 44ra, FLG 419 fol. 78vb, Escorial h-I-14 fol. 150rb, and Escorial M-II-6 fol. 95^{v}. The account in BMP 9 (fol. 23vb) is incomplete.

44   An analogue to this relationship can be found in the addendum to the *Legenda aurea* in a section dealing with the Last Supper, but as this was not subsequently reworked into Castilian, it cannot necessarily be regarded as an influence: 'Tertio lavit pedes spiritualiter aqua sui sanguinis, de quo dicitur Apocal. II: laverunt stolas suas in sanguine agni et dealbaverunt eas. Ex quo magis sanguis Christi dealbare dicitur, videtur, quod habet virtutem lactis et sanguinis. Lac enim est sanguis in uberibus excoctus. Sanguis autem Christi fuit excoctus in corpore suo

A second source of scriptural authority is 1 Peter 2:2-3, which presents believers as newborn babies and knowledge as milk. The mysterious and magical nature of this relationship is reflected in hagiography in references to nursing and the transference not simply of nourishment, but knowledge and protection. A striking example can be found in the legend of Saint Odilia, where the breasts of her wet-nurse are found incorrupt eighty years after her death. The assumption in this instance is that interaction produces an element of symbiosis which leads to mutual enrichment. A different version of this relationship, with a sickly infant unable to take the breast, appears in the legend of Saint Ulrich, which like that of Odilia, was appended to a number of later versions of the *Legenda* but was not subsequently reworked into Castilian.[45]

Other texts, in contrast, were reworked, and notable in this respect is Saint Nicholas, who displays evidence of saintly behaviour from infancy by refusing to accept the breast more than once on Wednesdays and Fridays.[46] Related examples can be found in the reading for Mary Magdalene, where she saves a nursing infant and its mother from death at sea, and in the legend of Saint George, where the King laments the fact that he will not see grandchildren suckling at his daughter's breast. The most mysterious and intriguing example, however, is that of Saint Giles, who is nursed by a doe while living in the wilderness. This leads to an element of human-animal reciprocity, for when the doe is hunted, Giles repays his debt by coming to its protection. For this reason he is regarded even today as a patron of nursing mothers.[47]

---

et in corde nostro, in corpore suo fuit excoctus igne amoris sui, qui tam vehementer in corpore, suo ebullit, quia aperto latere cum impetus emanavit. In corde autem nostro sunt duo ubera, scilicet intellectus et affectas. Dicitur autem exeoqui in ubera intellecus per meditationem et in ubere affectus per devotionem, et sic sanguis Christi in suo corpore et in nostro corpore per meditationem et affectionem vertitur in albedinem et animas nostras dealbat et mundat. Apocalyps. I: lavit nos a peccatis nostris in sanguine suo' (Graesse 1846: 930).

45   For Odilia, see Graesse 1846: 876-77, and for Ulrich, 1846: 877-79.

46   See Escorial h-III-22 fol. 20vb (Compilation A), and BMP 9 fol. 2^r, FLG 419 fol. 213vb, Escorial K-II-12 fol. 9rb, and Escorial h-I-14 fol. 8rb (Compilation B). For a discussion of other types of refusal, see Bynum 1987: 214-15.

47   See BNM 12689 fols 62vb-63ra, and for Compilation B: FLG 419 fol. 196ra, Escorial K-II-12 fol. 183rb, and Escorial h-I-14 fol. 240va.

This, of course, duplicates one of the roles of Agatha, who is most commonly revered in popular tradition in her paradoxical capacity as virginal bride of Christ and patron saint of nursing mothers and nursemaids, all of whom were expected on her feast day (5 February) to ask her for healthy breasts and a bountiful supply of milk. The most tangible textual evidence of this twofold function can be seen in her words to Quintianus, for having seen her breast severed, she upbraids him for his cruelty, characterizing herself in the process as a paradoxical amalgam of virgin, mother, and sexualized celestial bride:[48]

> Tirano cruel e malo, ¿cómo non as vergueña de cortar en la fenbra lo que mamaste en tu madre mesma? Yo he otras tetas entregas en la mi alma que consagré al Señor desde la mi niñez, e con ellas dó yo a los mis sesos fartura de leche.

Agatha in this respect stands specifically as a surrogate of Mary, reserving the nourishing milk of her breasts for the benefit of Christ alone.

In the light of this multiple function, the severing of the breast can be interpreted in a number of distinct but interrelated ways. In basic terms, the descent into violence can be seen partly as a by-product of the Roman judicial system, but also partly as a result of frustration, disbelief, and an inability on the part of the Roman authorities to envision an alternative to their control. It is for this reason that their power decays into violence, in this way establishing an impression throughout the texts of failing political control and domination. This, of course, is exacerbated by Agatha's skilful manipulation of rhetoric, and the way in which she sexualizes her relationship to Christ, presenting him not simply as a deity, but a superior romantic rival. The introduction of this frame of reference confounds the inquisitor's intellectual limitations, and in a conspicuously sexualized attack (bred of fear and confusion), he launches an assault on her breast, a mysterious and quintessentially female organ, revered throughout the ages for its erotic and life-giving qualities. His triumph, however, is short-lived, for as Agatha spends the

---

48 *Istoria*, 91-94. See also: *Passión* (59-62), *Vida* (62-64), and *Vida de la virgen* (56-59).

night in prison, it is restored by none other than Saint Peter. In this way it comes to stand partly as an image of the life-giving nourishment of Christian souls, and partly of its potential or temporary denial.

It is perhaps for this reason that we can understand why Agatha becomes such an attractive model for Lucy to emulate. The bond between them is presented throughout the texts as one of sisterly devotion; Agatha even addresses Lucy specifically as 'hermana'. From the relationship between the two female saints, the focus is amplified to include Lucy's mother, a character referred to in some texts by name (Euthicia), and in others, purely in terms of maternal function. The curing of Euthicia's haemorrhage focuses the reader's attention on questions of gynaecology, bringing the female sexual organ to the forefront of the narrative. This, however, is soon counterbalanced by a reminder of the life-giving quality of the breast, as it is Lucy's wetnurse (rather than mother) who assists her in the hoodwinking of her husband-to-be. The fact that she is unnamed, of course, is symbolic of her function—and it is in the light of such conspicuously female connections that the texts can most profitably be read.

These are not tales of defeminization or of becoming male, but the power of female virtue and the series of complex and paradoxical ways in which the manifold mysteries of womanhood intersect with aspects of traditional Christian dogma and teaching. With Lucy, of course, the process is taken a stage further, as the narrative focuses specifically on questions of female empathy and complicity. This can be seen not just internally in relation to the trinity of female protagonists of which she is part, but in the way in which her bond with Agatha is used and adapted in order to fashion an overarching conceptual frame. It is partly for this reason that the legends have had such a powerful and lasting effect on believers, for by exploring the paradox of womanhood in such a direct and engaging way, they present Agatha and Lucy as figures worthy not simply of admiration, but ultimately, of emulation.

7
Critical Editions

Editorial Criteria

THE CRITICAL EDITIONS PRESENTED in this Chapter are derived from transcriptions undertaken *in situ* and revised thereafter in conjunction with microfilm copies. Scribal abbreviations have been resolved and are indicated by the use of italics. The random distribution of *i/j* and *u/v* has been regularized, while word-initial *ff-*, *rr-*, and *ss-* are transcribed as *f-*, *r-*, and *s-*. The consonant *ç* is retained before *a*, *o*, and *u*, but is otherwise transcribed as *c*. Tironian signs and *et* are transcribed as *e*.

Accentuation follows modern practice, except for those that have been added to medieval forms to avoid confusion. These include *ál* ('otra cosa'), *dó* ('doy'), *fuése* ('se fue'), *só* ('soy'), and *ý* ('allí'). Accents are also included on the tonic forms of *nós* and *vós* and on archaic imperfect verb endings (*-ié*).

Word division follows modern practice, with the exception of elided compounds such as 'deste' and 'quel' (which are recorded as they appear) and enclitic verb-prounoun compounds such as 'mandóle', 'díxole', and 'respondióle', which are written out as a single form. Punctuation has been supplied and capitalization altered to make it conform to modern practice.

Changes of folio are indicated in brackets, with superscript *ra/rb* and *va/vb* designating recto and verso column divisions. A vertical bar (|) indicates a change of folio within a single word. Variant readings and departures from the base texts are listed in the critical apparatus.

The abbreviation *om.* indicates that a reading does not appear in a manuscript, and [-], that it falls in a lacuna.

The seven manuscripts are identified in the critical apparatus as follows: *A* (Escorial h-III-22), *B* (Biblioteca Nacional 12688), *C* (Fundación Lázaro Galdiano 419), *D* (Biblioteca Menéndez Pelayo 9), *E* (Escorial K-II-12), *F* (Escorial h-I-14), and *G* (Escorial M-II-6).

Text I
La istoria de la bienaventurada Santa Ágata
(Escorial h-III-22 and BNM 12688)

[fol. 171ʳᵃ] Aquí comiença la istoria de la bienaventurada Santa Ágata Ágata quiere dezir 'santa de Dios'. E segunt dize Sant Crisóstomo, tres cosas fazen al onbre santo: conviene saber, la linpieza del coraçón e la presencia del Spíritu Santo e la muchedunbre de las buenas obras. E todas estas tres cosas fueron conplidamente en Santa Ágata. E aun Ágata quiere dezir 'deesa sin tierra'; conviene saber, syn amor de las cosas terrenales. E aun Ágata quiere dezir 'fabladora conplida e acabada'. E aquesto paresce asaz claramente en sus respuestas. E a|un [fol. 171ʳᵇ] Ágata quiere dezir 'servidunbre mayor'. E aquesto paresce asaz claramente en la respuesta que dio a Quinciano, diziendo: 'Aquella es grant nobleza en la qual es provada la servidunbre de Jhesu Christo.' E aun Ágata quiere dezir 'acabada solepnemente'. E esto paresce asaz claramente en el su enterramiento, que fue acabado de los ángeles.

E aquesta santa virgen fue en Cecilia en la cibdat de Catania, noble e fermosa por linaje e por cuerpo, mas mucho más noble e fermosa por alma. E aquesta santa virgen sirvió sienpre al Salvador en toda santidat. E Quinciano, un cónsul que era en Cecilia, era de vil linaje e luxurioso e avariento e adorador de los ýdolos, e deseava mucho prender a Santa Ágata. Por que fuese temido, aunque era de baxo linaje, quería prender a muger tan noble e de tan [fol. 171ᵛᵃ] alto linaje, e cobdiciava mucho conplir con ella su luxuria porque era donzella de grant fermosura, e deseava aver sus riquezas sy non quisiese adorar los ýdolos.

E fízola prender e traer delante sý. E como la fallase muy firme e non movible de su entinción, diola a guardar a una mala muger que avía nonbre Afrodisan, que tenía nueve fijas que eran todas malas mugeres, por que mudase el su coraçón de la entinción de la christiandat e la ynclinase a aver ayuntamiento con él. E Afrodisan tóvola consigo treynta días e trabajava mucho por la mudar de su entinción, a las vezes prometiéndole cosas muy alegres, a las vezes amenazándola con tormentos muy fuertes. E oyendo estas cosas Santa Ágata de Afrodisan e de sus fijas, díxoles: 'El mi coraçón está asentado sobre piedra muy firme, e está funda|do [fol. 171vb] sobre Jhesu Christo, fijo de Dios bivo. E las vuestras palabras son asý como viento, e los vuestros prometimientos son así como lluvias que fallescen de ligero, e los vuestros espantos son así como ríos que pasan arrebatados. E non podrán derribar los cimientos de mi casa porque están asentados sobre piedra de grant firmeza.' E llorava cada día e rogava al Señor que conpliese el su deseo e la fiziese venir a la gloria del martirio. E veyendo Afrodisan la fortaleza del su coraçón, fuése para Quinciano, pasados los treynta días, e díxole: 'Más aýna podrían ser molidos los guijarros e tornado el fierro así como plomo blando, que ser apartada esta donzella de la su creencia.'

E oyendo esto, Quinciano mandóla traer delante sý. E asentóse en su silla e díxole: '¿De qué condición eres tú?' E respondióle Santa Ágata e dixo: 'Non so|lamente [fol. 172ra] só libre, mas aun de muy noble linaje, segunt lo demuestra todo el parentesco que yo tengo.' E díxole Quinciano: 'Si eres libre e noble, ¿por qué te demuestras en las costunbres aver persona de sierva?' E respondióle Santa Ágata e dixo: 'Muéstrome tener persona de sierva porque só sierva de Jhesu Christo, fijo de Dios bivo.' E díxole Quinciano: 'Si libre eres e noble como dizes, ¿en qué manera te afirmas ser sierva?' E respondióle Santa Ágata e dixo: 'La clarydat de la nobleza se demuestra en la servidunbre de Jhesu Christo, criador del syglo.' E díxole Quinciano: '¡Conviene escoger de dos cosas la una: o ofrescer sacreficio a los dioses non mortales o sofrir muchos tormentos e grandes!' E respondióle Santa Ágata e dixo: '¡Tales seades tú e tu muger qual fue el tu dios Jú|piter!' [fol. 172rb] E oyendo esto, Quinciano mandóla ferir a palmadas e díxole: '¡Non te deves atrever a ynjuriar locamente al juez!' E respondióle Santa Ágata e dixo: 'Mucho me maravillo de ty, que te tienes por onbre sabio e te crees ser ynjuriado porque te digo que agora fueses tal como aquél a quien te ynclinas a adorar. E si tú e tu muger non deseades remedar la vida de aquél que adorades por dios, ¿en qué manera te ynclinas a le sacreficar e onrrar? Ca si Júpiter es tu dios, non te desee mal mas bien, conviene saber que fueses semejante a él. E si aborresces de le semejar, ¿por qué me costriñes a lo adorar? Ca sy aborresces la su conpañía, eso mesmo sientes que yo siento, e non deves querer que yo le ofresca encienso.' E díxole Quinciano: '¿Para qué me detienes [fol. 172va] en palabras demasiadas? ¡O sacrefica a los dioses o te faré morir a tormentos de grandes dolores!' E respondióle Santa Ágata e dixo: 'Si me amenazas que me echarás a las vestias bravas, oyendo el nonbre de Jhesu Christo serán amansadas. E sy me amenazas que me quemarás en el fuego, los ángeles me enbiarán rocío saludable del cielo. E si me amenazas con otros tormentos, yo he comigo el Spíritu Santo, que me da esfuerço e me librará dellos.' E oyendo esto, Quinciano mandóla levar a la cárcel, ca lo confondía por palabras delante de todos los que allí estavan. E Santa Ágata fuése muy alegre e gloriándose a la cárcel como sy fuera conbidada a manjares muy delectables. E encomendava al Señor la su batalla con oraciones muy afincadas.

    E otro día mandóla Quinciano traer delante sý e díxole: [fol. 172vb] '¡Niega a Jhesu Christo crucificado e adora a los dioses muy altos!' E como Santa Ágata non lo quisiese fazer, mandóla atormentar muy gravemente en un tormento que era llamado cavallejo. E estando allí Santa Ágata, dixo a Quinciano: 'Así me deleyto yo en aquestas penas en que estó, como el que oye algunt buen mensaje, o vee al que mucho desea veer, o falla thesoros muy presciosos. Ca non puede ser metido el trigo en el alfolí si non fuere primero la paja trillada e alinpiada. E así la mi alma non podrá entrar en el Paraýso del mi Dios con el vencimiento de martirio si non fuere atormentado con toda diligiencia el mi cuerpo de los tus carniceros.' E oyendo esto, Quinciano mandóla atormentar cruelmente en la una teta; e después, mandógela cortar. E [fol. 173ra] desque fue cortada, díxole Santa Ágata: 'Tirano cruel e malo, ¿cómo non as vergueña de cortar en la fenbra lo que mamaste en tu madre mesma? Yo he otras tetas entregas en la mi alma que consagré al Señor desde la mi niñez, e con ellas dó yo a los mis sesos fartura de leche.'

    E oyendo esto, Quinciano mandóla tornar a la cárcel. E defendió que non fuese cirugiano alguno a la melezinar e que non le diesen a comer nin a bever. E acerca de la medianoche vino a ella un viejo de grant reverencia, e venía delante dél un moçuelo con una facha ardiendo. E traýa muchas e diversas melezinas. E díxole: 'Aqueste cónsul loco, Quinciano, te ha mucho atormentado, mas más atormentaste tú a él con tus respuestas sabias e enseñadas. E aunque él te fizo cortar la teta, la su [fol. 173ʳᵇ] alegría se le tornará en amargura e tristeza. E yo aý estava quando te la cortavan e vi que tu teta podía bien sanar. E por ende vengo agora a te la melezinar.' E respondióle Santa Ágata e dixo: 'Yo nunca puse en mi cuerpo melezina carnal, e mucho sería a mí grant torpedat quebrantar agora lo que he guardado fasta aquí por la gracia divinal.' E díxole el viejo: 'Fija mía, yo christiano só, e non ayas vergueña.' E respondióle Santa Ágata e dixo: 'Yo non he por qué aver vergueña, como tú seas viejo e de grant hedat, e yo esté llagada de tan grant crueldat, que non avría onbre que me pudiese en este estado cobdiciar. Mas fágote muchas gracias, señor padre, porque te plogo de aver de mí cuydado e me venir a vesitar.' E díxole el viejo: '¿E por qué non quieres que te ponga melezina en tu teta?' E respondióle Santa Ágata e [fol. 173ᵛᵃ] dixo: 'Yo he por físico al mi señor Jhesu Christo, e quando a él plaze, él sana todas las enfermedades e llagas por sola su palabra. E si quisiere, él me puede sanar.' E oyendo esto, el viejo sonrrióse e dixo: 'E yo, fija, el su apóstol só, e él me enbió a ty. E sepas que en el su nonbre eres sana.' E luego desapareció el apóstol Sant Pedro. E catándose Santa Ágata, fallóse toda sana e tornada la teta a los pechos. E derribóse en tierra, faziendo gracias al señor Jhesu Christo e al apóstol Sant Pedro. E veyendo las guardas en la cárcel tan grand claridat, dieron a foyr e dexaron la puerta abierta. E quedó allí uno e començóle a rogar que se fuese. E respondióle ella e dixo: 'Non quiera Dios que yo dé a foyr e pierda la corona de la paciencia, e ponga a mis guardas en tribulación e angustia de las sus ánimas.'

E dende a quatro días, mandóla Quinciano traer delante sý e [fol. 173ᵛᵇ] díxole que adorase a los dioses por que non sufriese otros tormentos mayores. E respondióle Santa Ágata e dixo: 'Tus palabras son locas e vanas e desiguales e ensuzian el ayre, ca ¿cómo quieres tú, mezquino syn seso e sin entendimiento, que adore las piedras e dexe de adorar al Criador que me fizo?' E díxole Quinciano: '¿Quién te sanó?' E respondióle Santa Ágata e dixo: 'Sanóme Jhesu Christo, fijo de Dios bivo.' E díxole Quinciano: '¿Aún te atreves a nonbrar a Jhesu Christo, non queriendo yo oýr el su nonbre?' E respondióle Santa Ágata e dixo: 'Llamaré a Jhesu Christo con el coraçón e con la boca demientra biviere.' E díxole Quinciano: '¡Agora veré yo sy te sanará el tu Christo!' E mandó derramar tejas agudas e menudas, e traer brasas encendidas e bolcarla sobre ellas. E fue fecho luego un grant movimiento de la tierra e movió toda la cibdat. [fol. 174^(ra)] E cayó parte de la casa ado estava Quinciano asentado a judgar e mató a dos consejeros e amigos de Quinciano. E allegóse todo el pueblo e dezía a grandes bozes a Quinciano que por los agravios e tormentos syn justicia que dava a Santa Ágata viniera aquel movimiento de la tierra. E Quinciano, aviendo grant temor de la una parte del movimiento de la tierra, e de la otra parte de la discordia del pueblo, mandó tornar a la cárcel a Santa Ágata. E Santa Ágata, entrando en la cárcel, oró al Señor e dixo: 'Señor Jhesu Christo, que me criaste e me guardaste desde la mi niñez, e me feziste trabajar varonilmente en la mi mancebía, e quitaste de mí el amor del siglo, e apartaste el mi cuerpo de todo ensuziamiento, e me feziste vencer los tormentos de los carniceros (el fierro e las prisiones e el fuego), e me diste virtud de paciencia entre los tormentos, ruégo|te [fol. 174^(rb)] que rescibas agora el mi espíritu, ca tiempo es, Señor, que me mandes dexar aqueste siglo e yr a la tu misericordia.' E como ella dixiese aquestas cosas con grant devoción e con grant voz, dio el spíritu al Señor en el año de la su encarnación de dozientos e treynta e tres, a cinco días de febrero, seyendo Decio enperador.

E los christianos tomaron el su santo cuerpo e ungiéronlo con unguentos, e pusiéronlo en un monumento nuevo. E como lo pusiesen en el monumento, vino un mancebo vestido de vestiduras de seda, e venían con él más de cien moços fermosos e blancos quales non fueran vistos en toda aquella tierra. E entró a aquel logar ado enterravan el cuerpo de la santa virgen e puso a la cabeçera del sepulcro una tabla de mármol pequeña en que estava escripto: 'Aquesta donzella avía alma santa e voluntaria, e dio a Dios onrra e a la tierra libramiento.' E estovo allí fasta que fue cerrado el sepulcro con toda di|ligiencia. [fol. 174^(va)] E fuése luego dende, e non paresció más en toda aquella tierra. E sin alguna dubda es de creer que fue el su ángel. E después que fue aqueste miraglo publicado, començaron los gentiles e los judíos a onrrar aquel logar ado estava el su cuerpo enterrado.

170 E después de aquesto, yva Quinciano a buscar e tomar la riqueza de Santa Ágata e a prender a todos sus parientes. E pasando por una puente, començaron dos cavallos a relinchar e rifar entre sý, e a lançar coces. E uno dellos diole un bocado, e otro diole una coz e echólo en medio del río. E afogóse luego. E nunca pudo ser fallado su cuerpo.

175 E dende a un año del día que fue martiriada Santa Ágata, salió el fuego de un monte grande que es acerca de la cibdat de Catania e arde sienpre, e quemó las tierras e las piedras e llegó a la cibdat con llama muy brava. E los gentilles [fol. 174vb] descendieron del monte e fueron al sepulcro de Santa Ágata. E tomaron el paño que estava sobre
180 su sepulcro e pusiéronlo contra el fuego. E cesó luego el fuego e non fue más adelante.

E de aquesta santa virgen dize Sant Anbrosio en el Profacio: 'Aquésta fue virgen noble e bienaventurada, que meresció dar a su Señor gloria de loor por sangre de martirio leal. Aquésta es santa clara e
185 gloriosa, ennoblecida de dos fermosuras de grant prescio, porque entre la aspereza e graveza de los tormentos meresció ser vesitada e sanada del apóstol Sant Pedro. E subió al cielo a casar con Jhesu Christo, su esposo e medianero, e meresció aver servicios singulares en el su enterramiento, demostrando el coro de los ángeles la santidat de la su
190 alma e el libramiento de la tierra.'

Aquý acaba la ystoria de la bienaventurada Santa Ágata a onrra e gloria del Nuestro Reden|tor, [fol. 175ra] el qual con el Padre e con el Spíritu Santo bive para syenpre un Dios. Amén.

Critical Apparatus

Incipit] Aquí comiença la istoria de la bienaventurada *A*: Declaración del nonbre de *B*
6] syn amor *A*: *om. B*
14] E *A*: Síguese su istoria *B*
15] mas *B*: e mas *A*

16] E aquesta *A*: Esta *B*
19] quería prender: prendiendo *AB*
20] e *A*: *om. B* // cobdiciava: cobdiciando *AB* // 'mucho' (*A*) added in margin
21] grant *A*: tanta *B*
22] deseava: deseando *AB*
25] que eran *A*: *om. B*
29] muy *A*: *om. B*
43] sý *A*: de sý *B*
44] condición *A*: condiciones *B*
48] e dixo *B*: *om. A*
49] tener *A*: temer *B*
53] Conviene *A*: Conviénete de *B*
59-60] te crees: creer *A*; creerte *B*
67] detienes *A*: tienes *B*
71] sy *A*: *om. B* // quemarás *A*: echarás *B*
75] confondía *A*: ofendía *B*
77] E *B*: *om. A*
83] yo *A*: ya *B* // aquestas *A*: estas *B*
84] mensaje *A*: mensajero *B*
84-85] el trigo *A*: *om. B*
87] alma *A*: ánima *B*
88] de *A*: del *B* // toda *A*: *om. B*
90] la *A*: *om. B*
94] a los mis sesos fartura *A*: fartura a los mis huesos *B*
100] atormentaste *A*: atormentas (?) *B*
119] sana *A*: santa e sana *B*
122] puerta *B*: *om. A*
123] ella *A*: *om. B*
125] las sus ánimas *B*: la su ánima *A*
128] mayores *A*: *om. B*
137] agudas e menudas *A*: menudas agudas *B* // brasas *B*: blasas *A*
145] a la cárcel a Santa Ágata *A*: a Santa Ágatha a la cárcel *B*
147] desde *A*: de *B*
149] cuerpo *B*: coraçón *A*
155] tres *B*: tres años *A*

159] vestido *A*: *om. B*
168] onrrar *A*: honrrar mucho *B*
170] la riqueza *A*: las riquezas *B*
171] una *B*: la *A*
175] del: el *AB*
180] su sepulcro *A*: el sepulcro de Santa Ágatha *B*
184] Aqu*é*sta es sa*n*ta *A*: E aquesta santa es *B*
191] acaba *A*: se acaba *B*

Text II
La pasión de Santa Luzía
(Escorial h-III-22 and BNM 12688)

[fol. 36rb] De la pasió*n* de Santa Luzía

Lucía es dicha de 'luz'. E la luz ha fermosura en el acatamiento porque segunt dize Sant Anbrosio, de la natura de la luz es que sea deleĉtable de acatar, e que eſtienda los sus rayos syn se ensuziar, ca non se ensuzia q*u*anto quier que se eſtienda sob*re* algunas cosas suzias. E aun de la natura de la luz es endereſçar los sus rayos sin torcer, e pasar luengo eſpacio syn tardança. E por aqueſto es demoſtrado que Santa Lucía ovo fermosura de virginidat syn corrupción, e derrama|miento [fol. 36va] de la su claridat sin suziedad de amor, e endereſçamiento a Dios de la su entinción sin algunt torcimiento. E aun ovo luengo rayo de obra continua e buena sin tardança de nigligiencia. E aun Lucía quiere dezir 'carrera de luz'.

    E eſta santa virgen fue natural de Çaragoça de Cecilia e de noble linaje. E oyendo la fama de Santa Ágata q*ue* se derramava por toda Cecilia, fue a vesitar el su sepulcro con su madre, Euticia, que avía quatro años que tenía fluxo de sangre e non podía sanar por mucho que los físicos trabajavan por la remediar. E como a la misa se leyese el evangelio que dize de cómo sanó el Señor a la muger que tenía fluxo de sangre doze años avía, díxole Santa Lucía: 'Madre mía, sy creyes a eſtas cosas que agora son leýdas, creet [fol. 36vb] que Santa Ágata eſtá sienpre presente delan*te* aquél por cuyo amor rescibió muerte; e llega al su sepulcro creyendo firmemente e rescebirás luego sanidat conplidamen*te*.'

    E desque se fueron todos los que ende eſtavan, q*u*edaron allí Santa Lucía e su madre, Euticia, e ynclináronse a orar amas al sepulcro de Santa Ágata. E adurmióse Santa Lucía e aparescióle Santa Ágata en medio de los ángeles, apostada de piedras presciosas e de vestiduras muy fermosas. E díxole: 'Hermana mía Lucía, virgen devota al Señor, ¿por qué me demandas lo que puedes dar a tu madre? Ahé que tu madre es sana por tu fee.' E despertando Santa Lucía, dixo a su madre: 'Madre mía, ya eres sana. E por ende ruégote, por amor de aquélla que te ganó salud por sus oraciones, que de aquí adelante non me [fol. 37ra] nonbres a mi esposo más, e que des a los pobres todo lo que me avías de dar para casar.' E respondióle la madre e díxole: 'Fija, cubre primero mis ojos e después faz lo que quisieres de todo lo que quedare después de mi muerte.' E díxole Santa Lucía: 'Madre mía, lo que dieres después de la muerte, non lo darás si non porque non lo podrás contigo levar. E por ende dalo mientra bives e has sanidat por que ayas gualardón en el regno celestial.'

E como se tornasen para su casa, partían con los pobres largamente e acorrían a sus nescesidades alegremente. E oyendo dezir el esposo que su esposa vendía todo lo que su madre avía, vínolo a preguntar a una ama que criara a su esposa. E ella respondióle sabiamente e díxole: 'Tu esposa ha fallado otra heredat mucho [fol. 37rb] mejor e querríala conprar para sí e en su nonbre, e vende algunas cosas de las de su madre para la poder aver.' E el esposo, creyendo esto, començó a la ayudar a vender, creyendo ser verdat lo que le dixiera la ama que criara a su esposa, e que quería conprar alguna heredat tenporal. E desque fueron vendidas todas las cosas e dadas a los pobres, vídose engañado el esposo e fízola enplazar delante un juez que avía nonbre Pasqual. E quexóse della, diziendo que era christiana e bivía contra las leyes romanas.

E oyendo esto, el juez don Pasqual mandó que ofresciese sacreficios a los dioses. E respondió Santa Lucía e dixo: 'El sacreficio aplazible a Dios es vesitar a los pobres e acorrerlos en sus nescesidades, e porque ya non he otra cosa que le pueda ofrescer, ofresco a mi mesma a él.' [fol. 37va] E díxole don Pasqual: 'Estas palabras puedes tú dezir a otro christiano que es tan loco como tú, mas non a mí, que guardo las leyes e mandamientos de los señores del ynperio.' E respondióle Santa Lucía e dixo: 'Si tú guardas las leyes de tus príncipes, así guardo yo la ley del mi Dios. E si tú temes al enperador, yo temo a Dios. E sy tú non quieres ofender a tus señores, yo non quiero ofender a mi Señor. E si tú deseas plazer al enperador, yo deseo plazer al mi Salvador. E por ende faz todo lo que quisieres, que yo non faré si non lo que entendiere.' E díxole don Pasqual: 'Agora que has despendido tu patrimonio con los amadores de tu corrupción, fablas así como muger pública que non ha vergueña nin temor.' E respondióle Santa Lucía e dixo: 'Yo puse mi patrimonio en logar seguro e nunca conoscí [fol. 37vb] corronpedores de mi cuerpo nin de mi alma.' E díxole don Pasqual: '¿E quáles son los corronpedores del cuerpo e del alma?' E respondióle Santa Lucía e dixo: 'Vós sodes los corronpedores del alma, que amonestades a los onbres que dexen a su Criador. E los corronpedores del cuerpo son los que anteponen la delectación corporal a la delectación que sienpre ha de durar.'

E díxole don Pasqual: '¡Cesarán las palabras quando viniéramos a los açotes e a las llagas!' E respondióle Santa Lucía e dixo: '¡Non pueden cesar las palabras de Dios!' E díxole don Pasqual: 'Segunt esto, ¿tú eres Dios?' E respondióle Santa Lucía e dixo: 'Non só yo Dios, mas só sierva de Dios. E él dixo que quando estoviésemos delante los reyes e de los juezes, non oviésemos cuydado de pensar lo que avíamos de fablar, que él nos diría lo que oviése|mos [fol. 38ra] a dezir, e que non seríamos nós los que fablávamos, mas el Spíritu Santo que fablaría en nós.' E díxole don Pasqual: 'Pues segunt esto, ¿en ti está el Spíritu Santo?' E respondióle Santa Lucía e dixo: 'El apóstol dixo que los que biven castamente son tenplo del Spíritu Santo.' E díxole don Pasqual: 'Yo te faré levar al logar de las mugeres públicas e faré corronper la tu castidat, e fuyrá de ty el Spíritu Santo.' E respondióle Santa Lucía e dixo: 'Non puede ser ensuziado el cuerpo si non dé consentimiento de la voluntad de la razón. E si me fizieres corronper contra mi voluntad, doblarás a mí la corona de la mi castidat. E non podrás ynclinar la mi voluntad a consentir a la suziedat, ca tienes en tu mano el mi cuerpo mas non tienes la mi alma en tu poderío. E por ende, ¡non tardes de fa|zer [fol. 38rb] lo que quisieres, e comiença así como fijo del diablo a poner en obra los tus malos deseos, e a me dar qualesquier tormentos!'

E oyendo esto, don Pasqual fizo venir muchos rufianes e mandóles que conbidasen el pueblo a la su castidat e durmiesen con ella fasta que la dexasen por muerta. E queriéndola levar los rufianes al burdel, asieron della, e de tan grant peso la fizo ser el Sp*íri*tu Santo que non la pudiero*n* mover. E mandó don Pasq*ua*l que le atasen los pies e las manos con sogas e tirasen dellas mill onbres, mas non la pudieron mover. E fizo traer muchos pares de bueyes e fízolos atar a las sogas e tyrar, mas non la pudiero*n* mover punto nin más. E fizo llamar a unos enca*n*tadores para que la fiziesen mover con sus encantamentos, mas non pudieron. E veyendo esto, [fol. 38va] el juez don Pasqual dixo a la santa virgen: '¿Qué encantamentos son éstos, que sabes que non puedes ser movida de mill onbres nin de mill pares de buey*e*s?' E respondióle Santa Lucía e dixo: 'Non son aquéstos -que yo sé- encantamentos nin maleficios, mas beneficios del mi Señor Jh*es*u *Chris*to. E si añadieres otros diez mill pares de bueyes para tyrar, non me podrás mover nin levar.' E pensando don Pasqual que con azeyte podría fazer fuyr al diablo e desatar aquellos encantamentos, mandó echar azeyte encima della. E como non la pudiesen mover con todo esto, començó a se ensangustiar mucho más, e fizo encender grant fuego enderredor della, e mandó echar sobre ella pez e resina e azeyte. E díxole Santa Luzía: 'Yo he ganado del mi Señor espacio para el mi martirio por que quite el temor [fol. 38vb] de la pasión a los fieles e la voz de alegría a los ynfieles.'

E veyendo los amigos del juez que se ensangustiava mucho don Pasq*ua*l, mandáronle meter una espada por la garganta. E Santa Lucía, non perdiendo por esto la fabla, dixo a los que allí estavan: 'Dígovos de donde vós podedes alegrar, ca ya es dada paz a la eglesia porque el enperador Maximiano fue oy muerto, e Diocleciano fue echado del inperio. E asý como por mi hermana Santa Ágata es anparada la cibdat de Catania, asý será anparada por mí aquesta cibdat Ciracusana.'

E como aun la santa v*ir*gen fablase estas cosas, llegaron unos cavalleros romanos e prendiero*n* a don Pasqual. E lleváronlo a Roma a los senadores, ca oyeran dezir que robava toda la tierra de Cecilia. E como llegase a Roma, fue acusado delante de los se|nadores; [fol. 38vb] e fue fallado culpado de las acusaciones, e fue mandado descabeçar. E la virgen bienaventurada Santa Lucía no*n* se movió del logar adonde estava, nin dio el alma fasta que vinieron los clérigos e le dieron el sacramento del cuerpo del Señor. E desque fue muerta, fiziéronle en aquel logar una eglesya, e enterráronla en ella.

Aquí acaba la vida de la bienaventurada Santa Lucía a honrra e gloria del Nuestro Salvador, el qual con el Padre e con el Spíritu Santo bive e regna un Dios por todos los siglos. AMÉN.

Critical Apparatus

Incipit] De la pasión de Santa Luzía *A*: Aquí comiença la istoria de la bienaventurada Santa Luzía, virgen. Declaración de su nonbre *B*
2] E *A*: Ca *B*
4] sus *A*: *om. B*
5] estienda *B*: estiende *A*
9] suziedat *B*: suzidat *A*
10] torcimiento *A*: torcimiento de coraçón *B*
10-11] E aun ovo luengo rayo de obra continua e buena sin tardança de nigligiencia *A*: *om. B*
13] E *A*: *om. B* // Çaragoça *A*: la cibdat de Çaragoça *B*
20] creet *A*: cree *B*
21] presente *A*: *om. B*
27] piedras *A*: muchas piedras *B*
28] mía *B*: *om. A*
29] dar *A*: dar luego *B* // Ahé *A*: E ahé *B*
33] me *A*: a mí *B*
34] respondióle *B*: respondió *A*
35] quedare *A*: te quedare *B*
45] e *B*: *om. A*
47] la *A*: el *B*
50] un *A*: el *B*
52] sacreficios *A*: sacrificio *B*
54] a *B*: *om. A*
59] Si *A*: *om. B*
62] plazer *A*: a plazer *B*
64] don *A*: *om. B*
65] corrupción *A*: coraçón e corrupción *B*

66] respondióle *A*: respondió *B*
68] alma *A*: ánima *B*
69] alma *A*: ánima *B* // respondióle *A*: respondió *B*
72] corporal *A*: tenporal *B*
77] yo *A*: *om. B*
79] pensar *A*: pensar que es *B*
84] dixo *A*: dize *B* // díxole *B*: dixo *A*
90] tu *A*: la tu *B*
97] ser *A*: *om. B*
100] atar *A*: acatar *B*
105] respondióle *A*: respondió *B*
106] yo *A*: *om. B*
108] otros *A*: otras *B*
111] pudiesen *B*: pudiese *A* // esto *A*: eso *B*
116] ensangustiava *A*: santiguaba *B*
121] mi *A*: *om. B*
125] robava *A*: robara *B*
126] de *A*: *om. B*
133-35] Aquí acaba la vida de la bienaventurada Santa Lucía a honrra e gloria del Nuestro Salvador, el qual con el padre e con el Spíritu Santo bive e regna un Dios por todos los siglos. Amén. *B*: *om. A*

Text III
La passión de Santa Águeda
(Fundación Lázaro Galdiano 419, Biblioteca Menéndez Pelayo 9, and Escorial K-II-12)

[fol. 26^(vb)] La passión de Santa Águeda, virgen e mártir
Santa Águeda, virgen, fue fija dalgo, muy fermosa en el cuerpo e más en el alma. E onrrava sienpre a Dios en la cibdat de Atritanea con toda su santidat. E Quinciano, el adelantado de Cicilia, porque era omne villano e luxorioso e escasso e sirvía de grado a los ýdolos, parescíale que non enbargante que él era villano, que prendiendo a Santa Águeda, que le avrían todos miedo así como si fuesse fidalgo. E porque era luxurioso, queríase fartar de su fermosura. E porque era avariento, quería tomar sus riquezas. E porque era ydolatra, quería que sacrificasse los ýdolos.

E por ende fízola adozir ante sí. E después que fue aducha, él cognosció su talante, que non quería fazer nada de lo que él quería. E mandóla dar a una mala muger que dizían Afrodisa, que avía nueve fijas tan malas como ella, e que en xxx días mudasse su coraçón: la una vegada prometiéndole cosas buenas, e la otra vegada espantándola con cosas ásperas. E asý esperavan que la podrían [fol. 27^(ra)] trastornar. E díxoles Santa Águeda: 'La mi voluntad está asý afirmada e raygada en Jhesu Christo, que vuestras palabras non valen nada, e vuestras promissiones son como luvia, e vuestros spantos son como ríos. Ca comoquier que estas cosas lidien contra mí, el cimiento de la mi casa non puede caher, ca está afirmado sobre piedra.' E diziendo esto, llorava cada día e rogava a Dios, desseando venir a la gloria del martirio. E veyendo Afrodisa que la non podía trastornar, dixo a Quinciano: 'Más de ligero se podrían amollentar las piedras e el fierro tornarse en plomo

blando que trastornar la voluntad desta niña de la fe de Jhesu Christo.'
    Entonce Quinciano fízola adozir ante sý e díxole: '¿Quién eres tú?' E díxole ella: 'Muger fija dalgo e muy noble, segund que dizen mis parientes.' E díxole Quinciano: 'Si tú eres fija dalgo, ¿por qué te muestras e te das por villana en tus fechos?' E respondió ella: 'Porque só sierva de Jhesu Christo: por esso me muestro por villana.' E díxole Quinciano: 'Sy tú eres fija dalgo, ¿por qué te llamas sierva?' E respondió ella: 'Ésta es muy grand virtud do se [fol. 27rb] prueva el servicio de Jhesu Christo.' E díxole Quinciano: '¡Escoje qual más quisieres: o sacrifica a los dioses o sufre muchos tormentos!' E díxole Águeda: '¡Sea tu muger como es la tu diosa Venus, e tú tal como el tu dios Júpiter!' Entonce Quinciano diole muchas palmadas, diziéndole: '¡Non quieras denostar al alcalde!' E respondió Águeda: 'Maravíllome mucho como tan sabio como tú tomeste tan grand locura que digas que aquestos son los mis dioses e non quieres tú nin tu muger semejarles. E dizes que te fago tuerto porque te digo que bivas así como ellos. Ca si son dioses, querrán tu bien; mas pues que aborresces su conpañía, quieras semejar a mí.' E dixo Quinciano: '¿Por qué andamos en tantas palabras? ¡O sacrifica a los dioses o fazerte he matar muy atormentada!' E respondió Águeda: 'Sy me pusieres entre las bestias crueles, nonbrando a Jhesu Christo fazerse han mansas. E si me metieres en el fuego, los ángeles de Dios enbiarán rocío del cielo e matarlo han. E si me llagares e me atormentares, el Spíritu Santo, por quien menosprecio todas las tus amenazas, te confrondrá.' Entonce mandóla levar a la cárcel porque lo confondía por placer. E ella yva muy alegre como si fuesse conbidada a buen comer. E acomendava a Dios su lid.
    E otro día díxole [fol. 27va] Quinciano: '¡Niega a Jhesu Christo e adora los dioses!' E diziendo que non quería, mandóla atar e dar torcejones. E díxole Águeda: 'Agora tomo sabor en estas penas, asý como quien oye buen mensajero, o quien le vee al que ha tienpo que le desea, o quien falla muchos thesoros. Ca non pueden poner el trigo en el alfolí si non fuere la caña fuertemente quebrantada e toda menuda. Así la mi alma non puede entrar en paraýso con palma de martirio si non fizieres el mi cuerpo despedaşcar.' Entonce ensañósse Quinciano e mandóle tajar la teta. E díxole Águeda: 'O omne cruel, sin piadat e

falsso, ¿non oviste vergüença de tajar en mí lo que tú mameste en tu madre? Enpero yo tengo otras tetas enteras de dentro en mi alma de que se crian todos los mis sesos. E los ofrescí a Dios de pequeña.'

Entonce mandóla tornar a la cárcel. E defendió que ningund físico non entrasse a ella e non le diessen a comer pan nin agua. E a la medianoche vino un omne anciano a ella, e yva ante él un niño que levava lunbre e traýa muchas medecinas. E díxole: 'Maguer este adelantado loco te quebrantó los mienbros con tormentos, más lo atormentaste tú. Enpero que él te tajó la teta e te atormentó en ella, más es él atormentado e amargado. E porque lo sofriste en paciencia, vy que la tu teta podría muy bien sanar.' E dixo Águeda: 'Nunca fiz melezina carnal al [fol. 27vb] mi cuerpo, e seméjame a mí muy sin guisado que lo que guardé fasta aquí que lo pierda agora.' E díxole el anciano: 'Fija, yo christiano soy, e de mí non ayas ninguna vergüença.' E dixo Águeda: '¿Por qué avré de ti vergüença, ca eres viejo e anciano, e yo soy tan malamente despedaçada que non ha omne en el mundo que en mí tomasse plazer? Enpero gradézcotelo mucho, padre señor, porque quesiste aver cuydado de mí.' E díxole él: '¿Por qué non quieres que te sane?' E respondióle ella: 'Porque el Nuestro Señor Jhesu Christo solamente por la palabra sana todas las cosas e las aduze a su estado. E éste me puede sanar sy quisiere.' E díxole el anciano, riyéndosse: 'Yo soy el apóstol Sant Pedro e él me enbió a ti. E sepas que en el su nonbre serás sana.' E desaparesció a la sazón Sant Pedro. E Santa Águeda cayó en tierra. E agradeciéndogelo mucho, fallósse bien sana e la teta entera en sus pechos. E las guardas, espantadas de la lunbre grande que vieron, fuyeron e dexaron la cárcel abierta. E dixéronle algunos que se fuesse. E dixo ella: 'Non lo quiera Dios que yo fuya e que pierda la corona que he ganado, e que sean las guardas por mí malandantes.'

E después díxole Quinciano que adorasse los dioses en tal que non su|friesse [fol. 28ra] mayores penas. E díxole Águeda: '¡Las tus palabras son locas e vanas e ensuzian el ayre! Mesquino sin seso e syn entendimiento, ¿por qué quieres que adore las piedras e dexe de adorar a Dios del cielo que me sanó?' E díxole Quinciano: '¿Aún osas nonbrar a Jhesu Christo, que yo non quiero oýr?' E dixo Águeda: 'Mientra que viviere, sienpre llamaré a Jhesu Christo en la boca e en el coraçón.' E díxole Quinciano: '¡Agora veré si te sanará Jhesu Christo!' E mandó esparzir muchos tiestos quebrantados e poner carvones encendidos sobre los tiestos; e ella desnuda, que la enbolviessen en ellos. E demientra que lo fazían, tremió mucha la tierra en manera que esgrimió toda la cibdat. E cayó una partida de la pared e mató a dos consejeros de Quinciano. Entonce todo el pueblo fuésse para él dando bozes, diziendo: '¡Tales cosas sofrimos porque fazes mal a Santa Águeda!' Entonce Quinciano, temiendo de una parte el tremor de la tierra, e de la otra el pueblo, mandóla aun poner en la cárcel. E Santa Águeda rogó a Dios, diziendo asý: 'Señor Jhesu Christo, que me crieste e sienpre me guardeste que el mi cuerpo fuesse linpio, e que me diste fuerça que pudiese sofryr estos tormentos, e me diste paciencia en ellos, resci|be [fol. 28rb] la mi ánima e mándame venir a la tu gloria.' E esto diziendo, dio grand boz e salióssele el ánima.

E los christianos tomaron el su cuerpo e enbolviéronlo en muchas espeçias, e pusiéronlo en su sepulcro. Entonce vino un mancebo vestido de paños de sirgo, e con él más de cient omnes muy fermosos e honrrados, todos vestidos de blanco, que nunca fueron vistos en aquella tierra. E vino al su cuerpo e púsole una tabla de mármol a la su cabeça. E nunca más lo vieron. E fallaron escripto en aquella tabla: '¡Aquésta ovo alma santa e rescibió de grado martirio por amor de Dios, e diole honrra que le franqueó su tierra!' E quando supieron este miraglo, gentiles e judíos honrravan sienpre su sepulcro.

E demientra que Quinciano fue a buscar sus riquezas, estavan dos cavallos ante sý, el uno resinchando e el otro lançando las coces. E con muessos echáronlo en el río e murió.

E a cabo de un año que ella finó, ronpióse un grand monte cerca de la cibdat. E salió dél grant fuego en manera que regalava las piedras e la tierra e vinía muy atrevidamente contra la cibdat. Entonce grand conpaña de los paganos descendieron del monte e fuyeron al sepulcro. E tomaron un velo que estava sobrel altar e pusiéronlo contra el fuego. E estovo quedo e non fue más adelante.

Critical Apparatus

Incipit] La passión de Santa Águeda virgen e mártir *C*: De Santa Águeda virgen cuya fiesta es el día v de febrer[-] *D*; De Santa Ágada *E*

2] virgen *CD*: fue virgen *E* // fue fija dalgo muy fermosa *D*: muy fermosa *C*; fija dalgo fermosa *E* // cuerpo *CE*: [-] *D*

3] más *D*: muy fija dalgo e más fermosa *C*; mucho más *E* // alma *CD*: ánima *E* // E *D*: *om.* *CE* // honrrava *C*: onrrava e sirvié *D*; orava *E*

4] su *C*: *om.* *DE* // el *CD*: *om.* *E*

5] e escaso *CD*: *om.* *E* // sirvía *C*: sirvié *DE*

6] parescíale *C*: semejával *DE* // non enbargante que él era villano que *C*: *om.* *DE* // prendiendo *CD*: sy prendiese *E*

7] que le avrían *C*: pero que era villano quel abrién *D*; enpero que serié villano que le avrién *E* // todos *CD*: *om.* *E* // así *C*: *om.* *DE* // si fuesse *C*: a *DE*

8] queríase fartar *C*: querié fartarse *D*; querié se fazer *E* // su *CD*: *om.* *E*

9] quería *CE*: querié *D* // sus *CD*: las sus *E* // ydolatra *D*: ydolatría *CE* // quería *CE*: querié *D*

10] sacrificasse *C*: sacrificase a *D*; adorase *E*

11] fízola *CD*: mandóla *E* // E después que fue aducha e *CD*: e *E*

11-12] él cognosció *CD*: sopo *E*

12] su talante *DE*: *om.* *C* // que *CD*: en como *E* // quería *CE*: querié *D* // fazer nada *C*: nada fazer *D*; fazer ninguna cosa *E* // quería *C*: asmava *DE* // E *C*: *om.* *DE*

13] dizían *CE*: dizién *D* // que avía *C*: que avié *D*; e a *E* // nueve *CD*: diez *E* // tan *CD*: suyas que eran tan *E* // e que *C*: que *D*; por tal que sy quiera *E* // mudasse *C*: mudasen *DE*

14-15] la una vegada prometiéndole *CD*: e de primero acometiénla *E*

15] cosas buenas *C*: buenas cosas *D*; muchas cosas buenas *E* // la otra vegada *CE*: otra *D*

15-16] espantándola con cosas ásperas e asý esperavan *C*: espantávanla esperavan *D*; amenazándola pensando *E*

16] podrían *CE*: podrién *D*

17] díxoles Santa *CD*: *om.* *E* // está asý *CD*: está assí *E* // afirmada e raygada *C*: raygada e afirmada *D*; afirmada e arraygada *E*

18] en *CD*: en el amor de *E* // vuestras *CD*: las vuestras *E* // e *CD*: nin las *E*

19] son *CD*: q*ue* son *E* // luvia *CD*: llama *E* // como *CD*: bien como *E* // ríos *DE*: rayos *C* // ca *CE*: q*ue D*

20] lidien *CD*: lidian *E*

21] ca está afirmado sobre piedra *C*: *om. DE*

22] cada día *CD*: e todo el día llorava *E* // venir a *C*: *om. DE*

23] la no*n* *CE*: no*n* la *D* // podía *C*: podié *DE* // trastornar *CE*: tornar *D*

24] amollentar *CD*: enblandar *E* // tornarse *CD*: e tornarse *E* // en *CE*: *om. D*

25] trastornar *CD*: no*n* trastornar *E* // voluntad *CD*: fe *E* // de la fe *CD*: *om. E*

27] E díxole ella *CD*: Respondió *E* // Muger *CD*: Yo só muger *E* // noble *C*: noble por linage *D*: noble de lynaje *E* // dize*n* *CE*: dize*n* todos *D*

28] eres fija dalgo *CD*: muge*r* fija dalgo eres *E*

29] muestras e te das *CD*: demuestras *E* // en *CD*: en todas *E* // fechos *C*: costu*n*bres *DE* // E respondió *C*: Respondiól *DE*

30] só *CE*: só yo *D* // E *CE*: *om. D*

31] Sy *CD*: Sy si *E* // tú *CE*: *om. D* // eres fija dalgo *CD*: muger fija dalgo eres *E* // te *CD*: te muestras e te *E* // sierva *CD*: sierva de Jh*e*su Ch*ris*to *E* // E *CE*: *om. D* // respondió *C*: Respondiól *DE*

32] Ésta es muy grand virtud *CD*: Éste es el linaje muy grande *E*

32-33] Jhesu Ch*ris*to *CD*: Dios *E*

33-34] a los dioses *C*: los dios *D*; los ýdolos *E*

34] sufre *CD*: toma *E* // E díxole *C*: Díxol *D*; Respondiól *E* // tu *CD*: la tu *E*

35] como *CD*: tal sy como *E* // es *C*: *om. DE* // la tu diosa *CD*: deesa *E* // el *DE*: *om. C* // Entonce *CE*: E entonce *D*

36] diole *C*: ma*n*dól dar *DE* // quieras *C*: quieras ser muy garida en *D*; seas garrida en *E*

37] al *CE*: el *D* // E respondió Águeda: Maravíllome mucho *C*: Maravíllome mucho dixo Águeda *D*; Respondió Sa*n*ta Ágada: Maravíllome mucho *E* // como *C*: porq*ue DE* // sabio *C*: sabio om*n*e *DE*

38] tomeste *E*: porque cognosces *CD* // que digas *C*: que dizes *D*; porq*ue* dizes *E* // que *D*: *om. CE* // son los *E*: *om. CD*

39] mis dioses *C*: [-] dioses *D*; mis dios *E* // E *DE*: *om. C* // semejarles *CE*: semejarlos *D* // e dizes *E*: en diziendo *CD* // te *E*: *om. CD*

40] Ca *C*: *om. D*; e *E* // dioses *C*: dios *DE*

41] que *CE*: *om*. *D*
41-42] q*u*ieras semejar a mí *CD*: avrás de semejarlos *E*
42] E dixo *C*: Díxol *DE* // tantas *DE*: tan tantas *C*
43] a *CD*: *om*. *E* // dioses *C*: dios *DE* // fazerte he matar muy *C*: faze*r*te matar *D*; te faré morir *E* // E *C*: *om*. *DE* // re∫pondió *CD*: Re∫pondiól *E*
44] Sy me pusieres *CD*: Poniéndome *E* // crueles *CD*: bravas *E*
45] mansas *CD*: mansos *E* // E *C*: *om*. *DE* // me *CD*: me tú *E*
46] enbiará*n* rocío del cielo *CD*: dar me an esfuerço *E* // E *CE*: *om*. *D* // e *C*: o *DE*
47] por q*u*ien *E*: te confondrá por q*u*ien *C*; por q*u*e *D* // meno∫precio *C*: de∫precio *D*; yo de∫precio *E*
47-48] las tus amenazas *CD*: amenazas *E*
48] te confondrá *D*: *om*. *C*; ese me guardará *E*
49] co*n*fondía *C*: cofondié *DE* // por *DE*: en la *C* // placer: plaça *CDE* // muy alegre *C*: muy leda e muy gozosa *D*; muy alegre e muy leda *E* // como *C*: bie*n* como *DE*
50] buen comer *CD*: buena yantar *E* // su *CD*: toda su *E*
51] E *CD*: *om*. *E*
52] dioses *C*: dios *DE* // E diziendo que *CD*: E ella *E* // quería *C*: q*u*erié *D*; q*u*eriendo *E*
52-53] atar e dar torcejones *CD*: dar torme*n*tos e açotes *E*
53] díxole *CD*: dezía Sa*n*ta *E* // Agora *CE*: *om*. *D*
54] quien oye *CD*: aq*u*el que viene *E*
54-55] o quien le vee al que ha tie*n*po que le *C*: a q*u*al viene e que a tie*n*po q*u*al *D*; si a tie*n*po qu*e*l *E*
55] o *C*: o a *D*; o como *E* // muchos *CD*: grandes *E* // pueden *CE*: puede *D*
56] alforí *C*: alfolí o en orrno *D*; orrno *E* // fuertemente *E*: p*r*imera p*r*imero *C*; *om*. *D* // menuda *C*: fecha paja *D*; fecha menuda *E*
58] fizieres el mi *C*: fizieres todo el mío *D*; fuere todo el *E* // de∫pedasçar *CD*: desmigajado *E* // ensañósse Qui*n*ciano *CD*: Quinciano muy sañudo *E*
59] e *CD*: *om*. *E* // la teta *C*: las tetas *DE* // díxole *CD*: díxol Sa*n*ta *E* // O *CE*: *om*. *D* // sin *CD*: e syn *E*
60] e falsso *CD*: *om*. *E* // en *CD*: a *E* // tú *CE*: *om*. *D*
61] Enp*er*o *CD*: Enp*er*o q*u*e *E* // enteras *CD*: *om*. *E* // de *C*: *om*. *DE* // mi *C*: la mi *DE*

61-62] de que se crian *CD*: donde se goviernan *E*
62] mis *CE*: míos *D* // sesos *CD*: huesos *E* // e los ofrescí a Dios de pequeña *CD*: e estas ofrescí de pequeñuela a Dios *E*
63] mandóla *CD*: mandóla Quinciano *E* // tornar a *CD*: meter en *E*
64] e non le diessen a comer *CD*: nin le diesen *E* // a *CD*: cerca de *E*
65] vino *CD*: vino a ella *E* // omne *CD*: *om*. *E* // a ella *CD*: *om*. *E* // ante él *CD*: delante dél *E*
66] que *E*: e *CD* // traýa *C*: aduzié *D*; *om*. *E* // e díxole *CD*: diziéndol *E* // Maguer *C*: Maguer que *D*; Ágada enpero que *E* // *D ends
67] loco *C*: *om*. *E* // los mienbros *C*: *om*. *E*
67-68 más lo atormentaste tú *C*: tú mal le atormenteste en qual respondiste contra su voluntad *E*
68] que él *C*: aunque te atormentó en que *E* // la teta e te atormentó en ella *C*: las tetas *E*
69] más *E*: enpero más *C* // es él *C*: *om*. *E* // e amargado *C*: quedó él e más amargo *E*
70] vy que *C*: ven acá por que pueda *E* // podría muy *C*: *om*. *E* // dixo *C*: respondiól *E*
70-71] fiz melezina carnal *C*: melezina de carne fiz *E*
71] mi *C*: mío *E* // e seméjame a mí *C*: ca me semeja *E*
72] guisado *C*: guisa *E* // que lo que guardé fasta aquí que lo pierda *C*: ca pues que fasta oy non lo guarde que lo guarde *E*
73] ayas ninguna verguença *C*: tomes vengança *E*
74] dixo *C*: respondiól Santa *E* // de ti verguença *C*: vengança de ty *E* // ca *C*: ca tú *E* // e anciano *C*: *om*. *DE*
75] despedaçada *C*: e tan despedaçada *E* // en el *C*: del *E*
76] en *C*: de *E* // tomasse *C*: tome *E*
77] Por *C*: Enpero por *E*
78] E respondióle ella *C*: *om*. *E* // el Nuestro Señor *C*: he al mi señor *E*
79] solamente por la palabra sana *C*: por sanador e sana por palabra *E*
80] puede *C*: puede a mí bien *E* // riyéndosse *C*: como reyendo *E*
80-81] Yo soy el apóstol *C*: E yo su apóstol só *E*
81] Sant Pedro *C*: e me dizen Pedro *E* // a ti *C*: acá *E*
82] a la sazón *C*: luego el apóstol *E* // cayó *C*: cayó luego *E*

83] agradeciéndogelo C: gradesciólo E // fallósse bien C: a Dios e fue luego E // la teta entera C: las tetas entregas E
84-85] espantadas de la lunbre grande que vieron fuyeron C: de la cárcel fueron todos maravillados de tan grant lunbre como vieran E
85] dixiéronle C: fuxieron e rogávanla E
86] yo C: *om. E* // e que C: por do E
87] he ganado e que C: tengo ganada E // guardas C: *om. E*
88] después C: después desto E // díxole C: mandól E // dioses C: ýdolos E // en tal C: por E
89] E díxole C: Respondiól Santa E
90] ensuzian C: suzias e E // mesquino C: e mezquino loco e E
92] de adorar a E: a C // del cielo C: verdadero E
93] que yo non quiero oýr C: fijo de Dios E // E dixo Águeda C: *om. E*
94] Mientra C: demientra E // viviere C: yo vesquiere E
94-95] llamaré a Jhesu Christo en la boca e en el coraçón C: le llamaré con la mi boca e con el mi coraçón Jhesu Christo E
95] E díxole C: Dixo E
96] E C: Estonce E // esparzir C: poner E
97] ella desnuda C: mandó que la desnudasen e E
98] mucha C: *om. E*
99] esgrimió C: se entremició E // cayó una partida de la pared C: cayeron muchas paredes E // mató a C: mataron E
100] consejeros C: mensageros E // Entonce C: E E // fuésse C: se fue E // él C: Quinciano E
101] diziendo C: e diziendo E
101-02] Santa Águeda C: esta Ágada sin razón E
102] una C: la una E
103] otra C: otra parte E // pueblo C: pueblo que serié contra él E // aun C: *om. E* // en C: como de cabo en E
103-04] Santa Águeda C: ella E
104] rogó a Dios C: rogando E // diziendo C: a Dios dezía E // crieste C: guieste E
105] sienpre C: *om. E* // fuesse C: sienpre fuese E
106] fuerça C: sienpre fuerça e vertud E // sofryr C: vencer E // e C: e sofrirlos e E

107] rescibe *C*: toma *E* // ánima *C*: alma *E* // mándame *C*: mándala *E* // venir *C*: yr *E*
107-08] esto diziendo *C*: ella deziendo esto *E*
108] grand *C*: muy grant *E* // salióssele el ánima *C*: salió el ánima del cuerpo *E*
110] pusiéronlo *C*: poniéndolo *E* // su *C*: el *E* // Entonce vino *C*: afevos *E*
111] vestido de *C*: de *E* // sirgo *C*: sirgo vestido *E*
112] e honrrados *C*: *om. E* // todos vestidos de blanco *C*: e vestidos de vestidos de vestiduras blancas *E* // que *C*: quales *E* // vistos *C*: vestidos *E*
113] vino *C*: venieron *E* // su *C*: *om. E* // púsole *C*: posiéronle *E* // a la *C*: sobre *E*
114] nunca más *C*: jamás nunca *E* // lo *C*: los *E* // fallaron escripto en aquella tabla *C*: en esta tabla eran escriptas estas cosas *E*
115] Aquésta *C*: Este cuerpo *E*
115-16] por amor de Dios *C*: *om. E*
116] diole *C*: diol Dios *E* // que le *C*: e *E* // su *C*: la su *E*
116-17] supieron este miraglo gentiles e *C*: los gentiles sopieron este miraglo e aun los *E*
117] sienpre *C*: *om. E* // su *C*: el su *E*
118] a *C*: *om. E* // estavan *C*: venieron *E*
119] ante sý *C*: *om. E* // el uno *E*: *om. C* // e el otro lançando *E*: alçaron *C* // las *C*: *om. E*
119-20] con muesos *E*: *om. C*
120] echáronlo en el río e murió *C*: lançáronlo en un río *E*
121] a cabo de un año que ella finó *E*: *om. C* // ronpiósse *C*: corrunpióse *E* // grand monte *C*: un monte grande *E*
122] salió *C*: salía *E* // grant *C*: un grant *E*
123] muy atrevidamente *C*: *om. E*
123-24] grand conpaña *C*: una grant conpañía *E*
124] paganos *C*: gentiles *E* // sepulcro *C*: monimento de Santa Gadea *E*
125] altar *C*: su cuerpo *E*
126] estovo quedo e *C*: luego quedó que *E* // adelante *E*: adelante e cessó luego *C*

Text IV
La vida de Santa Lucía
(Fundación Lázaro Galdiano 419, Biblioteca Menéndez Pelayo 9, and Escorial K-II-12)

[fol. 8ᵛᵇ] Santa Lucía, virgen
Santa Lucía fue virgen fija dalgo, natural de Siracusana. E oyó dezir la fama de Santa Águeda que corría por toda Cecilia e fuésse para el su sepulcro con su madre, que avía corrimiento de sangre bien avía
5 catorze años e non podía sanar dello. E mientra que dezían la missa, acaesció que leyan aquel evangelio en que cuenta que Nuestro Señor Jhesu Christo sanó una muger desta enfermedat. E entonce dixo Santa Lucía a su madre: 'Sy creyeres estas cosas que leen agora, cree que Santa Águeda sienpre tiene delante sý aquél por cuyo amor sufrió muerte e
10 passión. Mas si lo creyeres, tañe el sepulcro e serás a la sazón sana e alegre.'

E después desto fuéronse todos e fincaron Santa Lucía e su madre. E adormescióse Lucía e vido en medio de los ángeles estar a Santa Águeda cubierta de vestiduras e piedras preciosas. E díxole: 'Mi
15 hermana Lucía, virgen devota a Dios, ¿por qué me demandas que sane a tu madre, lo que tú puedes bien fazer? E por la tu grand fe es sana.' E dixo Santa Lucía a su madre: 'Sepas, madre, que por las oraciones de Santa Ágada eres sana. Ruégote, por amor de aquél que te sanó, que nunca de oy más me digas de fechos de casamiento, mas todo lo que me
20 dieres en logar de arras, dalo a los pobres.' E díxole su madre: 'Cierra los mis [fol. 9ʳᵃ] ojos primeramente e después faz lo que quisieres de todas mis riquezas.' E dixo Lucía: 'Lo que después que mueres das, por esso lo das, porque non lo puedes levar contigo. E por ende dalo

mientra que bives e avrás por ello merced.'

E después que tornaron, começaron a vender quanto avían e darlo a los pobres. E en este comedio sópolo el esposo e demandó a su ama que qué era aquello. E respondióle como sabia diziendo: 'Tu esposa falló otra heredat más provechosa que quiere conprar en tu nonbre e por ende paresce que vende algunas cosas.' E el loco pensando que era alguna heredat deste mundo, así mesmo començó a vender. E después que fue todo vendido e dado a pobres, su esposo adúxola a juyzio antel alcalde Pascual.

E començóla a conbidar que sacrificasse a los ýdolos. E respondióle ella: 'El sacrificio que plaze a Dios es vesitar a los pobres e fazerles limosnas, e porque yo non he otra cosa que le ofrezca, dóte a mí mesma, que me le ofrezcas.' E díxole Pascual: 'A los christianos locos deves e puedes dezir estas palabras, e non a mí, que guardo la ley de los enperadores.' E dixo Lucía: 'Tú guardas los decretos de los príncipes e yo guardo la ley de Jhesu Christo. Tú as miedo a los príncipes e yo he miedo a Dios. Tú no les quieres fazer pesar nin yo a Dios. Tú deseas de les fazer plazer e yo a Dios. E pues que asý es, faz tu pro e yo faré el mío.' E díxole Pascual: 'Desgastaste tu patrimonio con los garçones e por ende fablas [fol. 9ʳᵇ] como mala muger.' E díxole Lucía: 'Yo puse mi patrimonio en lugar seguro e nunca sope que era corronpimiento de voluntad nin de cuerpo.' E respondióle Pascual: '¿Quién son los corronpedores del ánima e del cuerpo?' E díxole Lucía: 'Los corronpedores del alma sodes los que vos trabajades que las almas se partan de Dios. Los del cuerpo son los que aman más las cosas tenporales que las celestiales.'

E dixo Pascual: '¿Qué darán las palabras quando rescibieres las feridas?' E díxole Lucía: 'Las palabras de Dios non pueden cessar.' E dixo Pascual: '¿E tú eres Dios?' Respondió Lucía: 'Yo só vassalla de Dios que dixo: "Quando estoviéredes ante los reyes o príncipes non pensaredes como devedes fablar, ca yo fablaré por vos". E Sant Paulo dixo: "Vos sodes casa de Spíritu Santo".' E dixo Pascual: '¿El Spíritu Santo es en ti?' E dixo Lucía: 'Todos aquellos que biven en castidat son tenplo de Spíritu Santo.' E díxole Pascual: 'Yo te faré llevar al logar de las malas mugeres por tal que te corronpan e pierdas el Spíritu Santo.'

E dixo Lucía: 'Nunca se ensuzia el alma si la voluntad non consiente, ca si me fizieres corronper e yo non consiento, yo avré la corona de la castidat doblada. E la voluntad nunca la podrás adozir que consienta en pecado. Evaste aquí el mi cuerpo presto para rescebir tormento. ¿Para qué estás tardando? ¡Comiença ya, fijo del diablo, e cunple la pena que se ha de tornar sobre ty!'

Estonce Pascual fizo venir los garçones e díxoles: 'Conbidat todo el pueblo e tanto la escarnesced fasta que la matedes.' E ellos queriéndola levar al dicho lugar non [fol. 9va] pudieron, ca el Spíritu Santo la fizo asý pesada que la non pudieron levar nin mover. E fizo venir Pascual mill omnes e atáronle los pies e las manos e non la pudieron mover tanpoco como ante. E mandó venir Pascual mill yuntas de bueyes mas non la pudieron mover. E mandó venir los encantadores mas non la pudieron mover con sus encantamientos. Estonces dixo Pascual: '¿Qué son estos encantamientos, que tantos millares de bueyes e de omnes non han podido mover una niña?' E dixo Lucía: 'Non son encantamentos, mas beneficios de Jhesu Christo. Enpero si me aduxieres otros mill omnes, non me podrán mover más que ante.' E pensó Pascual segund infinta de algunos que se desatarían estos malificios con agua. E mandóle echar agua de suso. Enpero asý non la pudieron mover tan poco como ante. E por ende fue muy cuytado e mandó encender muy grand fuego enderedor della, e esparzir pez e resina e ollio ferviente sobre ella. E dixo Lucía: 'Demando treguas de mi martirio por tal que ninguno non tema la mi passión e los que creyeren en Dios ayan alegría.'

E veyendo los amigos de Pascual que él tomava por esto grand pesar, firiéronla en la garganta con una espada. E ella non perdió la palabra, mas dixo: 'Dígovos buenas nuevas: que avredes paz, ca el enperador Maximiano es muerto e el enperador Diocleciano es desterrado. E bien como Santa Águeda defiende la cibdat de Quitanea, bien asý he yo de rogar por la cibdat de Siracusana.'

E en tanto que la virgen [fol. 9va] esto fablava, afevos los sayones de los romanos do yvan. E prendieron a Pascual e aduxiéronlo preso antel enperador porque avía robado toda la provincia e algo avían dicho al enperador. E así lo levaron preso a Roma. E los senadores de los romanos dieron sentencia que lo descabeçasen por los males que fiziera.

E la virgen Santa Lucía non se movió del lugar do la firieron, nin morió fasta que los capellanes vinieron a comulgarla. E la enterraron en esse mesmo logar. E quantos ende estavan loaron mucho a Dios. E fizieron ý noble iglesia.

Critical Apparatus

Incipit] Santa Lucía virgen *C*: [-] Lucía *D*; De Santa Luzía *E*
2] Santa *CE*: Así fue que Santa *D* // fue *CE*: *om*. *D* // virgen fija dalgo *CD*: fue de Siracusana *E* // natural de Siracusana *C*: na[-] *D*; fija dalgo virgen *E* // E *CE*: [-] *D* // oyó *C*: [-] *D*; oyendo *E* // dezir *C*: [-] *D*; *om*. *E*
3] la fama de Santa *CE*: [-] *D* // corría *C*: corrié *DE* // e *CD*: *om*. *E* // el *C*: [-] *D*; *om*. *E*
4] su sepulcro con su madre que *CE*: [-] *D* // avía *C*: [-] *D*; avié *E* // corrimiento *C*: [-]cia *D*; correncia *E* // avía *CD*: avié *E*
5] podía sanar *CE*: [-] *D* // dello *C*: [-] *D*; della *E* // E *CE*: [-] *D* // mientra *C*: [-] *D*; demientra *E* // missa *CE*: [-] *D*
6] acaesció *C*: [-]escióse *D*; acaescióse *E* // en *CD*: *om*. *E* // que *CD*: como *E* // Nuestro Señor *C*: *om*. *DE*
7] enfermedat *CE*: enfermed[-] *D* // E *C*: *om*. *DE* // Santa *CD*: *om*. *E*
8] creyeres *CE*: creyes *D* // estas cosas *CD*: aquellas palabras *E* // leen agora *C*: leyeron agora *D*; agora dixeron en el evangelio *E* // cree *DE*: creý *C*
9] tiene *C*: tien[-] *D*; tien *E* // delante *C*: [-] *D*; ante *E* // sufrió *CE*: recibió *D*
9-10] muerte e passión *CD*: passión e muerte *E* //
10] Mas *CD*: *om*. *E* // creyeres *CD*: crees *E* // el *C*: el su *D*; en el *E* // serás *CD*: a la sazón serás *E* // a la sazón *C*: luego *D*; *om*. *E*
12] E *C*: *om*. *DE*; después *CD*: *om*. *E* // desto *CD*: desto todo *E* // Santa *C*: *om*. *DE*
13] en medio de los ángeles *CD*: *om*. *E* // estar *CE*: *om*. *D*
14] cubierta *C*: estar cubierta *D*; en medio de los ángeles cobierta *E* // vestiduras e *C*: de *DE*
15] virgen *CD*: *om*. *E* // sane *CD*: dé sanidat *E*
16] bien *CD*: om *E* // E *CD*: Ca *E* // grand *CE*: gr[-] *D* // sana *CD*: sana tu madre *E*

17] Santa *CD*: *om. E*
17-18] Sepas madre q*ue* por las oraciones de Sa*n*ta Ágada eres sana. *D*: *om. CE*
18] por *CE*: por madre *D* // aq*u*él *CD*: aq*u*élla *E*
19] más *CD*: además *E* // de fechos *C*: fecho *D*; de fecho *E* // lo q*ue CD*: q*u*anto *E*
20] dieres *C*: dariés *D*; has a dar *E* // logar de *CE*: *om. D*
21] los mis ojos pr*i*meramente *CD*: pr*i*mero los los mis ojos *E* // faz lo que quisieres *CE*: lo q*ue* q*u*isieres faz *D*
22] mis *CE*: n*ue*śtras *D* // dixo *C*: díxol *DE* // Lo que *CD*: *om. E* // que mueres das *C*: q*u*i[-]res dar *D*; q*ue* vos morieredes q*ue* no*n* agora *E*
23] esso *CD*: esto no*n E* // q*ue* non lo puedes *C*: q*ue* no lo puedes *D*; lo das por no*n* lo *E*
24] mientra *CE*: mie*n*tre *D* // bives *C*: bive[-] *D*; vesquieres *E* // e avrás *CE*: [-] *D* // por ello *CD*: salud *E*
25] E *CD*: Por ende *E* // q*ue CD*: *om. E* // comença*ro*n *CE*: a su casa comença*ro*n *D* // a *CD*: de *E* // q*u*anto *CD*: cada día q*u*anto *E* // avía*n CE*: avié*n D*
26] los pobres *CE*: [-] *D* // E *CE*: *om. D* // el *CD*: su *E* // eśposo *CE*: eśposo de Sa*n*ta Lucía *D*
27] q*u*e qué *D*: que q*u*erié *C*; q*u*é *E* // aquello *CD*: esto *E* // E *CD*: E ella *E* // como sabia *CE*: [-]bia *D* // diziendo *C*: *om. DE* // Tu eśposa *C*: e su eśposa *D*; que su eśposo que *E*
28] falló *C*: fallara *D*; fall*ar*an *E* // p*ro*vechosa *CD*: conplida e más ap*ro*vechosa *E* // quiere *C*: q*u*i[si]ere *D*; la q*u*ería *E* // en tu nonbre *C*: p*ar*a sí *DE*
29] ende *CE*: esso *D* // paresce *C*: semeja *D*; seméjame *E* // vende *CE*: [-] *D* // E *CD*: *om. E* // pensando *CE*: creýa *D*
30] así mesmo *C*: otrosí *D*; e otrosý *E* // començó *CD*: en el comie*n*ço *E* // a *C*: él a *D*; de *E*
31] todo *CD*: *om. E* // dado *CD*: dado todo *E* // su eśposo *CD*: *om. E* // adúxola *CE*: q*u*ando lo sopo adúxola *D* // a juyzio *CD*: *om. E* // antel *CE*: d*e*lante el *D*
32] al*ca*lde Pascual *C*: alcalde P*as*cual *D*; al*ca*lde don Pascual su eśposo en juyzio e acusóla que era *Christ*iana e q*ue* yva contra la ley de los enp*er*adores *E*
33] començóla *CD*: don Pascual començóla *E* // a *CD*: de *E*
34] que *CD*: co*n* q*ue E* // plaze *DE*: a plaze *C* // a *CE*: *om. D* // pobres *CD*: enfermos *E* // fazerles *CD*: darles *E*
35] limosnas *C*: almosnas *D*; lymosna *E* // que *CE*: ende *D* // yo *CD*: *om. E* // otra *CD*: yo otra *E* // que le ofrezca *CD*: *om. E* // dóte *C*: ofrezcol *D*; dole e ofréscole *E*

36] que me le ofrezcas *C*: en sacrificio *D*; *om. E* // A los *chris*tianos locos *CD*: Estas palabras locas e vanas a los *christ*ianos *E*
37] deves e *C*: *om. DE* // puedes *C*: las puedes *D*; las podedes *E* // estas palabras *C*: essas cosas *D*; *om. E* // e *CE*: q*ue D*
38] dixo *C*: díxol *DE* // los decretos *CD*: la ley *E* // pr*í*ncipes *CD*: t*u*s enp*er*adores *E*
39] guardo *CD*: q*ue* guardo *E* // Jhes*u* Chris*t*o *CD*: Chris*t*o mi señor *E* // los *CD*: los tus *E*
40] he miedo *CD*: *om. E* // Tú no les q*u*ieres faz*er* pesar ni*n* yo a Dios *D*: *om. C*; Tú no*n* les q*u*ieras fazer pesar ni*n* yo a Dios *E*
41] E *C*: *om. DE* // faz *C*: tu faz *DE* // tu pro *CD*: lo tuyo *E*
42] faré *DE*: fará *C* // Desgastaste *C*: Desgastes *D*; Desgasteste *E*
44] puse *C*: pus *D*; pues *E* // patrimonio *E*: matrimonio *C*; [-]tr*i*mo*n*io *D*
45] respondióle *C*: respondió *D*; díxol *E*
46] Quién *CD*: Qu*á*les *E* // los *CD*: *om. E* // ánima *C*: cuerpo *DE* // cuerpo *C*: alma *D*; ánima *E*
47] del alma *CD*: de los cuerpos *E* // los *CD*: aq*u*ellos *E* // al*m*as *CD*: ánimas q*ue E*
48] los *CD*: aq*u*ellos *E*
49] te*n*porales *CD*: terrenales *E*
50] dixo *C*: díxol *DE* // q*u*ando *CD*: q*ue* non *E*
51] E *CD*: *om. E*
52] dixo *CE*: díxol *D* // E *C*: Pues *DE* // Respondió *CD*: Dixo *E* // Yo *C*: *om. DE*
53] estovieredes *C*: estudieres *DE* // o *C*: e los *D*; e ante los *E*
54] devedes *CD*: avedes de *E* // Santo *CE*: [-] *D* // E *C*: *om. D*
55] dixo P*a*scu*a*l *CD*: *om. E* // El *C*: Pues el *D*; *om. E*
55-56] Sp*í*ritu S*a*n*t*o *CD*: *om. E*
56] E *C*: *om. DE* // Santo *CE*: S[-] *D* // E díxole *CE*: Dixo *D* // llevar *CD*: venir *E* // por tal *C*: en tal *D*; por *E*
pierdas *CD*: perderás *E*
59] E *CD*: *om. E* // dixo *C*: díxol *DE* // Nu*n*ca *CD*: Non *E* // ensuzia *CD*: ensuziará *E* // alma *CD*: mi cuerpo *E*
60] corronper e yo non consie*n*to *CE*: [-] *D* // yo *C*: [-] *D*; *om. E*
60-61] avré la corona de la castidat doblada e *CE*: [-] *D* // la *C*: [-] *D*; la mi *E*
61-62] voluntad nu*n*ca la podrás adozir que consienta en pecado *CE*: [-] *D*
62] Evaste *CE*: [-] *D* // aquí *C*: [-] *D*; *om. E* // el mi cuerpo *CE*: [-] *D* // presto *C*: [-] *D*; do está presto *E* // p*ar*a rescebir tormento *CE*: [-] *D*
63] para *E*: *om. C*; [-] *D* // estás tardando *CE*: [-] *D* // Comie*n*ça ya *CE*: [-] *D*

// fijo del diablo *DE*: de perdición *C*

63-64] e cunple la pena que se ha de tornar sobre ti *C*: [-] *D*; para qué estas asý cunple las tus sañas que tus deseas *E*

65] Estonce Pascual fizo venir *CE*: [-] *D* // los *C*: [-] *D*; ante sý todos *E* // garçones e *CE*: [-] *D* // díxoles *C*: [-] *D*; dixo *E* // Conbidat *CE*: [-] *D*

66] escarnesced *CE*: escarne[-] *D* // fasta que la matedes *CE*: [-] *D*

66-67] E ellos queriéndola levar al dicho lugar *CE*: [-] *D*

67] asý *CD*: tan *E*

68] que la non pudieron levar *CE*: [-] *D* // nin mover *C*: [-] *D*; nin solamente non la podieron mover *E* // E fizo *CE*: [-] *D* // venir Pascual *C*: [-] *D*; Pascual venir *E* // mill *CE*: [-] *D*

69] omnes *CE*: [-]nes *D* // e atáronle los pies e las manos e *CD*: om. *E* // e *CD*: mas *E* // pudieron *CE*: p[-] *D* // mover *CE*: [-]over *D* // tanpoco *E*: a tanpoco *C*; om. *D*

70] como *CE*: om. *D* // ante *C*: om. *D*; antes *E*

70-71] mandó venir Pascual mill yuntas de bueyes mas non la pudieron mover *C*: [-]es e atar con muchas sogas mas non la pudie[-] tan poco com[-] *D*; om. *E*

71] E *CE*: [-] *D* // mandó *C*: [-] *D*; fizo *E* // venir los *CE*: [-] *D* // encantadores *CE*: [-]ncantadores *D* // mas *C*: e *D*; om. *E*

71-72] non la pudieron mover con sus encantamientos *C*: non pudieron moverla con sus enc[-] *D*; que la moviesen con sus encantamientos enpero non podieron *E*

72] Estonces *C*: Estonce *D*; E estonce *E* // Pascual *CE*: [-] *D*

71-72] Qué son estos *CE*: esto[-] *D* // encantamientos *CE*: [-] *D* // de bueyes e de omnes *C*: de omnes *D*; om. *E*

73] han podido *C*: pudieron *D*; pueden *E*

74] una niña *CE*: u[-] *D* // E *C*: [-] *D*; om. *E*

75] beneficios *CD*: son beneficios *E* // Jhesu Christo *CD*: Dios *E* // Enpero si me aduxieres *CD*: ca tú aunque me adugas *E* // mill omnes *C*: diez mi[-] *D*; diez mill *E*

76] podrán *CD*: podrás *E* // más que *CD*: tanpoco como *E* // pensó *C*: mandó *D*; afinó *E*

77] ques desatarían *D*: que se desataría *C*; que desatarié *E* // estos *DE*: om. *C* // malificios *E*: om. *C*; ma[-]icios *D* // agua *C*: lavadura *D*; levadura *E*

77-78] E mandóle echar agua de suso *C*: E mandóla lavar *D*; Entonce la mandó levar *E*

78] enpero asý *C*: mas *D*; enpero asý nin asý *E* // mover tan poco *C*: mover a tan poco *D*; levar *E*

78-79] como ante *CD*: antes *E*
79] e *CD*: e por ende *E* // ma*n*dó encender *D*: mandó encender muy cuytado e mandó encender *C*; mandó encender e fazer *E*
80] esparzir *CE*: derramar *D* // pez e resina e ollio ferviente *C*: pez e resina e azeyte [-]rvie*n*te *D*; olio e resina e pez ferviente *E* // sobre *CE*: en somo *D* // E *CD*: Estonce *E*
81] Dema*n*do *CD*: Demande *E* // treguas de *CD*: tregua del *E*
83] E *C*: *om. DE* // los amigos de *C*: las amigos de *D*; las amarguras q*ue E* // que él *C*: q*ue D*; *om. E* // grand pesar *CD*: *om. E*
84] una espada *C*: un cuchiello *D*; un cochiello *E* // E ella non *CD*: Enp*er*o nunca ella *E* // perdió *CD*: per|perdio *E* // palabra *CD*: fabla *E*
85] nuevas *DE*: dueñas *C* // ca *C*: q*ue D*; ay*n*a ca *E* // el enp*er*ador *CD*: *om. E*
86] dest*er*rado *CE*: desterra[-] *D*
88] Siracusana *CE*: Si[-]sana *D*
89] E en ta*n*to *C*: E demie*n*tre *D*; Demientra *E* // afevos *C*: ahévos *D*; afevos do venién *E*
90] do yvan *C*: do vinía*n D*; *om. E* // prendieron *C*: p*r*isie[-] *D*; presiero*n E* // a Pascual *CE*: *om. D* // aduxiéronlo *CD*: leváronlo *E*
91] toda la p*r*ovincia *CD*: la tierra e toda la cibdat de Provincia *E*
91-92] e algo avían dicho al enp*er*ador: e aglo avían dicho al enp*er*ador *C*; e q*ue* lo oyera el emp*er*a[-] *D*; q*ue* lo oyera el enp*er*ador *E*
92] e *CE*: *om. D* // lo levaron preso *C*: aduxiéro*n*lo *DE* // senadores *CD*: sañadores *E* // de *D*: e *CE*
93] que lo descabeçase*n C*: q*ue* lo descabeças[-] *D*; contra el q*ue* le descabeçasen *E* // por los *CE*: [-] *D* // males *CE*: [-]les *D*
94] E *C*: *om. DE* // del lugar *CD*: de los logares *E* // firieron *CD*: fezieron *E*
95] capellanes *CE*: [-] *D*
95-96] E la ent*er*raron en esse mesmo logar e q*u*antos ende estava*n* loaron mucho a Dios *C*: E q*u*antos ý estava*n* loaro*n* a Dios e luego finó e enterráro*n*la en esse [-] *D*; E q*u*antos aý estava*n* loaron mucho a Dios e enterraro*n* el cuerpo de la virgen en ese mismo logar *E*
96] E *CE*: [-] *D*
97] noble *CD*: muy noble *E*

Text V
La vida de Santa Águeda
(Escorial h-I-14)

[fol. 61ra] Capítulo XXIII de la vida de Santa Águeda
Santa Águeda era niña fija dalgo, e muy fermosa en el cuerpo e más fermosa en el alma. E rogava sienpre a Dios e era en la cibdat de Acatania con toda su santidat. E Quinciano, el adelantado de Cecilia,
5 porque era omne villano e luxorioso e escaso e sirvié de grado a los ýdolos, semejával que tomando él a Santa Águeda, que le averían todos miedo como a fijo dalgo. E porque era luxorioso, quería fartarse [fol. 61rb] de su fermosura. E porque era avariento, quería tomar sus riquezas. E porque era ydolatra, quería que sacrificase a los ýdolos.

10 E por ende fízola traer ante sí. E después que fue traýda, conoció el su talante, que non quería fazer nada de lo que él asmava. E mandóla dar a una mala muger que dizían Efrodizia, que avía nueve fijas que eran tan malas como ella, e que en treynta días mudasen su coraçón. E ellas la una vegada le prometían buenas cosas, e la otra la espantavan
15 e esperavan que la podrién trastornar. Estonce díxoles Santa Águeda: '¿En qué estades? Que la voluntat está así arraygada e afirmada en Jhesu Christo, que todas vuestras promessas son así como la luvia, e vuestros espantos son así como ríos, que comoquier que estas cosas lidien contra mí, el cimiento de la mi casa non puede caer.' E diziendo esto,
20 llorava cada día e rogava a Dios, deseando venir a la gloria de martirio. E viendo esto Efrodisia que non la podía trastornar, dixo a Quinciano: 'Así dígote que más de ligero se podrían las piedras [fol. 61va] e el fierro torrnarse en polvo muy blando, ante que trastornar esta niña de la fe de Jhesu Christo.'

25 Estonces Quinciano fízola traer ante sí e díxole: '¿Quién eres tú?' E díxole Santa Águeda: 'Yo só fija dalgo e muy noble por linage, segunt

que dizen mis parientes.' E díxole Quinciano: 'Si tú eres fija dalgo, ¿por qué te demuestras e te das por villana en tu costunbre?' E respondióle ella: 'Porque só sierva de Jhesu Christo: por eso me muestro por villana.'
E díxole fuertemente Quinciano: 'Si eres fija dalgo, ¿por qué te llamas sierva?' E respondió ella: 'Ésta es muy grant gracia do se prueva el servicio de Jhesu Christo.' Estonces dixo Quinciano: '¡De dos cosas faz la una: o sacrifica los ýdolos o sufre muchos tormentos!' E díxole Santa Águeda: '¡Sea tu muger tal qual como es la tu deesa Venus, e tú como el tu dios Júpiter!' Estonces Quinciano mandóle dar muchas palmadas e díxole: '¡Non quieras ser muy garrida en denostar el alcalde!' Respondió Santa Águeda: 'Maravíllome mucho porque tan grant [fol. 61vb] sabio como tú, porque conosciste a tan grant locura, que dizes a los maderos que son tus dioses. E dizes que tú e tu muger non queredes semejar a ellos. E dizes que te fablo mal porque digo que bivas así como ellos. Ca si son dioses, querán el tu bien, mas aborresces su conpaña; quieras pues semejar a mí.' E díxole Quinciano: '¿Por qué andas en tantas palabras? ¡O sacrifica los dioses o fazerte he morir atormentada!' E respondió Santa Águeda: 'Si me pusieres entre las bestias crueles, nonbrando a Jhesu Christo fazerse han mansas. Si me metieres en el fuego, los ángeles del cielo enbiarán rocío del cielo e matarlo han. Si me atares o ligares e me atormentares, sanarme ha el Spíritu Santo porque desprecio todas tus menazas.' Estonces mandóla Quinciano levar a la cárcel porque le confondía por placer. E ella yva muy leda e muy gozosa, bien como si fuese conbidada a buen comer. E demandava a Dios su lid.

E otro día Quinciano mandóla traer ante sí. E díxole Quinciano: '¡Niega a [fol. 62ra] Dios e adora los ýdolos!' E ella diziendo que non quería, mandóla aspar e darle torcejones. E díxole Santa Águeda: 'Agora tomo yo muy grant sabor en estas penas, como quien oye buen mensagero, o quien le vee como quando ha tienpo que le desea, o quien falla muchos e grandes thesoros. Ca saben que non pueden poner el trigo en el alfolí o en el orno si non fuere la su caña quebrantada toda e fecha paja. E así la mi ánima non puede entrar en Paraýso con palma de martirio si non fuere el mi cuerpo despedaçado.' Estonces ensañóse Quinciano e mandóle cortarla una teta. E díxole Santa Águeda:

'¿Cómo cruel, sin piedat e falso, non oviste vergüença de tajar en mí lo que tú mameste en tu madre? Enpero yo tengo otras tetas de dentro en la mi alma. E las ofrescí de pequeña a Dios.'

65 Estonces Quinciano mandóla poner en la cárcel. E defendió que ningunt físico que non entrase a ella e que le non diesen de comer nada. E cerca la medianoche vino a ella un omne anciano, e yva antél un niño [fol. 62ʳᵇ] que levava lunbre e trayánle muchas melezinas. E dixo: 'Empero que este adelantado loco te fizo mal e te quebrantó con
70 muchos tormentos, tú más le atormenteste. Empero que él te tajó la tu teta e te atormentó en ella, más él es atormentado e amargo. E porque lo sofriste en grant paciencia, vi que la tu teta podrié bien sanar.' E dixo Santa Águeda: 'Nunca melezina fize a mi cuerpo de carne, e seméjame muy sin justicia perder lo que guardé fasta agora.' E díxole el anciano:
75 'Fija, yo christiano só, e de mí non te temas de ninguna vergüença.' E díxole Santa Águeda: '¿E por que avría yo de ti vergüença, ca eres viejo e anciano, e yo só tan malamente despedaçada que non ay omne en el mundo que de mí tomase plazer? Enpero gradézcotelo mucho, padre señor, porque quisiste aver cuydado de mí.' E díxole él: '¿Por
80 qué non quieres que te sane?' Respondió ella: 'Porque Nuestro Señor Jhesu Christo es maestro que solamente por la palabra sana todas las enfermedades e las trae a su estado. E éste me puede sanar si quisiere.' [fol. 62ᵛᵃ] E díxole el anciano, riéndose: 'Yo só su apóstol e él me enbió a ti. E sepas que serás sana en el su nonbre.' E desaparesció el anciano
85 adesora. E éste fue el apóstol Sant Pedro. Estonces Santa Águeda fincó los ynojos en tierra e gradesciólo mucho a Dios. E fallóse toda sana e la teta entera en sus pechos. E las guardas todas fueron espantadas de la lunbre que vieron grande, e fuyeron e dexaron la cárcel abierta. E algunos rogávanla que se fuese. E dixo ella: 'Non lo quiera Dios que yo
90 fuya e que pierda la corona que he ganada del mi señor Jhesu Christo, e que sean las guardas por mí malandantes.'

E otro día dixo Quinciano que adorase los ýdolos por tal manera que non sufriese mayores penas. E díxole Santa Águeda: '¡Las tus palabras son locas e vanas e ensuzias todo el ayre! O mezquino sin seso
95 e sin entendimiento, ¿por qué quieres que adore las piedras e dexe a Dios del cielo que me sanó?' E díxole Quinciano: '¿Quién te sanó?'

E díxole Santa Águeda: 'Jhesu Christo, el fijo de Dios.' [fol. 62^(vb)] E díxole Quinciano: '¿Aún osas nonbrar a Jhesu Christo, que yo non quiero oýr?' E díxole Santa Águeda: 'Mientra que visquiere, sienpre llamaré a Jhesu Christo en la boca e en el coraçón.' E dixo Quinciano: '¡Agora veré si te sanará Jhesu Christo!' Estonce mandó traer e esparzir muchos tiestos quebrados e poner carbones encendidos en ellos; e ella desnuda, que la enbolviesen en ellos. E demientra que fazían esto, tremía la tierra muy fuertemente en manera que meneó toda la cibdat. E cayó muy grant partida de la cerca e mató a dos omnes consegeros de Quinciano. Estonces todo el pueblo fuése para Quinciano, dando bozes e diziendo así: '¡Tales cosas sufrimos por ti porque fazes mal a Águeda e sin razón!' Estonces Quinciano, temiéndose del temor de la tierra, e de la otra parte del pueblo, mandóla poner en la cárcel, do rogava a Dios Santa Águeda, diziendo así: 'Señor Jhesu Christo, que me crieste e sienpre me guardeste que el mi cuerpo fuese linpio, e me diste fuerça [fol. 63^(ra)] que pudiese sofrir estos tormentos, e me diste paciencia en ellos, toma la mi alma e mándame venir a la tu gloria.' E diziendo esto, dio una grant boz e salióle el alma.

Estonce los christianos tomaron el su cuerpo e enbolviéronlo en muchas especias, e pusiéronle en un sepulcro muy onrradamente. E en este comedio vino un mancebo vestido de paños de sirgo, e con él más de cient omnes muy fermosos e vestidos de paños blancos que nunca fueron vestidos en aquella tierra. E vinieron al sepulcro e pusieron una tabla de mármol a su cabeça. E nunca jamás los vieron. E fallaron escriptas en aquella tabla aquestas palabras: '¡O alma santa, rescibió martirio de grado por amor de Dios, e Dios diole onrra e franqueó su tierra!' E quando supieron este miraglo, los gentiles e los judíos onrravan mucho al su sepulcro.

E un día, mientra que Quinciano fue buscar las sus reliquias, levava dos cavallos ante sí. E los cavallos reninchando, alçáronse en coces e echáronle en el río. E el uno a coces e el otro a muesos, [fol. 62^(rb)] matáronlo.

E después, a cabo de un año que murió Santa Águeda, ronpióse un monte que era cerca de la cibdat de Acatania. E salió dende muy grant fuego en manera que regalava todas las piedras e la tierra e venía muy atrevidamente contra la cibdat. Estonce muy gra*n*t co*n*paña de paganos descendiero*n* del monte e fuyero*n* al sepulcro de Sa*n*ta Águeda. E tomaro*n* un velo q*ue* estava sobre el sepulcro. E luego q*ue*dó el fuego, q*ue* no*n* fue adelante.

En Acatania era un ob*is*po de s*an*ta vida e avía un palafrén a maravilla muy noble. E una vegada escapósele e fuésele áq*u*el q*ue* le g*u*ardava. E fuxó e metióse por la boca del infierrno. E él yva dando grandes bozes e entró en pos dél. E los diablos mostráro*n*le muchos cavallos e palafrenes e muchos manjares muy nobles. E en cabo de todo aq*ues*to, diéro*n*le su palafrén e una capa de oro bien cerrada e de dentro llena de fuego inferrnal. E dixéro*n*le q*ue* la presentase a su señor, el ob*is*po. E el ob*is*po entendiólo por Sp*íri*tu Santo e mandó a dos moros [fol. 62ᵛᵃ] q*ue* tomasen la capa, e q*ue* la fuesen echar en *e*l mar e q*ue* se viniesen. E ellos, co*n* cobdicia del oro, ronpiero*n* la capa e salió el fuego. E q*ue*mó a ellos e el agua e las piedras e las peña*s* e la t*ie*rra. E no*n* q*ue*dó fa*s*ta q*ue* sacaro*n* el velo de Sa*n*ta Águeda. E luego e*s*tudo q*ue*do, q*ue* no*n* fue más adelante.

Corrected Readings

6] semejával *DE*: e semejándole *F*; paresçíale *C*; e pensó *G*

9] ydolatra *D*: ydolatría *CEF*; ydolat*r*o *G*

12] que avía *CD*: e avía *EFG*

18] ríos *DEG*: rayos *CF*

34] como *CDEG*: se *F*

36] quieras *CD*: seas *EG*; quieres *F*

41] dioses *C*: dios *DEF*; *om. G* // querrán *CDE*: quería *F*; *om. G*

43] dioses *C*: dios *DEF*; ýdolos *G*

53] diziendo *CD*: *om. E*; dixo *F*; díxol *G*

69] te quebra*n*tó *CDEG*: quebrantar *F*

72] sofri*s*te *CDEG*: sofilte *F*

74] perder: *om. F* (cf. 'que lo pierda' *C*)

Text VI
La vida e passión de Santa Lucía
(Escorial h-I-14)

[fol. 12ʳᵇ] Capítulo cuarto de la vida e passión de Santa Lucía, virgen

Santa Lucía fue del lugar de Siracusano e fue fija dalgo e virgen. E oyó la devoción de Santa Gueda que era por toda Cicilia e fuése para el sepulcro con su madre, que avía correncia de sangre bien avía catorze años e non podía sanar por ninguna melezina que le fazían. E mientra que dezían misa, acaesció que dezían el evangelio que cuenta que Jhesu Christo sanó una muger que avía luengo tienpo esta enfermedat. E estonce dixo Santa Lucía a su madre: 'Si creyeres [fol. 12ᵛᵃ] estas palabras que agora fueron leýdas, cree que Santa Águeda siempre tenía ante sí aquél por cuyo amor ella rescibió pasión en el su cuerpo. E si lo creyeres, tañe el sepulcro de Santa Águeda e luego serás sana e alegre de tu dolencia.'

E después de todo esto fuéronse Santa Lucía e su madre. E dormiéronse amas a dos e Santa Lucía vio en medio de los ángeles a Santa Águeda estar cubierta de piedras preciosas. E díxole Santa Águeda estas palabras: 'Hermana Lucía, virgen devota a Dios, ¿por qué me mandas que dé sanidat a tu madre, lo que tú puedes luego fazer? Ca por la tu buena fe es sana tu madre.' Estonce dixo Lucía a su madre: 'Madre, sabe que eres sana. Ruégote, por amor de aquél que te sanó, que de oy adelante nunca me más digas de fechos de casamiento, mas todo lo que me darías en lugar de casamiento, dalo todo a pobres.' E díxole su madre: 'Cierra los mis ojos ante e después faz lo que quisieres de todas las mis riquezas.' E dixo Santa Lucía a su madre: 'Lo que después que tú murieres dieres, por esso lo darás, porque lo non podrás levar contigo. E por ende dalo mientra que bives e averás por ende merced.'

E por ende, deque torrnaron para su casa, començaron de vender cada día lo que tenían e darlo a los pobres. E en este [fol. 12ᵛᵇ] comedio sópolo el esposo de Santa Lucía e demandó a su ama que la criara que qué era esto, que ansí vendía todo lo que avía.' E respondióle ella e díxole como su esposa fallara otra heredat más provechosa e quería conprarla, e por ende vende algunas cosas de las que ha. E el loco creyólo, cuydando que alguna heredat era deste mundo. E otrosí començó él de vender de lo suyo e dárgelo para que conprase más. E después que fue todo vendido e dado a los pobres, su esposo tráxola a juyzio ante el alcalde don Pascual e acusóla como era christiana e fazía contra la ley de los emperadores.

E estonce don Pascual començóla de conbidar que adorase los ýdolos. E respondió ella e dixo esta razón: 'El sacrificio que plaze a Dios es visitar a los pobres e fazer limosna, e porque ya non tengo otra cosa de que le faga sacrificio, quiero fazerle sacrificio de mí misma.' E dixo Pascual: 'Estas razones a los christianos las di tú, e non a mí, que guardo la ley de los enperadores.' E díxole Santa Lucía: 'Tú guardas los decretos de los tus príncipes e enperadores e yo guardaré la ley de Jhesu Christo. E tú as miedo a los enperadores e yo a Dios. Tú non les fazes pesar nin yo a Dios. E tú deseas de les fazer plazer, [fol. 13ʳᵃ] yo a Dios. E pues así es, tú faz tu pro e yo faré la mía.' E díxole Pascual: 'Desgastaste tu patrimonio con los garçones, por ende fablas como mala muger.' E dixo Santa Lucía: 'Yo puse mi patrimonio en un lugar seguro e nunca sope que era corronpimiento nin de voluntad nin de fecho.' E preguntó Pascual: '¿Qué son los corronpedores del cuerpo e del ánima?' E dixo Santa Lucía: 'Los corronpedores del ánima sodes aquellos que vos trabajades que las ánimas se perezcan e se partan de Dios. Los corronpedores del cuerpo son los que aman más las cosas terrenales que las espirituales.'

E dixo Pascual: '¿Qué darán las tus razones quando sufrieres penas e las feridas?' E dixo Santa Lucía: 'Las palabras de Dios nunca pueden cesar.' Dixo Pascual: '¿Pues tú eres Dios?' Dixo Santa Lucía: 'Non só yo Dios, mas só sierva de Dios, que dixo estas palabras: "Quando estudieres ante los reyes e príncipes non pensedes qué digades, ca yo fablaré por vos". E Sant Pablo dixo: "Vos sodes e sabedes casa de

Spíritu Santo"'. E dixo Pascual: 'Yo te faré levar a la casa de las malas mugeres en tal manera que te corronpan e pierdas el Spíritu Santo.' E dixo Santa [fol. 13rb] Lucía: 'Nunca se ensuzia el ánima si la voluntad non lo consiente, e si me fizieres corronper sin consentimiento, averé la corona de la virginidat doblada e la voluntat non corronpida. Nin me podrás adozir que consienta en peccado. E evas mi cuerpo presto para sofrir tormentos. ¿Para qué estás tardando? ¡Comiença ya, fijo del diablo, e cunple las penas que tienes en el coraçón!'

E estonce Pascual fizo venir los garçones e mandólos que conbidasen todo el pueblo e que la escarnesciesen fasta que muriese. E ellos quisiéronla levar al dicho lugar mas non podieron, ca el Spíritu Santo la fazía pesada por que la non pudiesen levar. E fizo Pascual venir mill omnes e atáronla los pies e las manos mas non la podieron mover de aquel lugar tanpoco como ante. E mandó venir los encantadores que la moviesen con encantamentos mas non podieron. Estonce le dixo Pascual: '¿Qué son estos tus encantamentos, que tantos millares de omnes non pueden mover una niña?' Dixo Santa Lucía: 'Non son encantamentos mas beneficio de Dios. E aunque trayas otros mill, non podrán tanpoco como ante.' E pensó Pascual segunt [fol. 13va] enfinta que algunos sabidores desatarían estos maleficios con lavamiento. E mandóla lavar. Enpero que ansí non la pudieron tanpoco mover como ante. E por ende fue muy cuytado e mandó encender fuegos enderredor della, e esparzió pez e resina e olio ferviente sobrella. Dixo Lucía: 'Demando treguas del mi martirio por tal que ninguno non tema la mi passión e los que creen en Dios ayan alegría.'

Viéndolo esto los amigos de Pascual, que avían por ello grant pesar, firiéronla en la garganta con un cuchillo. E ella non perdió la palabra, mas dixo: 'Dígovos buenas nuevas: que avedes paz, ca el enperador Maximiano es muerto e Diocleciano desterrado.' E dixo Santa Lucía esta razón: 'Bien ansí como Santa Águeda defiende e guarda la cibdat de Quinorancia, bien ansí he yo de defender la cibdat de Siracusana.'

E mientra que la virgen esto fablava, ahévos do venía los sayones de los romanos. E prendieron a Pascual e traxiéronle preso antel enperador, porque avía robado toda la provincia. E los senadores de Roma dieron sentencia que le cortasen la cabeça por los [fol. 13vb] males que fiziera a la virgen. E ella non se movió del lugar do la firieron, nin murió fasta que los capellanes vinieron a comulgarla. E quantos ý estavan dieron muchas gracias a Dios. E enterráronla bien en ese mesmo lugar. E fizieron ý noble eglesia.

Corrected Readings

8] madre *CDE*: padre *F*
9] cree *DE*: creý *C*; e cree *F*
13] fuéronse *CDE*: fuése *F*
28] el *CD*: su *EF*
47] patrimonio *CDE*: matrimonio *F*
48] patrimonio *CE*: [-]trimonio *D*; matrimonio *F*
50] corronpedores *CDE*: corronpunientes *F*
60] casa *CDE*: cosa *F*
67] Para *E*: *om. CF*; [-] *D*
94] porque *CDE*: que *F*

Text VII
La vida de la virgen señora Santa Águeda
(Escorial M-II-6)

[fol. 24ʳ] La vida de la virgen señora Santa Águeda, la qual fue de la cibdad de Catania

Santa Águeda era niña fija dalgo, fermosa en el cuerpo, más fermosa en el alma. E rogava sienpre a Dios en la cibdad de Catania en toda santidad. E Quinciano, el adelantado de Cicilia, porque era villano, quería que todos le oviessen miedo. Ca era luxurioso e escasso e servía de grado a los ýdolos, pensó que si él tomasse a Santa Águeda por muger, quel avrían todos miedo como a fidalgo. E porque era luxorioso, queríase fartar de su fermosura. E porque era avariento, quería tomar las sus riquezas. E porque era ydolatro, quería que ella adorasse los ýdolos.

E fízola traher delante sí. E sopo su talanto, que non quería adorar los ýdolos nin fazer nada de lo que él asmava. E mandóla dar a una mala muger que llamavan Frodisia, e avía diez fijos que eran tan malos como ella. E esto fazía él por que fasta treynta días mudasse el coraçón a Santa Águeda. E a las vegadas prometiéle muchas cosas, e a las vegadas amenázavanla e espantávanla con tormentos, cuydando que la podrién trastornar. E díxoles Águeda: 'Sabed que la mi voluntad es assí firmada e raygada con Jhesu Christo, que vuestras amenazas non valen nada, e vuestras promissiones son como llama, e vuestros espantos son assí como ríos, que comoquier que estas cosas lidien contra mí, por esso el cimiento de la mi casa non puede caer.' E cada día llorava Santa Águeda con grand deseo por venir a la iglesia de Dios. E veyendo Frodissia que la non podía tornar, dixo a Quinciano: 'Más de ligero se podrían tornar las piedras blandas e el fierro plomo [fol. 24ᵛ] que trastornar el coraçón de esta niña de la fe de Jhesu Christo.'

E luego Quinciano fízola traher ante sí e díxol: '¿Quién eres tú?' E ella le dixo: 'Yo só muger fija dalgo e muy noble de linage, segunt que dizen mis parientes.' E díxol Quinciano: 'Si tú eres muy fija dalgo, ¿por qué te demuestras en tus costunbres en darte por villana?' E dixo ella: 'Porque só sierva de Jhesu Christo: por esso me muestro por villana.' E díxol Quinciano: 'Si tú eres libre, ¿por qué te demuestras por sierva?' E dixo ella: 'Non ay ninguno que pueda ser libre si primeramente non serviere al mi señor Jhesu Christo.' E díxol Quinciano: '¡Escoge qual quisieres: o sacrifica los ýdolos o recibe grandes tormentos!' E díxol Águeda: '¡Tal sea la tu muger como es la tu deessa Venus, e tú tal seas como el tu dios Júpiter!' E mandól dar muchas palmadas e díxol: '¡Non seas mucho garrida que denuestas al juez!' E díxol Águeda: 'Maravíllome mucho porque tan sabio como tú tomaste tan grand locura, diziendo que non querías semejar al tu dios e mandas a mí quel adore.' E díxol Quinciano: '¿Por qué andamos en muchas palabras? ¡Sacrifica los ýdolos o muere a tormentos!' E díxol Águeda: 'Si tú me pusieres entre las bestias crueles, yo llamando a Jhesu Christo luego serán mansas. E si me pusieres en el fuego, los ángeles de Dios a matarlo han. E si me llagas e me atormentas, el Spíritu Santo sanarme ha. E por esto non precio nada tus tormentos.' E mandó que la levassen a la cárcel. E ella yva tan alegre como si la levasen a buen comer.

E otro día díxol Quinciano: '¡Niega a Jhesu Christo e adora los ýdolos!' E ella díxol que non quería e mandóla aspar e dar torcejones. E dixo Águeda: 'Agora tomo yo sabor en estas penas, assí como quien oye buen mensagero, o vee al que a tienpo desea ver, o como quien falla muchos thesoros. E sabed que non pueden [fol. 25ʳ] poner el trigo en el alfolí si non fuesse primero quebrada la su caña e toda fecha paja. E assí la mi alma non puede entrar en el Paraýso si non fuesse el mi cuerpo primero menuzado e quebrantado con palma de martirio.' E asañóse Quinciano e mandól tajar las tetas. E díxol Águeda: 'O omne falso e cruel, malo sin piadad, ¿non oviste vergüença de tajar en mí lo que tú mameste de tu madre? Pero yo tengo otras tetas entregas en la mi alma do se crian todos los mis deseos. E los ofrecí de pequeña a Dios.'

E luego la mandó meter en la cárcel. E defendió que ningunt físico non entrasse a ella e non le diessen a comer nin a bever. E contra la medianoche vino un omne antiguo e anciano, e yva con él un niño que levava lunbre e traýa muchas melezinas. E díxol: 'Maguer que este adelantado loco te quebrantó con tormentos, mucho más atormenteste tú a él. E maguer que te tajó las tetas e te amargó, mucho más amargo finca él. E porque lo sofriste en paciencia, só aquí venido por sanar tus tetas.' E díxol Águeda: 'Yo nunca melezina fiz en el mi cuerpo, e paréceme ya sin guissa si lo agora fiziesse.' E díxole el anciano: 'Fija, yo christiano só, e non temas de mí en ninguna cosa.' E dixo Águeda: '¿Por qué avría yo de ti miedo, que tú eres viejo e anciano, e yo estó muy fuerte despedaçada que non ha omne en el mundo que de mí tomasse plazer? Pero agradézcote mucho porque quisiste aver cuydado de mí.' E díxole él: '¿Por qué non quieres que te sane?' E ella dixo: 'Porque Nuestro Señor non tan solamente de la su palabra sana todas las cosas e las trahe a su estado. E éste solo puede sanar a mí si él quisiere.' E díxol el anciano, riendo: 'Yo só el apóstol Sant Pedro.' E Santa Águeda cayó en tierra, gradeciól mucho a Dios, e fallóse toda sana e las tetas en su pecho. E las guardas espantáronse mucho de la grand claridad que vieron, e fuyeron e dexaron la cárcel abierta. E [fol. 25ᵛ] rogávanla algunos que se fuesse. E ella dixo: 'Non quiera Dios que yo esto faga e sean las guardas por mí malandantes, e yo pierda la corona que he ganado.'

E dixo Quinciano: 'Águeda, dime quál físico te sanó tan aýna de las llagas.' E díxol Águeda: 'Aquel físico sanó a mí que de la su palabra tan solamente puede sanar e fazer todas las cosas.' E dixo Quinciano: 'Si tú adoras los ýdolos, ya non sofrirás más penas.' E díxol Águeda: '¡Las tus palabras son locas e vanas e ensuzian todo el ayre! O mesquino loco e sin entendimiento, ¿por qué quieres que adore el ayre e las piedras e dexe a Dios del cielo que me sanó?' E dixo Quinciano: '¿Aún tú osas fablar de aquél que non querría oýr?' E díxol Águeda: 'Mientra visquiere, sienpre llamaré a Jhesu Christo en la mi boca e en el mi coraçón.' Estonce asañósse Quinciano e mandó esparzir muchos tiestos quebrados e poner carbones encendidos sobre ellos. E mandó que la enbolviessen en ellos toda fasta en los cabellos por ver si la sanaría

Jhesu Christo. E mientras esto fazían, tremió mucho la tierra en tal manera que se engrameó toda la cibdad. E cayeron muchas piedras en manera que mataron a dos consegeros de Quinciano. E todo el pueblo se fue para él e dixeron: '¡Tales cosas sofrimos porque matas a sin razón a Santa Águeda!' E Quinciano, temiendo la una parte del miedo del pueblo, mandóla poner en la cárcel. E Santa Águeda fizo su oración e dixo: 'Señor Jhesu Christo, que me crieste e me guardeste siempre el mi cuerpo que fuesse linpio, e me diste fuerça por do sufriesse estos tormentos, e diste paciencia en ellos, toma la mi alma e fazme venir a la tu gloria.' E diziendo esto, finósse e fuésse para la gloria de paraýso.

E los christianos tomaron el su cuerpo e enbolviéronlo en muchas specias, e pusiéronle en el sepulcro. E vino un mancebo vestido de paños de sirgo, e con él vinieron más de cient omnes [fol. 26ʳ] vestidos de nobles paños blancos, que nunca tales vestidos vieron en aquella tierra. E vinieron al sepulcro e pusieron una piedra sobre su cabeça. E nunca más vinieron hí. E fallaron escrito en aquella piedra: 'Esta ánima santa recibió martirio de grado, e Dios diole honrra e franqueóle su tierra.' E quando vieron este miraglo, judíos e gentiles todos honrravan su sepulcro.

E Quinciano cavalgó por yr buscar las riquezas de Santa Águeda e levávanle dos cavallos en diestro. E aquellos cavallos tornaron muy bravos para Quinciano, e el uno a coces e el otro a muessos, echáronlo en el río. E afogáronlo en el río.

E a cabo de un año, abrióse un grand monte cerca de la cibdad. E salía dél grande fuego de guissa que regalava las piedras e venía muy rezio contra la cibdad. E estonce grand conpaña de paganos decendieron del monte e fuyeron al sepulcro de Santa Águeda. E tomaron el velo de Santa Águeda que estava sobre el sepulcro e tornáronle contra el fuego. E el fuego non ovo poder de pasar más adelante.

Corrected Readings

7] ýdolos *CDEF*: ýdolos e *G*
43] crueles *CDF*: bravas *E*; crueles e *G*
68] paréceme: seméjame *CF*: me semeja *E*; parecerme *G* // díxole *CEF*: *om*. *G*
70] e anciano *CF*: *om*. *E*; anciano *G*
72] aver *CEF*: *om*. *G*
89] a *CEF*: *om*. *G*
92] esparzir *CF*: poner *E*; tener *G*
96] E *CE*: *om*. *F*; A *G*
112] judíos *CEF*: todos judíos *G*
116] e el *CEF*: el *G*
120] grand *CEF*: avía grand *G*

Appendix I

De sancta Agatha virgine

Agatha dicitur ab *agios*, quod est sanctus, et *theos* Deus, quasi sancta Dei. Tria enim sunt, sicut dicit Chrysostomus, quae sanctum faciunt, et illa perfecte fuerunt in ea, scilicet cordis munditia, spiritus sancti praesentia, bonorum operum affluentia. Vel dicitur ab *a*, quod est sine, et *geos* terra, et *theos* Deus, quasi Dea sine terra, id est, sine amore terrenorum. Vel ab *aga*, quod est loquens, et *thau* consummatio, quasi consummate et perfecte loquens, quod patet in suis responsis. Vel ab *agath*, quod est servitus, et *thaas* superior, quasi servitus superior: et hoc propter illud quod dixit: summa ingenuitas est ista etc. Vel ab *aga*, quod est solemnis, et *thau*, consummatio, quasi solemniter consummata, id est sepulta, quod patet in angelis, qui eam sepelierunt.

 Agatha virgo ingenua et corpore pulcherrima in urbe Cataniensium Deum semper in omni sanctitate colebat, Quintianus autem consularis Siciliae, cum esset ignobilis, libidinosus, avarus et ydolis deditus, beatam Agatham comprehendere nitebatur, ut quia erat ignobilis, comprehendendo nobilem timeretur, quia libidinosus, ejus pulchritudine frueretur, quia avarus, ejus divitias raperet, quia ydololatra, Diis eam faceret immolare, fecitque eam ad se adduci.

 Quae cum adducta esset et ejus immobile propositum cognovisset, tradidit eam cuidam meretrici, nomine Aphrodisiae et novem filiabus ejus ejusdem turpitudinis, ut per xxx dies suaderent et quomodo ejus animum immutarent. Et modo promittendo laeta modo terrendo aspera sperabant eam a bono proposito revocare, quibus beata Agatha dixit: 'Mens mea super petram solidata est et in Christo fundata, verba vestra venti sunt, promissiones vestrae pluviae, terrores vestri flumina sunt. Quae quantumvis impugnant, stat fundamentum domus meae, cadere non valebit.' Haec autem dicens flebat quotidie et orabat sitiens ad martirii palmam pervenire. Videns igitur Aphrodisia ipsam immobilem permanere dixit Quintiano: 'Facilius possunt saxa molliri et ferrum in plumbi mollitiem converti, quam ab intentione christiana mens istius puellae converti seu revocari.'

Tunc Quintianus fecit eam ad se adduci et ait illi: 'Cujus conditionis es?' Cui illa: 'Non solum ingenua, sed et spectabilis genere, ut omnis parentela mea testatur.' Cui Quintianus: 'Si ingenua es, cur moribus te servilem personam habere ostendis?' Illa respondit: 'Quia ancilla Christi sum, ideo servilem meam exhibeo personam.' Quintianus dixit: 'Si te ingenuam dicis, quomodo ancillam asseris?' Illa respondit: 'Summa ingenuitas est, in qua servitus Christi comprobatur.' Quintianus dixit: 'Elige quod volueris, aut scilicet Diis sacrificare aut diversa supplicia sustinere.' Cui Agatha: 'Sit talis uxor tua, qualis Venus Dea tua, et tu talis sis, qualis fuit Deus tuus Jupiter.' Tunc Quintianus jussit eam alapis caedi dicens: 'In injuriam judicis noli temerario ore garrire.' Agatha respondit: 'Miror te virum prudentem ad tantam stultitiam devolutum, ut illos dicas Deos tuos esse, quorum vitam non cupias tuam conjugem vel te imitari, ut dicas tibi injuriam fieri, si eorum vivas exemplo. Nam si Dei tui sunt boni, bonum tibi optavi, si autem exsecraris eorum consortia, mecum sentis.' Quintianus dixit: 'Quid mihi superfluus verborum cursus? Aut sacrifica Diis aut te faciam diversis suppliciis interire.' Agatha respondit: 'Si feras mihi promittas, audito Christi nomine mansuescunt, si ignem adhibeas, de coelo mihi rorem salvificum angeli ministrabunt, si plagas vel tormenta ingeras, habeo spiritum sanctum, per quem despicio universa.' Tunc jussit eam trahi ad carcerem, quia voce eum publice confundebat, ad quem laetissime et glorianter ibat et quasi ad epulas invitata agonem suum domino commendabat.

Sequenti die dixit ei Quintianus: 'Abnega Christum et adora Deos.' Quae cum renueret, jussit eam in equuleum suspendi et torqueri, dixitque Agatha: 'Ego in his poenis ita delector, sicut qui bonum nuntium audit aut qui videt, quem diu desideravit, aut qui multos thesauros invenit. Non enim potest triticum in horreum poni, nisi theca fuerit fortiter conculcata et in paleis redacta. Sic anima mea non potest intrare in paradisum cum palma martirii, nisi diligenter feceris corpus meum a carnificibus attrectari.' Tunc iratus Quintianus jussit ejus mamillam torqueri et tortam diutissime jussit abscidi. Cui Agatha: 'Impie crudelis et dire tyranne, non es confusus amputare in femina, quod ipse in matre suxisti? Ego habeo mamillas integras in anima mea, ex quibus nutrio omnes sensus meos, quas ab infantia domino consecravi.'

Tunc jussit eam in carcerem recipi prohibens ingressum medicorum et panem vel aquam sibi ab aliquo ministrari. Et ecce circa mediam noctem venit ad eam quidam senex, quem antecedebat puer luminis portitor, diversa secum ferens medicamenta et dixit ei: 'Licet consularis insanus tormentis te afflixerit, tu eum tuis responsis amplius afflixisti et licet ubera tua torserit, sed illius ubertas in amaritudinem convertetur, et quoniam ibi eram, quando hoc patiebaris, vidi, quia mamilla tua potest curam salutis suscipere.' Cui Agatha: 'Medicinam carnalem corpori meo nunquam exhibui, et turpe est, ut, quod tamdiu servavi, nunc perdam.' Dixit ei senex: 'Filia, ego christianus sum, ne verecunderis.' Cui Agatha: 'Et unde verecundari possum, cum tu sis senex et grandaevus, ego vero ita crudeliter lacerata, quod nemo de me possit concipere voluptatem. Sed ago tibi gratias, domine pater, quia sollicitudinem tuam mihi impendere dignatus es.' Cui ille: 'Et quare non permittis, ut curem te?' Agatha respondit: 'Quia habeo dominum Jesum Christum, qui solo verbo curat omnia et sermone restaurat universa. Hic si vult, potest me continuo curare.' Et subridens senior dixit: 'Et ego apostolus ejus sum et ipse me misit ad te et in nomine ejus scias te esse sanatam.' Et continuo Petrus apostolus disparuit. Et procidens beata Agatha gratias agens invenit se undique sanatam et mamillam suam pectori restitutam. Cum ergo ex immenso lumine custodes territi aufugissent et apertum carcerem reliquissent, rogant eam quidam, ut abiret. 'Absit', inquit, 'ut fugiam et coronam patientiae perdam et custodes meos tribulationibus tradam.'

Post dies quattuor dixit ei Quintianus: 'Ut Deos adoraret, ne graviora supplicia sustineret.' Cui Agatha: 'Verba tua fatua sunt et vana, aërem maculantia et iniqua. Miser sine intellectu, quomodo vis, ut lapides adorem et Deum coeli, qui me sanavit, dimittam?'

Quintianus dixit: 'Et quis te sanavit?' Cui Agatha: 'Christus filius Dei.' Quintianus dixit: 'Iterum tu Christum audes nominare, quem ego nolo audire?' Agatha dixit: 'Quamdiu vixero, Christum corde et labiis invocabo.' Quintianus dixit: 'Nunc videbo, si Christus te curabit.' Et jussit testas fractas spargi et sub testas carbones ignitos mitti et ipsam desuper nudo corpore volutari. Quod cum fieret, ecce terrae motus nimius factus est, qui totam civitatem ita concussit, ut palatium corruens duos consiliarios Quintiani opprimeret et omnis populus ad eum concurreret clamans, quod propter injustum Agathae cruciatum talia paterentur. Tunc Quintianus ex una parte terrae motum, ex alia seditionem populi metuens ipsam iterum in carcerem recipi jussit, ubi sic oravit dicens: 'Domine Jesu Christe, qui me creasti et ab infantia custodisti, qui corpus meum a pollutione servasti et a me amorem saeculi abstulisti, et qui tormenta me vincere fecisti et in iis virtutem patientiae tribuisti, accipe spiritum meum et jube me ad tuam misericordiam pervenire.' Haec cum orasset, cum ingenti voce spiritum tradidit circa annum domini CCLII sub Daciano imperatore.

Cum autem fideles cum aromatibus corpus ejus condirent et in sarcophago collocarent, quidam juvenis sericis indutus cum plus quam centum viris pulcherrimis et ornatis ac albis indutis, qui nunquam in illis partibus visi fuerant, ad corpus ejus venit et tabulam marmoream ad caput ejus ponens ab oculis omnium statim disparuit. Erat autem in praedicta tabula scriptum: 'Mentem sanctam, spontaneam, honorem Deo et patriae liberationem.' Quod sic intelligitur: 'Mentem sanctam habuit, spontaneam se obtulit, honorem Deo dedit et patriae liberationem fecit.' Et hoc miraculo divulgato etiam gentiles et Judaei sepulchrum ejus plurimum venerari coeperunt.

Quintianus autem, dum ad ejus investigandas divitias pergeret, duobus equis inter se fremitum dantibus calcesque jactantibus unus eum morsu appetiit, alter calce percussum in flumine projecit, ita quod corpus ejus nusquam potuit inveniri.

Revoluto anno circa diem natalis ejus mons quidam maximus circa civitatem ruptus eructavit incendium, quod quasi torrens de monte descendens et saxa terramque liquefaciens ad urbem cum magno impetu veniebat. Tunc paganorum multitudo descendit de monte et ad sepulchrum ejus fugiens velum, unde coopertum erat sepulchrum, arripuit et ipsum statuit contra ignem statimque in die natalis ipsius virginis ignis stetit et ultra ullatenus non processit.

De hac virgine dicit Ambrosius in praefatione: 'O felix et inclita virgo, quae meruit domini pro laude martirium fidelis sanguine clarificare suum. O illustris et gloriosa gemino illustrata decore, quae inter tormenta aspera cunctis praelata miraculis et mistico pollens suffragio apostoli meruit visitatione curari. Sic nuptam Christo susceperunt aethera, sic humani artus gloriosa fulgent obsequia, ut angelorum chorus sanctitatem mentis et patriae indicat liberationem.

Appendix II

De Sancta Lucia virgine

Lucia dicitur a *luce*. Lux enim habet pulchritudinem in aspectione, quia, ut dicit Ambrosius, lucis natura haec est, ut omnis in aspectu ejus gratia sit. Habet etiam diffusionem sine coinquinatione, quia per quaecunque immunda diffusa non coinquinatur; rectum incessum sine curvitate, longissimam lineam pertransit sine morosa dilatione. Per hoc ostenditur, quod beata virgo Lucia habuit decorem virginitatis sine aliqua corruptione, diffusionem caritatis sine aliquo immundo amore, rectum incessum intensionis in Deum sine aliqua obliquitate, longissimam lineam divinae operationis sine negligentiae tarditate. Vel Lucia dicitur quasi lucis via.

Lucia virgo Syracusana nobilis genere audiens famam sanctae Agathae per totam Siciliam divulgari, sepulchrum ejus adiit cum matre sua Euthicia annis quatuor fluxum sanguinis incurabiliter patiente. Inter ipsa igitur missarum solemnia contigit, ut illud evangelium legeretur, in quo dominus mulierem ab hac passione sanasse narratur. Tunc Lucia matri dixit: 'Si credis his quae leguntur, crede Agatham illum semper habere praesentem, pro cujus nomine sustinuit passionem: si ergo ejus sepulchrum credens contigeris, perfecta continuo sanitate gaudebis.'

Igitur recedentibus cunctis et matre et filia juxta sepulchrum in oratione exsistentibus Luciam somnus arripuit viditque Agatham in medio angelorum gemmis ornatam stantem et dicentem sibi: 'Soror mea Lucia, virgo Deo devota, quid a me petis, quod ipsa poteris praestare continuo matri tuae? Nam ecce per fidem tuam sanata est.' Evigilans autem Lucia matri suae dixit: 'Mater mea, ecce sanata es: per ipsam ergo te deprecor, quae suis orationibus te sanavit, ne mihi de caetero nomines sponsum, sed quidquid mihi datura eras pro dote, pauperibus elargire.' Cui mater ait: 'Tege prius oculos meos et quidquid volueris, de facultatibus facito.' Ad quam Lucia: 'Quod moriens das, ideo das, quia ferre tecum non potes: da mihi, dum vivis, et mercedem habebis.'

Cum ergo rediissent, fit quotidie distractio rerum et dantur in necessitatibus pauperum. Interea dum patrimonium distribuitur, ad sponsum notitia pervenit: requirit sponsus a nutrice de his. Respondit illa caute, quod utiliorem possessionem sponsa sua invenisset, quam suo volebat nomine comparare, et ideo videbatur aliquanta distrahere. Credidit stultus carnale commercium et coepit auctor esse vendentium. Venditis autem omnibus et pauperibus erogatis sponsus trahit eam coram Paschasio consulari, dicens eam christianam esse et contra leges agere Augustorum.

Invitante igitur Paschasio ad sacrificia ydolorum respondit: 'Sacrificium placens Deo est, visitare pauperes et eis in necessitatibus subvenire: et quia amplius non habeo, quid offeram, me ipsam sibi tribuo offerendam.' Cui Paschasius: 'Ista verba tibi simili stulto narrare poteris, mihi autem, qui principum decreta custodio, ista frustra persequeris.' Ad quem Lucia: 'Tu principum tuorum decreta custodis et ego Dei mei legem custodiam. Tu principes times et ego Deum timeo. Tu illos offendere non vis, et ego Deum offendere caveo. Tu illis placere desideras et ego ut Christo placeam concupisco. Tu ergo fac quod tibi utile esse cognosces et ego faciam, quod utile mihi esse perspexero.' Cui Paschasius: 'Patrimonium tuum cum corruptoribus expendisti et ideo quasi meretrix loqueris.' Cui Lucia: 'Patrimonium meum in tuto loco constitui, corruptores autem mentis et corporis nunquam scivi.' Respondit Paschasius: 'Qui sunt corruptores corporis et mentis?' Lucia dixit: 'Corruptores mentis vos estis, qui suadetis ut animae suum deserant creatorem. Corruptores vero corporis sunt, qui corporalem delectationem praeponunt epulis sempiternis.'

Paschasius dixit: 'Cessabunt verba, cum perventum fuerit ad verbera.' Cui Lucia dixit: 'Verba Dei cessare non possunt.' Cui Paschasius: 'Tu ergo Deus es?' Respondit Lucia: 'Ancilla Dei sum, qui dixit: "Cum steteritis ante reges et praesides, etc. Non enim vos estis etc.'" Paschasius dixit: 'In te ergo spiritus sanctus est?' Cui Lucia: 'Qui caste vivunt, templum spiritus sancti sunt.' Cui Paschasius: 'Ego faciam te duci ad lupanar, ut ibi violationem accipias et spiritum sanctum perdas.' Cui Lucia: 'Non inquinatur corpus nisi de consensu mentis, nam si me invitam violari feceris, castitas mihi duplicabitur ad coronam. Nunquam autem voluntatem meam ad consensum poteris provocare. Ecce corpus meum ad omne supplicium est paratum. Quid moraris? Incipe fili dyaboli desideria poenarum tuarum exercere.'

Tunc Paschasius lenones fecit venire, dicens iis: 'Invitate ad eam omnem populum et tamdiu illudatur, donec mortua nuntietur.' Volentes autem eam trahere, tanto pondere spiritus sanctus eam fixit, ut omnino eam movere nequirent. Fecitque Paschasius mille viros accedere et manus ejus et pedes ligare, sed eam nullatenus poterant movere; tunc et cum viris mille paria boum adhibuit, sed tamen virgo domini immobilis permansit. Vocatis autem magis, ut suis incantationibus moveretur, omnino moveri non potuit. Tunc dixit Paschasius: 'Quae sunt illa maleficia, quod una puella a mille viris non moveretur?' Lucia dixit: 'Non sunt ista maleficia, sed beneficia Christi. Porro si adhuc decem millia adhibueris, aeque ut primum immobilem me videbis.' Putans vero Paschasius secundum quorumdam figmenta, quod lotio fugarentur maleficia, jussit eam lotio perfundi, cumque nec sic moveri posset, angustiatus nimis copiosum ignem circa eam accendi picemque resinam et fervens oleum super eam fundi jussit. Dixitque Lucia: 'Inducias impetravi martirii mei, ut credentibus timorem auferam passionis et non credentibus vocem insultationis.'

Videntes autem amici Paschasii eum angustiari, in gutture ejus gladium immerserunt, quae nequaquam loquelam amittens dixit: 'Annuntio vobis pacem ecclesiae redditam Maximiano hodie mortuo et de regno suo Dyocletiano expulso, et sicut civitati Catanensi soror mea Agatha data est protectrix, sic et ego civitati Syracusanae concessa sum interventrix.'

Dum haec virgo loquitur, ecce ministri Romanorum veniunt, Paschasium apprehendunt, vinctum ad Caesarem secum ducunt. Audierat enim Caesar, quod universam provinciam fuerat depraedatus. Veniens ergo Romam et senatui accusatus pariter et convictus capitali sententia est punitus. Virgo vero Lucia de loco, in quo percussa est, mota non est nec spiritum tradidit, quoadusque sacerdotes venirent, et corpus domini ei traderent, et omnes astantes amen domino responderunt. In eodem loco autem est sepulta et ecclesia fabricata. Passa autem est tempore Constantini et Maxentii circa annos domini cccx.

APPENDIX III – COMPILATION B: CHECKLIST OF MANUSCRIPT FILIATIONS

Reading and Position in Voragine (*=interpolated reading)	BMP 8	BMP 9	FLG 419	Escorial K-II-12	Escorial h-I-14	Escorial M-II-6
[2] Andrew (30 Nov)	—	[1] fols 1ʳ–2ʳ	[1] fols 2ʳᵃ–5ʳᵇ	[1] fols 1ʳᵃ–5ʳᵃ	[1] fols 1ʳᵃ–4ᵛᵃ	—
[*] Barbara (4 Dec)	—	—	[11.53] fols 213ᵛᵇ–16ᵛᵇ	—	[2] fols 4ᵛᵃ–8ᵛᵇ	—
[3] Nicholas (6 Dec)	—	[2] fols 2ʳ–4ʳ	[2] fols 5ᵛᵇ–8ᵛᵃ	[3] fols 5ᵛᵃ–9ʳᵇ	[3] fols 8ᵛᵇ–12ʳᵇ	—
[*] Leocadia of Toledo (9 Dec)	—	—	—	[4] fols 9ʳᵇ–12ʳᵇ	—	—
[*] Eulalia of Merida (10 Dec)	—	—	—	[5] fols 12ʳᵇ–13ʳᵃ	—	—
[4] Lucy (13 Dec)	—	[3] fol. 4ʳ⁻ᵛ	[3] fols 8ᵛᵇ–9ᵛᵇ	[6] fols 13ʳᵃ–14ʳᵃ	[4] fols 12ʳᵇ–13ᵛᵇ	—
[5] Thomas the Apostle (21 Dec)	—	[6] fols 6ʳ–7ᵛ	[4] fols 9ᵛᵇ–12ʳᵃ	[7] fols 14ʳᵃ–15ʳᵇ	[5] fols 13ᵛᵇ–24ᵛᵃ	—
[6] The Nativity (25 Dec)	—	[7] fols 7ᵛ–8ᵛ	[11.1] fols 153ᵛᵃ–54ᵛᵃ	[8] fols 15ʳᵇ–18ʳᵃ	[6] fols 24ᵛᵃ–29ʳᵇ	—
[7] Anastasia (25 Dec)	—	—	—	[9] fols 18ʳᵃ–21ʳᵃ	—	—
[8] Stephen (26 Dec)	—	[4] fol. 4ᵛ	[5] fol. 12ᵛ⁻ᵃ	[10] fols 21ᵛᵃ–22ʳᵃ	[7] fols 29ʳᵇ–30ʳᵃ	—
[9] John the Apostle (27 Dec)	—	[5] fols 5ʳ–6ʳ	[6] fols 12ᵛᵃ–14ᵛᵃ	[11] fols 22ʳᵃ–24ᵛᵃ	[8] fols 30ʳᵃ–33ʳᵃ	—
[10] The Holy Innocents (28 Dec)	—	—	—	[12] fols 24ᵛᵃ–25ʳᵇ	[9] fol. 33ʳᵃ⁻ᵛᵃ	—
[11] Thomas of Canterbury (29 Dec)	—	—	—	—	[10] fols 33ᵛᵃ–39ʳᵇ	—
[12] Sylvester (31 Dec)	—	[9] fols 9ʳ–10ʳ	[8] fols 15ʳᵃ–17ʳᵃ	[13] fols 25ʳᵇ–27ᵛᵇ	[11] fols 39ᵛᵇ–42ᵛᵃ	[11.1] fols 50ʳ–53ʳ
[13] The Circumcision (1 Jan)	—	—	—	[17] fol. 33ʳᵃ⁻ᵇ	—	—
[14] The Epiphany (6 Jan)	—	[8] fols 8ᵛ–9ʳ	[7] fols 14ᵛᵃ–15ᵛᵇ	[18] fols 33ᵛᵇ–36ᵛᵇ	—	—
[21] Antony of Egypt (17 Jan)	—	[10] fols 10ʳ–11ʳ	[9] fols 17ʳᵇ–18ʳᵃ	[19] fols 36ᵛᵇ–37ᵛᵇ	[12] fols 42ᵛᵃ–43ᵛᵃ	—
[23] Sebastian (20 Jan)	—	[11] fols 11ʳ–12ʳ	[10] fols 18ʳᵃ–20ʳᵃ	[20] fols 37ᵛᵇ–40ʳᵇ	[13] fols 43ᵛᵃ–46ʳᵃ	—
[24] Agnes (21 Jan)	—	[12] fol. 12ʳ⁻ᵛ	[11] fols 20ʳᵃ–21ʳᵃ	[21] fols 40ʳᵇ–41ᵛᵃ	[14] fols 46ʳᵃ–47ᵛᵃ	—

Reading and Position in Voragine (*=interpolated reading)	BMP 8	BMP 9	FLG 419	Escorial K-II-12	Escorial h-I-14	Escorial M-II-6
[25] Vincent (22 Jan)	—	—	[12] fols 21ra–22rb	[22] fols 41va–43ra	[16] fols 49va–51rb	[II.36] fols 98vb–100^{r}
[26] Basil the Great (1 Jan)	—	[13] fols 12^{v}–13^{v}	[13] fols 22rb–23rb	[15] fols 29va–31rb	[15] fols 47va–49vb	[II.26] fols 82^{v}–84^{r}
[27] John the Almsgiver (23 Jan)	—	—	[II.2] fols 156ra–57va	[16] fols 31rb–33ra	[17] fols 49vb–53rb	[II.2] fols 53^{r}–54^{v}
[28] The Conversion of Saint Paul (25 Jan)	—	[14] fol. 13^{v}	[14] fols 23rb–24ra	[23] fol. 43^{ra-rb}	[18] fols 53rb–54	[II.3] fols 54^{r}–55^{r}
[30] Julian of Le Mans (27 Jan)	[26] fols 34rb–35ra	[26] fol. 19^{rb-vb}	[44] fols 67rb–69va	—	[19] fols 54ra–55rb	[1/11.4] fol. 19^{v}, 55^{r-v}
[36] Ignatius (1 Feb)	—	—	[II.3] fols 157va–58va	[24] fols 43vb–44va	[20] fols 55vb–57	[2] fols 19^{r}–20^{r}
[*] Brigit (1 Feb)	—	—	—	[25] fols 44va–45rb	—	[15] fols 55^{v}–59^{v}
[37] The Purification/Candlemas (2 Feb)	—	[15] fols 13^{v}, 15^{r}, 15^{v}	[15] fols 24ra–25va	[26] fols 45rb–47rb	[21] fols 57ra–59rb	[3] fols 20^{r}–22^{r}
[38] Blaise (3 Feb)	—	[17] fols 15^{r}, 14^{v}, 14^{r}	[16] fols 25va–26ra	[27] fols 47rb–48va	[22] fols 59rb–61ra	[4] fols 22^{r}–24^{r}
[39] Agatha (5 Feb)	—	[16] fol. 14^{r}	[17] fols 26vb–28vb	[28] fols 48va–50va	[23] fols 61ra–63vb	[5] fols 24^{r}–26^{r}
[41] Amand (6 Feb)	—	—	[II.4] fols 158va–59ra	[29] fols 50va–51ra	[24] fols 63vb–64rb	[6] fol. 26^{r-v}
[42] Valentine (14 Feb)	—	—	[II.5] fol. 159^{ra-rb}	[30] fol. 51^{ra-va}	[25] fol. 64^{rb-va}	[II.6] fols 59^{r}–60^{r}
[43] Juliana (16 Feb)	—	—	[II.6] fol. 159^{rb-vb}	[31] fols 51va–52rb	[26] fols 64va–65ra	[II.7] fols 60^{r}–61^{r}
[44] The Chair of Saint Peter (22 Feb)	[1] fol. 1^{ra-rb}	—	[18] fols 28va–29rb	[32] fols 52rb–53rb	[27] fols 65va–67ra	[7] fols 26^{r}–28^{r}
[45] Matthias (24 Feb)	[2] fols 1rb–2rb	—	[19] fols 29va–30vb	[33] fols 53vb–55	[28] fols 67ra–69va	[8] fols 28^{r}–30^{r}
[46] Gregory the Great (12 Mar)	[3] fols 4ra–6vb	—	[21] fols 31rb–34ra	[34] fols 55va–58rb	[29] fols 69rb–73ra	[9] fols 30^{r}–33^{v}
[47] Longinus (15 Mar)	[5] fols 2rb–3ra	[59] fols 55vb–57va	[20] fol. 31^{ra-rb}	[35] fol. 58^{vb-vb}	[30] fol. 73^{rb-vb}	[II.8] fol. 61^{r-v}
[49] Benedict (21 Mar)	[6] fols 6ra–9rb	—	[22] fols 34ra–36rb	[36] fols 58vb–61va	[31] fols 73ra–77ra	[II.9] fols 61^{v}–64^{r}
[50] Patrick (17 Mar)	[4/7] fols 3ra–4rb & 9rb–10rb	—	[23] fols 36rb–37rb	[37] fols 61va–62rb	[32] fols 77ra–79ra	[10] fols 33^{r}–34^{v}
[51] The Annunciation (25 Mar)	[8] fols 10rb–11va	—	[24] fols 37rb–38va	[38] fols 62vb–64rb	[33] fols 79rb–80vb	[11] fols 35^{r}–36^{r}
[53] The Passion (variable)	[9] fols 11va–13rb	—	[25] fols 38va–40rb	[39] fols 64rb–66rb	[34] fols 80vb–83va	[II.10] fols 64^{r}–65^{v}
[54] The Resurrection (variable)	[10] fols 13rb–14rb	—	[26] fols 40rb–42va	[40] fols 66rb–68^{ab}	[35] fols 83va–86ra	[II.11] fols 65^{v}–67^{r}

244

Reading and Position in Voragine (*=interpolated reading)	BMP 8	BMP 9	FLG 419	Escorial K-II-12	Escorial h-I-14	Escorial M-II-6
[55] Secundus (29 Mar)	—	—	—	[41] fols 68rb–69rb	[36] fols 86ra–87rb	[12] fols 36^v–37^v
[56] Mary of Egypt (2 Apr)	[11] fols 14vb–16ra	—	[27] fols 42ra–43rb	[42] fols 69rb–70vb	[37] fols 87rb–88vb	[13] fols 37^v–39^r
[57] Ambrose (4 Apr)	—	[60] fols 57ra–58vb	[28] fols 43rb–45ra	[43] fols 70vb–73ra	[38] fols 88vb–91va	[14] fols 39^v–41^v
[*] Toribius of Astorga (16 Apr)	—	—	—	[44] fol. 73$^{ra–rb}$	—	—
[58] George (23 Apr)	—	[61] fols 58vb–59va	[29] fols 45rb–47vb	[45] fols 73rb–75vb	[39] fols 91va–95ra	[15] fols 41^v–44^v
[59] Mark the Evangelist (25 Apr)	[12] fols 16ra–17ra	—	[30] fols 47vb–48vb	[46] fols 75vb–77ra	[40] fols 95ra–96rb	[16] fols 44^v–46^r
[60] Marcellinus (26 Apr)	—	—	[11.7] fols 159vb–60ra	[47] fol. 77$^{ra–rb}$	[41] fols 96rb–97ra	—
[61] Vitalis (28 Apr)	—	—	[11.8] fol. 160$^{ra–rb}$	[48] fol. 77$^{rb–vb}$	[42] fol. 97$^{ra–vb}$	—
[62] The Virgin of Antioch (29 Apr)	—	—	[11.9] fols 160rb–61va	[49] fols 77vb–79vb	[43] fols 97vb–99va	—
[63] Peter Martyr (29 Apr)	—	—	[11.10] fols 161va–65vb	[50] fols 79^v–85va	[44] fols 99va–107va	[11.12] fols 67^v–73^r
[*] Ildephonsus (23 Jan)	—	—	[11.11] fols 165vb–72va	—	—	—
[65] Philip the Apostle (1 May)	[13] fol. 17$^{ra–vb}$	—	[31] fols 48vb–49ra	[51] fols 85va–86ra	[45] fols 107va–108ra	[17] fol. 46$^{r–v}$
[67] James the Less (1 May)	[14] fols 17vb–22va	—	[32] fols 49ra–54ra	[52] fols 86ra–89ra	[46] fols 108ra–13ra	[18] fols 46^v–50^r
[68] The Finding of the Holy Cross (3 May)	[15] fols 22va–24va	—	[33] fols 54ra–56rb	[53] fols 89ra–91va	[47] fols 113ra–16rb	[11.13] fols 73^v–75^v
[69] Saint John before the Latin Gate (6 May)	[16] fols 24va–25ra	—	[34] fol. 56$^{rb–vb}$	[54] fols 91va–92ra	[48] fols 116ra–17rb	[11.14] fols 75^v–76^v
[70] The Litanies (3 days before Ascension)	[17] fols 25ra–26^r	—	[35] fols 56vb–58ra	[55] fols 92ra–93rb	[49] fols 117rb–19ra	[11.15] fols 76^v–77^v
[72] The Ascension (40 days after Resurrection)	[18] fols 26ra–27rb	[18] fol. 16^r	[36] fols 58ra–60ra	[56] fol. 93$^{rb–va}$	[50] fol. 119$^{ra–va}$	[11.16] fol. 77^r
[73] The Holy Spirit (50 days after Resurrection)	[19] fols 27rb–30ra	[19] fols 16^v–17^r	[37] fols 60ra–62rb	[57] fols 93va–94rb	[51] fols 119va–20ra	[11.17] fol. 77$^{r–v}$
[74] Gordianus and Epimachus (12 May)	—	—	—	[58] fol. 94ra	[52] fol. 120$^{ra–rb}$	—
[75] Nereus and Achilleus (12 May)	—	—	—	[59] fol. 94$^{ra–vb}$	[53] fols 120rb–21ra	—
[76] Pancratius (12 May)	—	—	—	[60] fols 94vb–95rb	[54] fols 121va–22rb	[11.18] fols 77^v–78^r
[77] Urban (25 May)	—	—	—	[61] fols 95vb–96ra	[55] fols 122va–23va	[11.19] fol. 78$^{r–v}$

Reading and Position in Voragine (*=interpolated reading)	BMP 8	BMP 9	FLG 419	Escorial K-II-12	Escorial h-I-14	Escorial M-II-6
[78] Petronilla (31 May)	[20] fol. 30^{ra-va}	[20] fol. 17^r	[38] fol. 62^{rb-vb}	[62] fol. 96^{ra-b}	[56] fols 123^{ra-vb}	[II.20] fols 78^v–79^r
[79] Peter the Exorcist (2 Jun)	[21] fol. 30va–31ra	[21] fol. 17^{r-v}	[39] fols 62vb–63va	[63] fols 96rb–97va	[57] fols 123vb–24vb	[II.21] fol. 79^{r-v}
[80] Primus and Felicianus (9 Jun)	[22] fol. 31^{ra-va}	[22] fol. 17^v	[40] fols 63va–64ra	[64] fol. 97^{ra-va}	[58] fols 124vb–25va	[II.22] fols 79^v–80^r
[81] Barnabas (11 Jun)	[23] fols 31va–32va	[23] fols 17^v–18va	[41] fols 64ra–65rb	[65] fols 97va–98rb	[59] fols 125va–27rb	[II.23] fols 80^r–81^r
[*] Anthony of Padua (13 Jun)	—	—	—	[66] fols 98rb–99rb	—	—
[82] Vitus and Modestus (15 Jun)	—	—	[II.12] fols 172va–73rb	[67] fols 99rb–100ra	[60] fols 127rb–28^{wa}	[II.24] fols 81^r–82^r
[83] Quiricus and Julitta (16 Jun)	[24] fols 32va–33rb	[24] fol. 18^{va-b}	[42] fols 65rb–66ra	[68] fol. 100^{ra-va}	[61] fols 128^{wa}–37va	[II.25] fol. 82^{r-v}
[84] Marina (18 Jun)	—	—	[II.13] fol. 173^{rb-va}	[69] fols 100va–01ra	[62] fols 137va–38rb	[II.27] fols 84^r–85^r
[85] Gervasius and Protasius (19 Jun)	[25] fols 33rb–34rb	[25] fols 18vb–19rb	[43] fols 66ra–67va	[70] fols 101ra–02va	[63] fols 138^{wa}–40ra	[II.28] fols 85^r–86^r
[86] The Birth of John the Baptist (24 Jun)	[27] fols 35va–37va	[27] fols 19vb–21va	[45] fols 69ra–71va	[71] fols 102va–03va	[64] fols 140ra–42va	[II.29] fols 86^r–87^v
[87] John and Paul (26 Jun)	[28] fol. 37^{va-b}	[28] fol. 21^{ra-vb}	[46] fols 71va–73rb	[72] fols 103va–05ra	[65] fols 142va–45ra	[II.30] fols 87^v–89^r
[*] Pelagius (26 Jun)	—	—	—	—	[66] fols 145rb–49rb	—
[88] Leo (28 Jun)	—	—	[II.14] fol. 173^{va-vb}	[73] fol. 105^{ra-va}	[67] fols 149rb–50rb	[II.31] fols 89^r–90^r
[89] Peter (29 Jun)	[29] fols 38rb–42va	[29] fols 21rb–23vb	[47] fols 73rb–76vb	[74] fols 105va–10va	[68] fols 150rb–57va	[II.32] fols 90^r–94^r
[90] Paul (30 Jun)	[30] fols 42va–44rb	[30] fol. 23vb	[48] fols 76vb–79va	—	[69] fols 157va–62vb	[II.33] fols 94^r–96^v
[91] Seven Brothers. Sons of Felicity (10 Jul)	—	—	[II.15] fols 173vb–74ra	[75] fol. 110^{va-vb}	[70] fols 162^{rb-vb}	[II.34] fols 96^v–97^v
[92] Theodora (12 Jul)	—	—	[II.16] fols 174ra–75rb	[76] fols 110vb–12va	[71] fols 162vb–66rb	[II.35] fols 97^v–98^v
[93] Margaret known as Marina (13 Jul)	[31] fols 45va–46rb	—	[49] fols 79va–81va	[77] fols 112va–13vb	[72] fols 166va–68^{wa}	[II.37] fols 100^v–101^r
[94] Alexis (17 Jul)	—	—	[II.17] fols 175rb–76vb	[78] fols 113vb–15va	[73] fols 168^{wa}–72va	[II.38] fols 101^v–103^v
[96] Mary Magdalene (22 Jul)	[32] fols 46vb–49vb	—	[50] fols 81va–86va	[79] fols 115va–20va	[74] fols 172vb–80rb	—
[97] Apollinaris (23 Jul)	—	—	[II.18] fols 176vb–77rb	[80] fols 120va–21vb	[75] fols 180rb–81vb	—
[98] Christina (24 Jul)	—	—	—	[81] fols 121va–22va	[76] fols 181vb–83^r	—

246

Reading and Position in Voragine (*=interpolated reading)	BMP 8	BMP 9	FLG 419	Escorial K-II-12	Escorial h-I-14	Escorial M-II-6
[99] James the Greater (25 Jul)	[33] fols 49rb–52rb	—	[51] fols 86va–90va	[82] fols 122va–26ra	[77] fols 183ra–90rb	—
[100] Christopher (25 Jul)	[34] fols 52va–55rb	—	[52] fols 90va–93ra	[83] fols 126ra–28va	[78] fols 190rb–93vb	—
[101] The Seven Sleepers (27 Jul)	—	[62] fols 59va–60ra	[53] fols 93ra–95rb	[84] fols 128va–30vb	[79] fols 193vb–96rb	—
[102] Nazarius and Celsus (28 Jul)	—	—	[II.19] fols 177vb–78vb	[85] fols 130vb–32ra	[80] fols 196rb–97vb	—
[103] Felix, Pope (29 Jul)	—	—	[II.20] fol. 178vb	[86] fol. 132^{ra-rb}	[81] fols 197vb–98va	—
[104] Simplicius and Faustinus (29 Jul)	—	—	[II.21] fol. 178^{vb-va}	[87] fol. 132^{rb-va}	[82] fol. 198^{va-va}	—
[105] Martha (29 Jul)	[35] fols 55rb–56vb	[31] fol. 24^{va-ra}	[54] fols 95rb–97va	[88] fols 132va–34rb	[83] fols 198va–200va	—
[106] Abdon and Sennen (30 Jul)	—	—	[56] fol. 100^{va-vb}	[89] fol. 134^{rb-va}	[84] fol. 200^{va-vb}	—
[107] Germain (31 Jul)	—	—	[II.23] fols 178vb–79vb	[90] fols 134va–36rb	[85] fols 200vb–02vb	—
[108] Eusebius (31 Jul)	—	—	[II.24] fols 179vb–80va	[91] fols 136rb–37ra	[86] fols 202vb–04ra	—
[109] The Holy Maccabees (1 Aug)	—	—	[II.25] fol. 180^{va-vb}	[92] fol. 137^{rb-va}	[87] fol. 204^{ra-rb}	—
[110] Peter in Chains (1 Aug)	[36] fols 56vb–58vb	[32] fols 24ra–25vb	[55] fols 97va–100va	[93] fols 137va–40rb	[88] fols 204rb–07vb	—
[111] Stephen, Pope (2 Aug)	[37] fols 58vb–59va	[33] fols 25vb–26ra	[56] fol. 100^{va-vb}	[94] fol. 140^{ra-va}	[89] fol. 207^{rb-va}	—
[112] The Finding of Saint Stephen (2 Aug)	[38] fols 59va–60va	[34] fol. 26^{ra-vb}	[57] fols 100vb–02vb	[95] fols 140va–42vb	[90] fols 207va–09va	—
[113] Dominic (4 Aug)	—	—	[II.26] fols 180vb–86va	[96] fols 142vb–50vb	[91] fols 209va–13vb	—
[114] Sixtus (6 Aug)	[39] fol. 60^{va-vb}	[35] fols 26vb–27ra	[58] fols 102vb–03va	[97] fols 150vb–51ra	[92] fols 213vb–14ra	—
[?] Mammes (7 Aug)	[40] fols 60vb–64rb	[36] fols 27ra–29va	[59] fols 103vb–07va	—	—	—
[115] Donatus (7 Aug)	—	—	[II.27] fols 186va–87ra	[98] fols 151ra–52ra	[93] fols 214ra–15ra	—
[116] Cyriacus and his Companions (8 Aug)	—	—	[II.28] fol. 187^{rb-va}	[99] fols 152ra–53ra	[94] fols 215ra–16ra	—
[117] Lawrence (10 Aug)	[41] fols 64rb–67ra	[37] fols 29va–30va	[60] fols 107va–10vb	[100] fols 153ra–56va	[95] fols 216ra–19va	—
[118] Hippolytus (13 Aug)	[42] fols 67ra–68ra	[38] fols 30va–31ra	[61] fols 110vb–11vb	[101] fols 156va–58ra	[96] fols 219va–20va	—
[119] The Assumption (15 Aug)	[43] fols 67ra–70vb	[39] fols 31rb–33ra	[62] fols 111vb–14$^{bu.vb}$	[102] fols 158ra–64rb	[97] fols 220va–24va	—

247

Reading and Position in Voragine (*=interpolated reading)	BMP 8	BMP 9	FLG 419	Escorial K-II-12	Escorial h-I-14	Escorial M-II-6
[120] Bernard (20 Aug)	—	—	[II.29] fols 187va–90rb	[103] fols 164rb–68va	[98] fols 224rb–27ra	—
[121] Timothy (22 Aug)	—	[40] fol. 33vb	[63] fol. 114$^{(ba)vb}$	[104] fol. 168^{va-vb}	[99] fol. 227^{ra-rb}	—
[122] Symphorian (22 Aug)	—	—	—	[105] fols 168vb–69ra	[100] fol 227^{rb-va}	—
[123] Bartholomew (24 Aug)	—	[41] fols 33vb–34rb	[64] fols 114$^{(ba)vb}$–16va	[106] fols 169ra–71rb	[101] fols 227va–29vb	—
[124] Augustine (28 Aug)	—	—	[II.30] fols 190va–93vb	[107] fols 171rb–77ra	[102] fols 229va–34ra	—
[125] Beheading of John the Baptist (29 Aug)	—	[42] fols 34vb–36ra	[65] fol. 116va–17rb	[108] fols 177ra–79va	[103] fols 234ra–36ra	—
[126] Felix and Adauctus (30 Aug)	—	—	[II.31] fol. 193^{rb-va}	[109] fol. 179^{va-b}	[104] fol. 236^{va-vb}	—
[127] Savinian and Savina (30 Aug)	—	—	[II.32] fols 193va–94vb	[110] fols 179vb–81ra	[105] fols 236vb–38va	—
[128] Lupus (1 Sep)	—	—	[II.33] fols 194va–95ra	[111] fol. 181^{ra-vb}	[106] fols 238va–39rb	—
[129] Mamertinus (4 Sept)	—	—	[II.34] fol. 195^{ra-b}	[112] fols 181vb–82vb	[107] fols 239rb–40rb	—
[130] Giles (1 Sep)	—	—	[II.35] fols 195vb–96ra	[113] fols 182vb–84ra	[108] fols 240rb–41vb	—
[*] Antoninus (2 Sep)	—	—	—	[114] fols 184ra–87va	[109] fols 241vb–45vb	—
[131] The Birth of the Virgin (8 Sep)	—	[43] fols 36ra–38^{vrb}	[66] fols 117va–22ra	[115] fols 187va–92va	[110] fols 245va–49va	—
[132] Cornelius and Cyprian (14 Sep)	—	[46] fol. 41rb	[69] fol. 125^{va-vb}	[120] fol. 198^{va-vb}	[115] fol. 257^{rb-va}	—
[133] Lambert (17 Sep)	—	—	[II.39] fols 198va–99ra	[122] fols 199vb–200rb	[117] fols 258vb–59va	—
[134] Adrian and his Companions (8 Sep)	—	—	[II.37] fols 196ra–97vb	[116] fols 192ra–94vb	[111] fols 249va–52ra	—
[135] Gorgonius and Dorotheus (8 Sep)	—	—	[II.36] fol. 196^{ra-rb}	[117] fol. 194^{rb-va}	[112] fol. 252^{ra-rb}	—
[136] Protus and Hyacinthus (11 Sep)	—	[44] fols 38vb–39vb	[67] fols 122ra–23rb	[118] fols 194va–96ra	[113] fols 252rb–54ra	—
[137] The Exaltation of the Holy Cross (14 Sep)	[44] fols 71ra–73rb	[45] fols 39vb–41rb	[68] fols 123rb–25va	[119] fols 196ra–98va	[114] fols 254rb–57ra	—
[139] Euphemia (16 Sep)	—	—	[II.38] fols 197vb–98vb	[121] fols 198vb–99vb	[116] fols 257va–58vb	—
[140] Matthew (21 Sep)	—	[47] fols 41va–42rb	[70] fols 125vb–27ra	[123] fols 200rb–201vb	[118] fols 259va–61ra	—
[141] Maurice and his Companions (22 Sep)	—	—	[II.40] fols 199va–200rb	—	[119] fols 261ra–63ra	—

248

Reading and Position in Voragine (*=interpolated reading)	BMP 8	BMP 9	FLG 419	Escorial K-II-12	Escorial h-I-14	Escorial M-II-6
[142] Justina (26 Sep)	–	–	[II.41] fols 200rb–01rb	–	[120] fols 265ra–65rb	–
[143] Cosmas and Damian (27 Sep)	–	–	[II.42] fols 201rb–02vb	–	[121] fols 265rb–66vb	–
[145] Michael the Archangel (29 Sep)	–	[48] fols 42rb–43rb	[71] fols 127ra–28va	–	[122] fols 266vb–68vb	–
[146] Jerome (30 Sep)	–	[63] fols 60vb–62ra	[72] fols 128va–30vb	–	[123] fols 268vb–70vb	–
[147] Remy (1 Oct)	–	–	[II.43] fols 202vb–03rb	–	[124] fols 270vb–71vb	–
[148] Leger (2 Oct)	–	–	[II.44] fol. 203^{rb-vb}	–	[125] fols 271vb–72ra	–
[149] Francis (4 Oct)	–	[49] fols 43rb–45rb	[73] fols 130vb–33va	–	[126] fols 272va–76ra	–
[150] Pelagia (8 Oct)	–	–	–	–	[127] fols 276ra–77	–
[151] Margaret (8 Oct)	–	–	[II.45] fols 203vb–04rb	–	[128] fol. 277^{vb-vb}	–
[152] Thais (8 Oct)	–	–	–	–	[129] fols 277vb–79ra	–
[153] Dionysius and his Companions (9 Oct)	–	–	[II.46] fols 204rb–06ra	–	[130] fols 279ra–81va	–
[154] Callistus (14 Oct)	–	–	–	–	[131] fol 281^{ra-va}	–
[155] Leonard (6 Nov)	–	–	[II.47] fols 206ra–07rb	–	[132] fols 281va–83rb	–
[156] Luke (18 Oct)	–	[50] fol. 45^{rb-vb}	[74] fols 133va–34rb	–	[133] fols 283rb–84rb	–
[157] Chrysanthus and Daria (25 Oct)	–	–	[II.48] fol. 207^{rb-vb}	[2] fol. 5^{ra-va}	[134] fols 284rb–85ra	–
[158] Ursula and the 11,000 Virgins (21 Oct)	–	–	[II.49] fols 207vb–09va	–	[135] fols 285rb–87ra	–
[159] Simon and Jude (28 Oct)	–	[51] fols 45vb–47ra	[75] fols 134va–36va	–	[136] fols 287ra–90ra	–
[160] Quentin (31 Oct)	–	–	–	–	[137] fol. 290^{ra-rb}	–
[161] Eustace (20 Sep)	–	–	–	–	[138] fols 290rb–93rb	–
[162] All Saints (1 Nov)	–	[52] fol. 47^{rb-vb}	[76] fols 136va–38ra	–	[139] fols 293rb–94vb	–
[163] All Souls (2 Nov)	–	[53] fols 47vb–48vb	[77] fols 138ra–41ra	–	[140] fols 294vb–97va	–
[164] The Four Crowned Martyrs (8 Nov)	–	–	–	–	[141] fol. 297va	–

Reading and Position in Voragine (*=interpolated reading)	BMP 8	BMP 9	FLG 419	Escorial K-II-12	Escorial h-I-14	Escorial M-II-6
[165] Theodore (9 Nov)	—	—	[1,50] fol. 212$^{\text{rb-va}}$	—	[142] fols 297va–98va	—
[166] Martin of Tours (12 Nov)	—	[54] fols 49ra–50rb	[78] fols 141ra–44ra	—	[143] fols 298va–301rb	—
[167] Brice (13 Nov)	—	[55] fol. 50$^{\text{rb-vb}}$	[79] fol. 144$^{\text{ra-va}}$	—	[144] fols 301rb–02ra	—
[169] Cecilia (22 Nov)	—	[56] fols 50vb–52va	[80] fols 144vb–47ra	—	[145] fols 302ra–04va	—
[170] Clement (23 Nov)	—	[57] fols 52va–55rb	[81] fols 147ra–51rb	—	[146] fols 304va–08vb	—
[171] Chrysogonus (24 Nov)	—	—	[1,51] fols 212va–13ra	—	[147] fols 308vb–09vb	—
[172] Catherine of Alexandria (25 Nov)	—	[58] fols 55rb–56rb	[82] fols 151rb–53va	—	[149] fols 310rb–12vb	—
[173] Saturninus and his Companions (29 Nov)	—	—	[1,52] fols 213$^{\text{ra-vb}}$	—	[148] fols 309vb–10rb	—
[174] James the Dismembered (27 Nov)	—	—	[1,54] fols 216vb–17rb	—	[150] fols 312vb–14rb	—
[*] Hilarion (21 Oct)	—	—	—	—	[151] fols 314rb–22vb	—

Works Cited

AHERN, John, 1981. 'Singing the Book: Orality in the Reception of Dante's *Comedy*', *Annals of Scholarship*, 2: 17-40.

ALEXIEVA, Bistra, 1997. 'There Must be Some System in this Madness: Metaphor, Polysemy and Wordplay in a Cognitive Linguistics Framework', in *Traductio: Essays on Punning and Translation*, ed. Dirk Delabastita, Collection Langues et Littératures, 2 (Manchester & Namur: St Jerome Publishing and Presses Universitaires de Namur), pp. 137-54.

ALTMAN, Charles F., 1975. 'Two Types of Opposition and the Structure of Latin Saints' Lives', *Medievalia et Humanistica*, new series 6: 1-11.

ALVAR, Manuel, ed., 1970-72. *'Vida de Santa María Egipciaca': estudios, vocabulario, edición de los textos*, Clásicos Hispánicos, 2.18-19 (Madrid: Consejo Superior de Investigaciones Científicas).

ÁLVAREZ PELLITERO, Ana María, 1991. 'La *Danza general de la Muerte*: entre el sermón y el teatro', *Bulletin Hispanique*, 93: 13-29.

ANSON, John, 1974. 'The Female Transvestite in Early Monasticism: The Origin and Development of a Motif', *Viator*, 5: 1-32.

ARENDT, Hannah, 1970. *On Violence* (London: Allen Lane).

ARTIGAS, Miguel, 1930. *Catálogo de los manuscritos de la Biblioteca de Menéndez Pelayo* (Santander: Sociedad Menéndez Pelayo).

ASTOR, James, 1989. 'The Breast as Part of the Whole: Theoretical Considerations Concerning Whole and Part Objects', *Journal of Analytic Psychology*, 34: 117-28.

ATKINSON, Clarissa W., 1983. *Mystic and Pilgrim: The 'Book' and the World of Margery Kempe* (Ithaca: Cornell University Press).

———, 1991. *The Oldest Vocation: Christian Motherhood in the Middle Ages* (Ithaca: Cornell University Press).

AVIGAD, N., 1977. 'Two Ammonite Seals Depicting the *Dea Nutrix*', *Bulletin of the American Schools of Oriental Research*, 225: 63-66.

BAÑOS VALLEJO, Fernando, 1995. '*La istoria de Sant Mamés*: un ejemplo de ficción (MS 8 de la Biblioteca Menéndez Pelayo)', in *Medioevo y literatura: Actas del V Congreso de la Asociación Hispánica de Literatura

Medieval (Granada, 27 septiembre—1 octubre 1993), ed. Juan Paredes, 4 vols (Granada: Universidad), 1, pp. 301-09.

———, 2000a. 'La leyenda de los santos: Flos Sanctorum del MS. 8 de la Biblioteca de Menéndez Pelayo', Boletín de la Biblioteca de Menéndez Pelayo, 76: 463-68.

———, 2000b. 'Manuscrito 8 de la Biblioteca de Menéndez Pelayo: peculiaridades de la version castellana de la Legenda aurea', in Actas del VIII Congreso Internacional de la Asociación Hispánica de Literatura Medieval: Santander, 22-26 de septiembre de 1999, ed. Margarita Freixas & Silvia Iriso (Santander: Consejería de Cultura del Gobierno de Cantabria, Año Jubilar Lebaniego, & Asociación Hispánica de Literatura Medieval), 1, pp. 279-89.

———, 2003. Las vidas de santos en la literatura medieval española, Colección Arcadia de las Letras, 17 (Madrid: Laberinto).

———, & Isabel URÍA MAQUA, ed., 2000. 'La leyenda de los santos': 'flos sanctorum' del ms. 8 de la Biblioteca Menéndez Pelayo, Estudios de Literatura y Pensamiento Hispánicos, 18 (Santander: Año Jubilar Lebaniego & Sociedad Menéndez Pelayo).

BATAILLON, Louis-Jacques, 1980. 'Approaches to the Study of Medieval Sermons', Leeds Studies in English, new series 11: 19-35.

BAYO, Juan Carlos, & Ian MICHAEL, ed., 2006. Gonzalo de Berceo, Milagros de Nuestra Señora, Clásicos Castalia, 288 (Madrid: Castalia).

BEER, Jeannette, 1989. 'Introduction', in her Medieval Translators and their Craft, Studies in Medieval Culture, 25 (Kalamazoo, MI: Medieval Institute Publications, Western Michigan University), pp. 1-7.

BERESFORD, Andrew M., 2001. '"Una oración, señora, que le dixeron que sabías, de Sancta Polonia para el dolor de las muelas": Celestina and the Legend of St Apollonia', Bulletin of Hispanic Studies, 78: 39-57.

———, 2003. 'Marianism, Misogyny, and Milk: The Cultural Significance of Saint Bernard of Clairvaux in Early Hispanic Literature', in Proceedings of the Twelfth Colloquium, ed. Alan Deyermond & Jane Whetnall, Papers of the Medieval Hispanic Research Seminar, 35 (London: Department of Hispanic Studies, Queen Mary, University of London), pp. 7-19

———, 2007a. The Legend of Saint Agnes in Medieval Castilian Literature, Papers of the Medieval Hispanic Research Seminar, 59 (London: Department of Hispanic Studies, Queen Mary, University of London).

———, 2007b. *The Legends of the Holy Harlots: Thaïs and Pelagia in Medieval Spanish Literature*, Colección Támesis, A238 (Woodbridge: Tamesis).

———, in press. 'A Sermon for the Feast of Saint Julian the Martyr', *Revista de Poética Medieval*.

———, in preparation. 'The Legend of Saint Paul of Thebes'.

BÉTÉROUS, P. V., 1975. 'A propos d'une des legendes mariales les plus répandues: le lait de la Vierge', *Bullétin de l'Association Guillaume Budé*, 4: 403-11.

BISSET, K. A., 1971. 'Who Were the Amazons?', *Greece & Rome*, second series 18: 150-51.

BOSS, Sarah Jane, 2000. *Empress and Handmaid: On Nature and Gender in the Cult of the Virgin Mary* (London: Cassell).

BOUREAU, Alain, & Benjamin SEMPLE, 1994. 'The Sacrality of One's Own Body in the Middle Ages', *Yale French Studies*, 86: 5-17.

BOWERSOCK, G. W., 1995. *Martyrdom and Rome*, The Wiles Lectures Given at the University of Belfast (Cambridge: University Press).

BOYER, Agustin, 1988. 'Estudio descriptivo del *Libro de las virtuosas e claras mugeres* de don Álvaro de Luna: fuentes, genero y ubicación en el debate feminista del siglo XV', PhD Thesis (Berkeley, California).

BRAY, Xavier, with Alfonso RODRÍGUEZ G. DE CEBALLOS, Daphne BARBOUR, & Judy OZONE, 2009. *The Sacred Made Real: Spanish Painting and Sculpture 1600-1700* (London: National Gallery).

BROOK, Leslie C., 1998. 'Jean de Meun: Translator of Hypothetical "Si" Clauses', in *The Medieval Translator (Traduire au Moyen Age)*, VI: *Proceedings of the International Conference of Göttingen, 22-25 July 1996 (Actes du Colloque Internacional de Gottingen, 22-25 juilliet 1996)*, ed. Roger Ellis, René Tixier, & Bernd Weitemeier (Turnhout: Brepols), pp. 175-93.

BROWN, Jonathan, 1991. *Zurbarán*, 2nd ed. (New York: Harry H. Abrams).

———, 1998. *Painting in Spain 1500-1700*, Pelican History of Art (Yale: University Press).

———, & Carmen GARRIDO, 1998. *Velázquez: The Technique of Genius* (New Haven: Yale University Press).

BROWN, Peter, 1988. *The Body and Society: Men, Women and Sexual Renunciation in Early Christianity* (New York: Columbia UP).

BRUSA, L., 1957. 'La tradizione del martirio di S. Lucia di Siracusa', *Archivio Storico Siciliano*, 3: 96-99.

BUCK, Carl D., 1889. 'On the Forms *ΑΡΤΕΜΙΣ, ΑΡΤΑΜΙΣ*', *American Journal of Philology*, 10: 463-66

BULLOUGH, Vern L., 1974. 'Transvestites in the Middle Ages', *American Journal of Sociology*, 79: 1381-94.

——, 1977. 'Sex Education in Medieval Christianity', *Journal of Sex Research*, 13: 185-96.

BURKE, James, F., 1980-81. 'The *Libro de buen amor* and the Medieval Meditative Sermon Tradition', *La Corónica*, 9 (Spring): 122-27.

——, 1998. *Desire Against the Law: The Juxtaposition of Contraries in Early Medieval Spanish Literature* (Stanford: University Press).

BURKE, Jill, 2006. 'Sex and Spirituality in 1500s Rome: Sebastiano del Piombo's *Martyrdom of Saint Agatha*', *The Art Bulletin*, 88: 482-96.

BURLEIGH, Gilbert R., Keith J. FITZPATRICK-MATTHEWS, & Miranda J. ALDHOUSE-GREEN, 2006. 'A *Dea Nutrix* Figurine from a Romano-British Cemetery at Baldock, Hertfordshire', *Britannia*, 37: 273-94.

BUTLER, Alban, 1903. *The Lives of the Fathers, Martyrs, and Other Principal Saints Compiled from Original Monuments and Other Authentic Records, Illustrated with the Remarks of Judicious Modern Critics and Historians*, 12 vols in 4 (New York: P. J. Kennedy).

BUXTON, Sarah, 2006. 'Saint Christopher in Medieval Spanish Literature', MA by Research (Durham University).

——, 2010. 'Military Martyrs in Medieval Castilian Literature', PhD Thesis (Durham University).

——, in preparation. 'The Legend of Saint George in BNM 10252'.

BYNUM, Caroline Walker, 1982. *Jesus as Mother: Studies in the Spirituality of the High Middle Ages* (Berkeley: University of California Press).

——, 1987. *Holy Feast and Holy Fast: The Religious Significance of Food to Medieval Women*, The New Historicism: Studies in Cultural Poetics, 1 (Berkeley: University of California Press).

——, 1990. 'Material Continuity, Personal Survival, and the Resurrection of the Body: A Scholastic Discussion in its Medieval and Modern Contexts', *History of Religions*, 30: 51-85.

BYRNE, Ryan, 2004. 'Lie Back and Think of Judah: The Reproductive Politics of Pillar Figurines', *Near Eastern Archaeology*, 67: 137-51.

CALVERAS, J., 1944a. 'Fray Gonzalo de Ocaña: traductor del *Flos Sanctorum* anónimo', *Analecta Sacra Tarraconensia*, 17: 206-08.

——, 1944b. 'Una traducción castellana del *Vita Christi* de Eximenis', *Analecta Sacra Tarraconensia*, 17: 208.

CANTERA, Francisco, 1958. 'Raquel e vidas', *Sefarad*, 18: 99-108.

CAPDEVILA, Miguel, 1949. *Iconografía de Santa Lucía*, Colección Publicaciones del Laboratorio del Norte de España, 18 (Barcelona: Laboratorio del Norte de España).

CARLÉ, Birte, 1980. 'Structural Patterns in the Legends of the Holy Women of Christianity', in *Aspects of Female Existence: Proceedings from the St. Gertrud Symposium 'Women in the Middle Ages', Copenhagen, September 1978*, ed. Birte Carlé et al. (Copenhagen: Gyldendal), pp. 79-86.

CARR, Dawson W., with Xavier BRAY, John H. ELLIOTT, Larry KEITH, & Javier PORTÚS, 2006. *Velázquez* (London: National Gallery).

CARRASCO, Magdalena, 1985. 'An Early Illustrated Manuscript of the Passion of St. Agatha', *Gesta*, 24: 19-32.

CASTILLO, Manuel, ed., 1908. *'Libro de las claras e virtuosos mugeres' por el condestable de Castilla, don Álvaro de Luna* (Toledo: Rafael G. Menor).

CASTRO, Manuel de, 1973. *Manuscritos franciscanos de la Biblioteca Nacional de Madrid* (Madrid: Servicio de Publicaciones del Ministerio de Educación y Ciencia Secretaría General Técnica).

CÁTEDRA, Pedro M., 1981. *Dos estudios sobre el sermón en la España medieval* (Bellaterra: Universidad Autónoma de Barcelona).

———, 1983-84. 'La predicacción castellana de San Vicente Ferrer', *Boletín de la Real Academia de Buenas Letras de Barcelona*, 39: 235-309.

———, 1986. 'La mujer en el sermón medieval: a través de textos españoles', in *La condición de la mujer en la Edad Media: Actas del Coloquio celebrado en la Casa de Velázquez, del 5 a 7 de noviembre de 1984* (Madrid: Casa de Velázquez & Universidad Complutense), pp. 39-50.

———, 1994. *Sermón, sociedad y literatura en la Edad Media: San Vicente Ferrer en Castilla, 1411-1412* (Salamanca: Junta de Castilla y León).

CAVINESS, Madeline H., 2001. *Visualizing Women in the Middle Ages: Sight, Spectacle, and the Scopic Economy* (Philadelphia: University of Pennsylvania Press).

CAZELLES, Brigitte, trans., 1991. *The Lady as Saint: A Collection of French Hagiographic Romances of the Thirteenth Century*, Middle Ages Series (Philadelphia: University of Pennsylvania Press).

CHAPMAN, Janet A., 1970. 'Juan Ruiz's Learned Sermon', in *'Libro de buen amor' Studies*, ed. G. B. Gybbon-Monypenny, Colección Tamesis, A12 (London: Tamesis), pp. 29-51.

CHAYTOR, H. J., 1945. *From Script to Print: An Introduction to Medieval Vernacular Literature* (Cambridge: W. Heffer).

CLOUD, David W., 2001. *Dynamic Equivalency: Death Knell of Pure Scripture* (Port Huron, MI: Way of Life Literature). First published in 1990.

CONNOLLY, Jane E., ed., 1990. *'Los miraglos de Santiago': Biblioteca Nacional de Madrid MS 10252*, Textos Recuperados, 5 (Salamanca: Universidad de Salamanca).

CONNOLLY, Margaret, 1994. 'Public Revisions or Private Responses? The Oddities of BL, Arundel MS 197, with Special Reference to Contemplations of the Dread and Love of God', *British Library Journal*, 20: 55-64.

——, 2003. 'Shaking the Language Tree: Translating the Word into the Vernacular in the Anglo-Norman *Miroir* and the Middle English *Mirror*', in *The Medieval Translator (Traduire au Moyen Age)*, VIII: *The Theory and Practice of Translation in the Middle Ages*, ed. Rosalynn Voaden, René Tixier, Teresa Sanchez Roura, & Jenny Rebecca Rytting (Turnhout: Brepols), pp. 17-27.

CONSTABLE, Olivia Remie, 1994. *Trade and Traders in Muslim Spain: The Commercial Realignment of the Iberian Peninsula, 900-1500*, Cambridge Studies in Medieval Life and Thought, 4th Series 24 (Cambridge: University Press).

CORMACK, Margaret, 2000. Review of Wolf 1997a, *Speculum*, 75: 733-35.

CORIA-SÁNCHEZ, Carlos M., 1998. 'Los tratados en defensa de las mujeres en la España medieval: tratados feministas?', *Publicación Feminista Mensual*, 22.184: 21-26.

CORTINA, Lynn Rice, 1972. 'Composition and Meaning of the *Vida de Santa María Egipciaca*', PhD thesis (Case Western Reserve University). *Dissertation Abstracts International*, 33 (1971-72), 1718A.

——, 1980. 'The Aesthetics of Morality: Two Portraits of Mary of Egypt in the *Vida de Santa María Egipciaca*', *Hispanic Journal*, 2.1: 41-45.

COSTANZA, S., 1957. 'Un *Martyrion* inedito di S. Lucia di Siracusa', *Archivio Storico Siciliano*, 3: 5-53.

CRACCO RUGGINI, Lelia, 1984. 'Christianisation in Sicily (IIIrd-IVth Century)', *Gerión*, 1: 219-34.

CROSBY, Ruth, 1936. 'Oral Delivery in the Middle Ages', *Speculum*, 11: 88-110.

——, 1938. 'Chaucer and the Custom of Oral Delivery', *Speculum*, 13: 413-32.

D'ARRIGO, Santo, 1985. *Il martirio di Sant' Agata nel quadro storico del suo tempo*, 2 vols (Catania: Istituto Catechistico Annunziazione di Maria, Università di Catania).

DAGENAIS, John, 1994. *The Ethics of Reading in Manuscript Culture: Glossing the 'Libro de buen amor'* (Princeton: University Press).

DAVIS, Kathleen, 1997. 'Signature in Translation', in *Traductio: Essays on Punning and Translation*, ed. Dirk Delabastita, Collection Langues et

Littératures, 2 (Manchester & Namur: St Jerome Publishing and Presses Universitaires de Namur), pp. 45-43.

DAVIS, Stephen J., 1998. 'Pilgrimage and the Cult of Saint Thecla in Late Antique Egypt', in *Pilgrimage and Holy Space in Late Antique Egypt*, ed. David Frankfurter, Religions in the Graeco-Roman World, 134 (Leiden: Brill), pp. 303-39.

———, 2001. *The Cult of Saint Thecla: A Tradition of Women's Piety in Late Antiquity*, Oxford Early Christian Studies (Oxford: University Press).

DELABASTITA, Dirk, 1994. 'Focus on the Pun: Wordplay as a Special Problem in Translation Studies', *Target*, 6: 223-43.

———, 1997. 'Introduction', in his *Traductio: Essays on Punning and Translation*, Collection Langues et Littératures, 2 (Manchester & Namur: St Jerome Publishing and Presses Universitaires de Namur), pp. 1-22.

DELCOURT, Marie, 1958. 'Le complexe de Diane dans l'hagiographie chrétienne', *Revue de l'Histoire des Religions*, 153: 1-33.

———, 1961. 'Female Saints in Masculine Clothing', in *Hermaphrodite: Myths and Rites of the Bisexual Figure in Classical Antiquity*, tr. Jennifer Nicholson (London: Studio Books), pp. 84-102.

DEMERSON, Paulette, 1984. 'La *Doncella a Dios* de Martín de Córdoba', *Bulletin Hispanique*, 86: 142-53.

DEYERMOND, Alan, 1973. 'Structural and Stylistic Patterns in the *Cantar de Mio Cid*', in *Medieval Studies in Honor of Robert White Linker*, ed. Brian Dutton, J. W. Hassell, & John Esten Keller (Madrid: Castalia), pp. 55-71.

———, 1974. '*Juglar*'s Repertoire or Sermon Notebook? The *Libro de buen amor* and a Manuscript Miscellany', *Bulletin of Hispanic Studies*, 51: 217-27.

———, 1976. 'Medieval Spanish Epic Cycles: Observations on their Formation and Development', *Kentucky Romance Quarterly*, 23: 281-303.

———, 1979-80. 'The Sermon and its Uses in Medieval Castilian Literature', *La Corónica*, 8: 127-45.

———, 1982. 'Cuentos orales y estructura formal en el *Libro de las tres razones* (*Libro de las armas*)', in *Don Juan Manuel: VII Centenario* (Murcia: Universidad & Academia Alfonso X el Sabio), pp. 75-87.

———, 1984. 'Problems of Language, Audience, and Arthurian Source in a Fifteenth-Century Castilian Sermon', in *Josep Maria Solà-Solé: Homage, homenaje, homenatge: miscelánea de estudios de amigos y discípulos*, ed. Antonio Torres Alcalá in collaboration with Victorio Agüera & Nathaniel B. Smith (Barcelona: Puvill Libros), pp. 43-54.

———, 1990. 'Lost Hagiography in Medieval Spanish: A Tentative Catalogue', in *Saints and their Authors: Studies in Medieval Hispanic Hagiography in Honor of John K. Walsh*, ed. Jane E. Connolly, Alan Deyermond, & Brian Dutton (Madison, WI: Hispanic Seminary of Medieval Studies), pp. 139-48.

Díaz y Díaz, Manuel C., 1990. 'Cuestiones en torno al culto de Santa Leocadia', in *Saints and their Authors: Studies in Medieval Hispanic Hagiography in Honor of John K. Walsh*, ed. Jane E. Connolly, Alan Deyermond, & Brian Dutton (Madison, WI: Hispanic Seminary of Medieval Studies), pp. 47-54.

Drewer, Lois, 1993. 'Margaret of Antioch the Demon-Slayer, East and West: The Iconography of the Predella of the Boston Mystic Marriage of St. Catherine', *Gesta*, 32: 11-20.

Dutton, Brian, ed., 1992. '*Vida de San Millán de la Cogolla*', in Gonzalo de Berceo, *Obra completa*, ed. Isabel Uría Maqua, Clásicos Castellanos, nueva serie [unnumbered] (Madrid: Espasa-Calpe), pp. 125-249.

Easton, Martha A., 1995. 'Saint Agatha and the Sanctification of Sexual Violence', *Studies in Iconography*, 16: 83-118.

Elliott, Alison Goddard, 1987. *Roads to Paradise: Reading the Lives of the Early Saints* (Hanover, NH: University Press of New England for Brown University Press).

Emmet, Dorothy, 1962. "'That's that'; Or Some Instances of Tautology', *Philosophy*, 139: 15-24.

Fábrega Grau, Ángel, 1957. *Santa Eulalia de Barcelona*, Publicaciones del Instituto de Estudios Eclesiásticos, 4 (Madrid: Iglesia Nacional Española).

Farmer, David Hugh, 1997. *The Oxford Dictionary of Saints*, Oxford Paperback Reference, 4th ed. (Oxford: University Press). First published 1984.

Faulhaber, Charles B., 1976. 'Some Private and Semi-Private Spanish Libraries: Travel Notes', *La Corónica*, 4: 81-90.

Ferrer, Ana, 2000. 'Santa Lucía: mediadora entre dos tiempos', *Opción*, 32: 9-34.

Fleming, John V., 1977. *An Introduction to the Franciscan Literature of the Middle Ages* (Chicago: Franciscan Herald Press).

Foster, David William, 1967. '*De Maria Egyptiaca* and the Medieval Figural Tradition', *Italica*, 44: 135-43.

———, 1970. *Christian Allegory in Early Hispanic Poetry*, Studies in Romance Languages, 4 (Lexington: University Press of Kentucky).

FOULCHÉ-DELBOSC, R., ed., 1912-15. *Cancionero castellano del siglo xv*, Nueva Biblioteca de Autores Españoles, 19 & 22 (Madrid: Ediorial Bailly-Bailliére).

———, & Jaume MASSÓ Y TORRENTS, ed., 1912. 'Cançoner sagrat de vides de sants': *segle xv* (Barcelona: Societat Catalana de Bibliòfils).

FRANCHINI, Enzo, 2001. *Los debates literarios en la Edad Media*, Colección Arcadia de las Letras, 9 (Madrid: Laberinto).

FRANCOMANO, Emily C., 2003. '"Lady, You Are Quite a Chatterbox": The Legend of St. Katherine of Alexandria: Wives' Words, and Women's Wisdom in MS Escorial h-I-13', in *Katherine of Alexandria: Texts and Contexts in Western Medieval Europe*, ed. Jacqueline Jenkins & Katherine J. Lewis, Medieval Women: Texts & Contexts, 8 (Turnhout: Brepols), pp. 131-52.

FREND, W. H. C., 1959. 'The Failure of the Persecutions in the Roman Empire', *Past & Present*, 16: 10-30.

———, 1965. *Martyrdom and Persecution in the Early Church: A Study of Conflict from the Maccabees to Donatus* (Oxford: Basil Blackwell).

FRENCH, Dorothea R., 1998. 'Maintaining Boundaries: The Status of Actresses in Early Christian Society', *Vigiliae Christianae*, 52: 293-318.

GAD, Tue, ed., 1961. *Legenden i dansk middelalder* (Copenhagen: Dansk Videnskabs Forlag).

GAIFFER, Baudouin de, 1945. 'Le légende de Sainte Julien l'Hospitalier', *Analecta Bollandiana*, 63: 144-219.

———, 1953. 'Les Sources latines d'un Miracle de Gautier de Coincy: L'Apparition de Ste Léocadie a S. Ildephonse', *Analecta Bollandiana*, 71: 100-32.

GALLOWAY, Andrew, 1994. 'Dream-Theory in the *Dream of the Rood* and *The Wanderer*', *Review of English Studies*, 45: 475-85.

GARANA, Ottavio, 1955. 'Santa Lucia di Siracusa: note agiografiche', *Archivio Storico Siciliano*, 1: 15-22.

GAVRONSKY, Serge, 1977. 'The Translator: From Piety to Cannibalism', *SubStance*, 6.16: 53-62.

GIROLAMI CHENEY, Liana de, 1986. 'The Cult of Saint Agatha', *Woman's Art Journal*, 17: 3-9.

GOLDBERG, Harriet, ed., 1974. *'Jardín de nobles donzellas', Fray Martín de Córdoba: A Critical Edition and Study*, North Carolina Studies in the Romance Languages and Literatures, 137 (Chapel Hill: Department of Romance Languages, University of North Carolina).

———, 1983. 'The Dream Report as a Literary Device in Medieval Hispanic Literature', *Hispania*, 66: 21-31.

González Palencia, Ángel, ed., 1942. 'La doncella que se sacó los ojos: para la leyenda de Santa Lucía', in *Estudios histórico-literarios*, II: *Historias y leyendas* (Madrid: Instituto Antonio de Nebrija & Consejo Superior de Investigaciones Científicas), pp. 9-75. First published in *Revista de la Biblioteca, Archivo y Museo del Ayuntamiento de Madrid*, 9 (1932): 181-200.

Graesse, Th., ed., 1846. Jacobi a Voragine, *'Legenda aurea': vulgo historia lombardica dicta* (Dresden: Librariae Arnoldianae).

Graham, Joseph F., 1981. 'Theory for Translation', in *Translation Spectrum: Essays in Theory and Practice*, ed. Marilyn Gaddis Rose (Albany: State University of New York Press), pp. 23-30.

Gravdal, Kathryn, 1991. *Ravishing Maidens: Writing Rape in Mediaeval French Literature and Law* (Philadelphia: University of Pennsylvania Press).

Green, D. H., 1990. 'Orality and Reading: The State of Research in Medieval Studies', *Speculum*, 65: 267-80.

Gurza, Esperanza, 1986. 'La oralidad y *La Celestina*', in *Renaissance and Golden Age Essays in Honor of D. W. McPheeters*, ed. Bruno M. Damiani (Potomac, MD: Scripta Humanistica), pp. 94-105.

Guterman, Simeon L., 1951. *Religious Toleration and Persecution in Ancient Rome* (London: Aiglon Press).

Gybbon-Monypenny, G. B., 1965. 'The Spanish *Mester de Clerecía* and its Intended Public: Remarks Concerning the Validity as Evidence of Passages of Direct Address to the Audience', in *Medieval Miscellany Presented to Eugène Vinaver by Pupils, Colleagues and Friends*, ed. F. Whitehead, A. H. Diverres, & F. E. Sutcliffe (Manchester: University Press), pp. 230-44.

Haliczer, Stephen, 2002. *Between Exaltation and Infamy: Female Mystics in the Golden Age of Spain* (Oxford: University Press).

Harvey, L. P., 1974. 'Oral Composition and the Performance of Novels of Chivalry in Spain', *Forum for Modern Language Studies*, 10: 270-86.

Hayne, Léonie, 1994. 'Thecla and the Church Fathers', *Vigiliae Christianae*, 48: 209-18.

Heffernan, Thomas J., 1988. *Sacred Biography: Saints and their Biographers in the Middle Ages* (Oxford: Oxford University Press).

Heller, L. G., 1974. 'Toward a General Typology of the Pun', *Language and Style*, 7: 271-82.

HERNÁNDEZ AMEZ, Vanesa, 2002-03. Mujer y santidad en el siglo XV: Álvaro de Luna y *El libro de las virtuosas e claras mugeres*', *Archivum*, 52-53: 255-88.

——, 2004-05. 'Las vidas de los mártires: modelos para imitar', *Archivum*, 54-55: 315-30.

——, 2008. *Descripción y filiación de los 'Flores sanctorum' medievales*, doctoral thesis published as CD (Oviedo: Universidad).

HIEATT, Constance B., 1967. *The Realism of Dream Visions: The Poetic Exploitation of the Dream-Experience in Chaucer and his Contemporaries*, De Proprietatibus Litterarum, Series Practica 2 (The Hague: Mouton).

HOTCHKISS, Valerie R., 1996. *Clothes Make the Man: Female Cross-Dressing in Medieval Europe* (New York: Garland).

HUGHES, Robert D., trans., 2008. *Francesc Eiximenis: An Anthology*, Colección Támesis, Serie B, Textos 50 (Woodbridge: Tamesis).

HUTCHINGS, P. Æ., 1964. 'Necessary Being and Some Types of Tautology', *Philosophy*, 39: 1-17.

JANTZEN, Grace M., 1995. *Power, Gender, and Christian Mysticism*, Cambridge Studies in Ideology and Religion (Cambridge: University Press).

JEFFREY, David L., 1975. 'Franciscan Spirituality and the Rise of Early English Drama', *Mosaic*, 8: 17-46.

JENKINS, Jacqueline, & Katherine J. LEWIS, ed. 2003. *St Katherine of Alexandria: Texts and Contexts in Western Europe*, Medieval Women: Texts and Contexts, 8 (Turnhout: Brepols).

JOHNSON, F. R., 1985. 'The English Cult of St Bridget of Sweden', *Analecta Bollandiana*, 103: 75-93.

JOSSET, Jacques, ed., 1981-84. Arcipreste de Hita, *Libro de Buen Amor*, Clásicos Castellanos, 14 & 17 (Madrid: Espasa-Calpe).

KARRAS, Ruth Mazo, 1996. *Common Women: Prostitution and Sexuality in Medieval England*, Studies in the History of Sexuality, 4 (Oxford: University Press).

KASSIER, Theodore L., 1972-73. 'The Rhetorical Devices of the Spanish *Vida de Santa María Egipciaca*', *Anuario de Estudios Medievales*, 8: 467-80.

KELCHNER, Georgia D., 1935. *Dreams in Old Norse Literature and their Affinities in Folklore* (Cambridge: University Press).

KIRK, Peter, 2005. 'Holy Communicative? Current Approaches to Bible Translation Worldwide', in *Translation and Religion: Holy Untranslatable?*, ed. Lynne Long, Topics in Translation, 28 (Clevedon: Multilingual Matters), pp. 89-101.

KLAPP, Orrin E., 1949. 'The Fool as Social Type', *American Journal of Sociology*, 55: 157-62.

KNUST, Hermann ed. 1890. *Geschichte der Legenden der h. Katharina von Alexandrien und der h. Maria Aegyptica* (Halle a.S.: M. Niemeyer).

KRUGER, Steven F., 1992. *Dreaming in the Middle Ages*, Cambridge Studies in Medieval Literature, 14 (Cambridge: University Press).

LACARRA, 1996. '*Enxenplo de un obispo que bivía deleitosamente*: la leyenda de Udo de Magdeburgo en la tradición peninsular', *Diablotexto*, 3: 173-86.

LANE FOX, Robin, 1986. *Pagans and Christians* (London: Viking).

LAWRANCE, Jeremy, 1984. 'Nueva luz sobre la biblioteca del Conde de Haro: inventario de 1455', *El Crotalón: Anuario de Filología Española*, 1: 1073-1111.

LEPPIHALME, Ritva, 1996. 'A Target-Culture Viewpoint on Allusive Wordplay', *The Translator*, 2: 199-218.

LEWISON, Edward F., 1950. 'Saint Agatha: The Patron Saint of Diseases of the Breast in Legend and Art', *Bulletin of the History of Medicine*, 24: 409-20.

LIDONNICI, Lynn R., 1992. 'The Images of Artemis Ephesia and Greco-Roman Worship: A Reconsideration', *Harvard Theological Review*, 85: 389-415.

LEWIS, Katherine J., 2000. *The Cult of St Katherine of Alexandria in Late Medieval England* (Woodbridge: Boydell & Brewer).

LLIGADAS, Josep, 2006. *Águeda y Lucía: las mártires del sur* (Barcelona: Centro de Pastoral Litúrgica).

LOMAX, Derek W., 1969. 'The Lateran Reforms and Spanish Literature', *Iberoromania*, 1: 299-313.

LOMBARDO, Luigi, 2007. 'L'occhio della Siracusana: analisi di un simbolo', in *Éthnos: Quaderno di Etnologia*, ed. Corrado di Pietro (Siracusa: Centro Studi di Tradizioni Popolari Turiddu Bella), pp. 36-55.

LONG, Lynne, 2005. 'Introduction: Translating Holy Texts', in her *Translation and Religion: Holy Untranslatable?*, Topics in Translation, 28 (Clevedon: Multilingual Matters), pp. 1-15.

LORD, Albert B., 1960. *The Singer of Tales* (Cambridge, MA: Harvard University Press).

LUCCA, Vittorio, 2007. 'Lucia, l'odissea di una Santa', in *Éthnos: Quaderno di Etnologia*, ed. Corrado di Pietro (Siracusa: Centro Studi di Tradizioni Popolari Turiddu Bella), pp. 20-27.

LUKES, Steven, 1974. *Power: A Radical View*, Studies in Sociology (London: Macmillan).

LUSIGNAN, Serge, 1997. 'Written French and Latin at the Court of France at the End of the Middle Ages', in *Translation Theory and Practice in the Middle Ages*, ed. Jeannette Beer, Studies in Medieval Culture, 38 (Kalamazoo, MI: Medieval Institute Publications, Western Michigan University), pp. 185-98.

LUTZKY, Harriet, 1998. 'Shadday as a Goddess Epithet', *Vetus Testamentum*, 48: 15-36,

LYNCH, Kathryn L., 1988. *The High Medieval Dream Vision: Poetry, Philosophy, and Literary Form* (Stanford: University Press).

MACBAIN, William, 1989. 'Five Old French Renderings of the *Passio Sancte Katerine Virginis*', in *Medieval Translators and their Craft*, ed. Jeannette Beer, Studies in Medieval Culture, 25 (Kalamazoo, MI: Medieval Institute Publications, Western Michigan University), pp. 41-65.

MACÍAS, José Manuel, trans., 1992. Santiago de la Vorágine, *La leyenda dorada*, 2 vols, Alianza Forma, 29-30 (Madrid: Alianza).

MAGENNIS, Hugh, 1996. '"Listen Now All and Understand": Adaptation of Hagiographical Material for Vernacular Audiences in the Old English Lives of St. Margaret', *Speculum*, 71: 27-42.

MALESANI, Maria Rosa, 2007. 'Santa Lucia di Maggio: una devozione siracusana che si rinnova nei secoli', in *Éthnos: Quaderno di Etnologia*, ed. Corrado di Pietro (Siracusa: Centro Studi di Tradizioni Popolari Turiddu Bella), pp. 28-35.

MANEIKIS KNIAZZEH, Charlotte S., & Edward J. NEUGAARD, ed., 1977. *'Vides de Sants Rosselloneses': text català del segle XIII*, Publicacions de la Fundació Salvador Vives Casajuana, 48, 51, & 53 (Barcelona: Fundació Salvador Vives Casajuana).

MARTÍN, José-Luis, 2003. *La mujer y el caballero: estudio y traducción de los textos de Francesc Eiximenis*, Textos y Comentarios, 2 (Barcelona: Edicions Universitat de Barcelona).

MEEKS, Wayne, 1974. 'Image of the Androgyne: Some Uses of a Symbol in Earliest Christianity', *History of Religions*, 3: 165-208.

MÉNENDEZ Y PELAYO, M., ed., 1891. *'Libro de las virtuosas e claras mujeres' el qual fizo e conpuso el condestable Don Álvaro de Luna, Maestre de la Orden de Santiago*, Sociedad de Bibliófilos Españoles, 28 (Madrid: Sociedad de Bibliófilos Españoles).

MCALLISTER, Patricia A., 1989. 'Apocryphal Narrative Elements in the *Genesis* of the Middle Low German *Historienbibel* Helmstedt 611.1', in *Medi-*

eval Translators and their Craft, ed. Jeannette Beer, Studies in Medieval Culture, 25 (Kalamazoo, MI: Medieval Institute Publications, Western Michigan University), pp. 81-92.

McLaughlin, Eleanor C., 1974. 'Equality of Souls, Inequality of Sexes: Woman in Medieval Theology', in *Religion and Sexism: Images of Women in the Jewish and Christian Traditions*, ed. Rosemary Radford Ruether (New York: Simon and Schuster), pp. 213-66

Michael, Ian, 1961. 'A Comparison of the Use of Epic Epithets in the *Poema de Mio Cid* and the *Libro de Alexandre*', *Bulletin of Hispanic Studies*, 38: 32-41.

Miles, Margaret, 1986. 'The Virgin's One Bare Breast: Female Nudity and Religious Meaning in Tuscan Early Renaissance Culture', in *The Female Body in Western Culture: Contemporary Perspectives*, ed. Susan Rubin Suleiman (Harvard: University Press), pp. 193-208.

Mohedano Hernández, José María, ed., 1951. *'El espéculo de los legos': texto inédito del siglo XV* (Madrid: Consejo Superior de Investigaciones Científicas).

Montaner, Alberto, ed., 1993. *Cantar de Mio Cid*, Biblioteca Clásica, 1 (Barcelona: Crítica).

Montgomery, Thomas, 1987. 'The Rhetoric of Solidarity in the *Poema del Cid*', *Modern Language Notes*, 102: 191-205.

Montoliu, Manuel de, 1959. *Eiximenis, Turmeda i l'inici de l'humanisme a Catalunya: Bernat Metge*, Les Grans Personalitats de la Literatura Catalana, 4 (Barcelona: Alpha).

Moore, John K. Jr., ed., 2008. *'Libro de los huéspedes' (Escorial MS h.I.13): A Critical Edition*, Medieval and Renaissance Texts and Studies, 349 (Tempe, AZ: Arizona Center for Medieval and Renaissance Studies).

Morreale, Margherita, 1996. 'Sobre San Vicente Ferrer y Pedro Cátedra, *Sermón, sociedad y literatura en la Edad Media: San Vicente Ferrer en Castilla*', *Bulletin of Hispanic Studies*, 73: 323-32.

Muessig, Carolyn, ed., 2002. *Preacher, Sermon and Audience in the Middle Ages*, A New History of the Sermon, 3 (Leiden: Brill).

Naguib, Saphinaz-Amal, 1994. 'The Martyr as Witness: Coptic and Copto-Arabic Hagiographies as Mediators of Religious Memory', *Numen*, 41: 223-54.

Nast, Heidi, & Steve Pile, 1998. *Places Through the Body* (London: Routledge).

NIDA, Eugene A., 1964. *Toward a Science of Translating, with Special Reference to Principles and Procedures Involved in Bible Translating* (Leiden: Brill).

———, & Charles R. TABER, 1969. *The Theory and Practice of Translation*, Helps for Translators, 8 (Leiden: Brill).

ONG, Walter J., 1982. *Orality and Literacy: The Technologizing of the Word*, New Accents (London: Methuen).

OWST, G. R., 1926. *Preaching in Medieval England: An Introduction to Sermon Manuscripts of the Period c. 1350-1450* (Cambridge: University Press).

PALLEY, Julian, 1983. *The Ambiguous Mirror: Dreams in Spanish Literature*, Albatrós Hispanófila, 27 (Valencia: Albatrós Ediciones; Chapel Hill: Hispanófila).

PENNY, Ralph, 1991. *A History of the Spanish Language* (Cambridge: University Press).

PETRUCCIONE, J., 1990. 'The Portrait of St Eulalia of Mérida in Prudentius' *Peristephanon* 3', *Analecta Bolandiana*, 108: 81-104.

———, 1991. 'The Persecutor's Envy and the Rise of the Martyr Cult: *Peristephanon* Hymns 1 and 4', *Vigiliae Christianae*, 45: 327-46.

———, 1995. 'The Martyr Death as Sacrifice: Prudentius, *Peristephanon* 4.9-72', 49: 245-57.

PEZZINI, Domenico, 1991. 'Brigittine Tracts of Spiritual Guidance in Fifteenth-Century England: A Study in Translation', in *The Medieval Translator II*, ed. Roger Ellis, Westfield Publications in Medieval Studies, 5 (London: Centre for Medieval Studies, Queen Mary and Westfield College, University of London), pp. 175-207.

———, 2003. 'How and Why a Translation May Be Revised: The Case of British Library, Arundel MS 197', in *The Medieval Translator (Traduire au Moyen Age)*, VIII: *The Theory and Practice of Translation in the Middle Ages*, ed. Rosalynn Voaden, René Tixier, Teresa Sanchez Roura, & Jenny Rebecca Rytting (Turnhout: Brepols), pp. 113-25.

POLECRITTI, Cynthia L., 2000. *Preaching Peace in Renaissance Italy: Saint Bernadino of Siena & his Audience* (Washington DC: The Catholic University of America Press).

POUCHELLE, Marie-Christine, 1976. 'Représentations du corps dans la *Légende dorée*', *Ethnologie Française*, 6: 293-308.

PRATT, Karen, 1989. 'Direct Speech: A Key to the German Adaptor's Art?', in *Medieval Translators and their Craft*, ed. Jeannette Beer, Studies in

Medieval Culture, 25 (Kalamazoo, MI: Medieval Institute Publications, Western Michigan University), pp. 213-46.

———, 1991. 'Medieval Attitudes to Translation and Adaptation: The Rhetorical Theory and the Poetic Practice', in *The Medieval Translator II*, ed. Roger Ellis, Westfield Publications in Medieval Studies, 5 (London: Centre for Medieval Studies, Queen Mary and Westfield College, University of London), pp. 1-27.

PRICKETT, Stephen, 1993. 'The Changing of the Host: Translation and Linguistic History', in *Translating Religious Texts: Translation, Transgression and Interpretation*, ed. David Jasper, Studies in Literature and Religion (London: Macmillan), pp. 4-20.

PRINCE, Dawn Ellen, 1993. 'A Fourteenth-Century Spanish Life of St Lawrence: Madrid, B.N. MS 10252', *La Corónica*, 21.2: 86-107.

PYM, Anthony, 1998. 'Translation History and the Manufacture of Paper', in *The Medieval Translator (Traduire au Moyen Age)*, VI: *Proceedings of the International Conference of Göttingen, 22-25 July 1996 (Actes du Colloque Internacional de Gottingen, 22-25 juilliet 1996)*, ed. Roger Ellis, René Tixier, & Bernd Weitemeier (Turnhout: Brepols), pp. 57-71.

RAUDINO, Maria Bella, 2007. 'Le divinità femminili a Siracusa da Demetra a S. Lucia', in *Éthnos: Quaderno di Etnologia*, ed. Corrado di Pietro (Siracusa: Centro Studi di Tradizioni Popolari Turiddu Bella), pp. 12-19.

REAMES, Sherry L., 1985. *The 'Legenda aurea': A Reexamination of its Paradoxical History* (Madison, WI: University of Wisconsin Press).

RENEVY, Denis, 1998. 'The Choices of the Compiler: Vernacular Hermeneutics in *A Talkyng of þe Loue of God*', in *The Medieval Translator (Traduire au Moyen Age)*, VI: *Proceedings of the International Conference of Göttingen, 22-25 July 1996 (Actes du Colloque Internacional de Gottingen, 22-25 juilliet 1996)*, ed. Roger Ellis, René Tixier, & Bernd Weitemeier (Turnhout: Brepols), pp. 232-53.

RESNICK, Seymour, 1956. '"Raquel e Vidas" and the Cid', *Hispania*, 39: 300-04.

RICH, Adrienne, 1983. *Compulsory Heterosexuality and Lesbian Existence* (London: Onlywomen Press).

ROBERTSON, Elizabeth, 1990. *Early English Devotional Prose and the Female Audience* (Knoxville: The University of Tennessee Press).

———, 1991. 'The Corporeality of Female Sanctity in *The Life of Saint Margaret*', in *Images of Sainthood in Medieval Europe*, ed. Renate Blumenfeld-Kosinski & Timea Szell (Ithaca: Cornell University Press), pp. 268-87.

ROBYNS, Clem, 1994. 'Translation and Discursive Identity', *Poetics Today*, 15: 405-28.
RODADO RUIZ, Ana Ma., 1990. 'La santidad femenina en la primitiva literatura española (siglos XIII-XIV)', *Cuadernos para Investigación de la Literatura Hispánica*, 13: 205-38.
ROMERO TOBAR, Leonardo, 1978-80. 'La *Vida de San Ildefonso* del Beneficiado de Úbeda: dos versiones inéditas', *Revista de Filología Española*, 60: 285-318.
——, 1984. 'Una versión medieval de la *Vida de San Ildefonso* (Escorial h.III.22)', *El Crotalón*, 1: 707-16.
RORDORF, Willy, 1986. 'Tradition and Composition in the *Acts of Thecla*: The State of the Question', *Semeia*, 38 (*The Apocryphal Acts of the Apostles*, ed. Dennis Ronald MacDonald): 43-52.
ROSS, Stephen David, 1981. 'Translation and Similarity', in *Translation Spectrum: Essays in Theory and Practice*, ed. Marilyn Gaddis Rose (Albany: State University of New York Press), pp. 8-22
RUFFINATTO, Aldo, ed. 1978. *La 'Vida de Santo Domingo de Silos' de Gonzalo de Berceo: estudio y edición crítica*, Colección Centro de Estudios Gonzalo de Berceo, 13 (Logroño: Instituto de Estudios Riojanos).
RYAN, William Granger, trans., 1993. Jacobus de Voragine, *The Golden Legend: Readings on the Saints*, 2 vols (Princeton: University Press).
SALISBURY, Joyce E., 1991. *Church Fathers, Independent Virgins* (New York: Verso).
SALOMONSKI, Eva, 1957. 'Raquel e Vidas', *Vox Romanica*, 15: 215-20.
SALVADOR MIGUEL, Nicasio, 1977. 'Reflexiones sobre el episodio de Rachel y Vidas en el *Cantar de Mio Cid*', *Revista de Filología Española*, 69: 183-223.
SANCHA, Fusto de, ed., 1855. *Romancero y cancionero sagrados: colección de poesías cristianas, morales y divinas sacadas de los obras de los mejores ingenios españoles*, Biblioteca de Autores Españoles, 35 (Madrid: M. Rivadeneyra).
SÁNCHEZ SÁNCHEZ, Manuel Ambrosio, ed., 1999. *Un sermonario castellano medieval: el ms. 1854 de la Biblioteca Universitaria de Salamanca*, 2 vols, Textos Recuperados, 19 (Salamanca: Universidad).
——, 2000. 'Vernacular Preaching in Spanish, Portuguese and Catalan', in *The Sermon*, ed. Beverley Mayne Kienzle (Turnhout: Brepols), pp. 759-858.

Sargent, Anne Marie, 1977. 'The Penitent Prostitute: The Tradition and Evolution of the Life of St Mary the Egyptian', PhD thesis (University of Michigan). *Dissertation Abstracts International*, 38 (1977-78): 1375-76A.

Scarborough, Connie L., 1994. 'Two Versions of the Life of Saint Mary the Egyptian: Lázaro Galdiano MS 419 and Menéndez Pelayo MS 8', *Anuario Medieval*, 6: 174-84.

——, 1995. 'The *Vida de Santa María Egipcíaca* and Julia Kristeva's Theory of Abjection', *Medievalia*, 20 (August): 14-19.

——, 1998. 'Santa María Egipcíaca: la vitalidad de la leyenda en castellano', in *Actas del XII Congreso Internacional de Hispanistas (Birmingham, 21-26 de agosto de 1995)*, 1: *Medieval y lingüística*, ed. Aengus Ward (Birmingham: Department of Hispanic Studies, University of Birmingham), pp. 302-10.

Scarry, Elaine, 1985. *The Body in Pain: The Making and Unmaking of the World* (Oxford: University Press).

Schiebinger, Londa, 1993. 'Why Mammals are Called Mammals: Gender Politics in Eighteenth-Century Natural History', *The American Historical Review*, 98: 382-411.

Schiff, Mario, 1905. *La Bibliothèque du Marquise de Santillane* (Paris: E. Bouillon).

Selman, Rebecca, 1998. 'Hearing Voices? Reading *Horologium Sapientiae* and *The Seven Poyntes of Trewe Wisdon*', in *The Medieval Translator (Traduire au Moyen Age)*, VI: *Proceedings of the International Conference of Göttingen, 22-25 July 1996 (Actes du Colloque Internacional de Gottingen, 22-25 juilliet 1996)*, ed. Roger Ellis, René Tixier, & Bernd Weitemeier (Turnhout: Brepols), pp. 254-69.

Semple, Benjamin, 1994. 'The Male Psyche and the Sacred Female Body in Marie de France and Christine de Pizan', *Yale French Studies*, 86: 164-86.

Seniff, Dennis P., 1987. 'Orality and Textuality in Medieval Castilian Prose', *Oral Tradition*, 2: 150-71.

Seybolt, Robert Francis, 1946a. 'Fifteenth-Century Editions of the *Legenda aurea*', *Speculum*, 21: 327-38.

——, 1946b. 'The *Legenda aurea*, the Bible, and *Historia scholastica*', *Speculum*, 21: 339-42.

Shewring, W. H., ed. & trans., 1931. *The Passion of Perpetua and Felicity: A New Edition and Translation of the Latin Text Together with the Sermons of Saint Augustine upon these Saints* (London: Sheed and Ward).

Smith, C. Colin, 1965. 'Did the Cid Repay the Jews?', *Romania*, 86: 520-38.

SOLOMON, Michael, 1995. 'Catarsis sexual: *La Vida de Santa María Egipciaca* y el texto higiénico', in *Erotismo en las letras hispánicas: aspectos, modos y fronteras*, ed. Luce López Baralt & Francisco Márquez Villanueva, Publicaciones de la *Nueva Revista de Filología Hispánica*, 7 (Mexico City: Colegio de México & Centro de Estudios Lingüísticos), pp. 425-37.

SPEARING, A. C., 1976. *Medieval Dream-Poetry* (Cambridge: University Press).

SPENCER, Frederic, 1889. 'The Legend of St. Margaret', *Modern Language Notes*, 4: 197-201.

———, 1890. 'The Margaret Legend', *Modern Language Notes*, 5: 61.

ST-JACQUES, Raymond C., 1989. 'The *Middle English Glossed Prose Psalter* and its French Source', in *Medieval Translators and their Craft*, ed. Jeannette Beer, Studies in Medieval Culture, 25 (Kalamazoo, MI: Medieval Institute Publications, Western Michigan University), pp. 135-54.

STANTON, Robert, 1997. 'The (M)other Tongue: Translation Theory and Old English', in *Translation Theory and Practice in the Middle Ages*, ed. Jeannette Beer, Studies in Medieval Culture, 38 (Kalamazoo, MI: Medieval Institute Publications, Western Michigan University), pp. 33-46.

STICCA, Sandro, 1988. *The 'Planctus Mariae' in the Dramatic Tradition of the Middle Ages*, tr. Joseph R. Berrigan (Athens, GA: University of Georgia Press).

STUART, Elizabeth, 1996. *Spitting at Dragons: Towards a Feminist Theology of Sainthood* (London: Mowbray).

SURTZ, Ronald E., 1983. 'The 'Franciscan Connection' in the Early Castilian Theater', *Bulletin of the Comediantes*, 35: 141-52.

TAYLOR, Barry, 1997. 'Cota, Poet of the Desert: Hermits and Scorpions in the *Diálogo entre el Amor y un viejo*', in *The Medieval Mind: Hispanic Studies in Honour of Alan Deyermond*, ed. Ian Macpherson and Ralph Penny, Colección Támesis, A170 (London: Tamesis), pp. 457-68.

TAYLOR, Robert, 1989. 'The Old French "Cistercian" Translations', in *Medieval Translators and their Craft*, ed. Jeannette Beer, Studies in Medieval Culture, 25 (Kalamazoo, MI: Medieval Institute Publications, Western Michigan University), pp. 67-80.

THOMPSON, Billy Bussell, 1990. '"Plumbei cordis, oris ferrei": la recepción de la teología de Jacobus a Voragine y su *Legenda aurea* en la Península', in *Saints and their Authors: Studies in Medieval Hispanic Hagiography in Honor of John K. Walsh*, ed. Jane E. Connolly, Alan Deyermond, & Brian Dutton (Madison, WI: Hispanic Seminary of Medieval Studies), pp. 97-106.

——, & John K. WALSH, ed., 1977. '*La vida de Santa María Egipçiaca*': *A Fourteenth-Century Translation of a Work by Paul the Deacon*, Exeter Hispanic Texts, 17 (Exeter: University).

——, & ——, 1986-87. 'Old Spanish Manuscripts of Prose Lives of the Saints and their Affiliations, I: Compilation *A* (The *Gran flos Sanctorum*)', *La Corónica*, 15: 17-28.

THOMPSON, Currie Kerr, 1976. 'The Use and Function of Dreaming in Four Novels by Emilio Pardo Bazán', *Hispania*, 59: 856-62.

TROTTER, D. A., 1998. 'Translations and Loan Words: Some Anglo-Norman Evidence', in *The Medieval Translator (Traduire au Moyen Age)*, VI: *Proceedings of the International Conference of Göttingen, 22-25 July 1996 (Actes du Colloque Internacional de Gottingen, 22-25 juilliet 1996)*, ed. Roger Ellis, René Tixier, & Bernd Weitemeier (Turnhout: Brepols), pp. 20-39.

TURNER, Ronney E., & Charles EDGLEY, 1980. 'Sociological Semanticide: On Reification, Tautology and the Destruction of Language', *Sociological Quarterly*, 21: 595-605.

TYMOCZKO, Maria, 1995. 'The Metonymics of Translating Marginalized Texts', *Comparative Literature*, 47: 11-24.

ULMER, Gregory, 1988. 'The Puncept in Grammatology', in *On Puns: The Foundation of Letters*, ed. Jonathan Culler (Oxford: Basil Blackwell), pp. 164-89.

URÍA, Isabel, ed., 1992. '*Poema de Santa Oria*', in Gonzalo de Berceo, *Obra completa*, ed. Isabel Uría Maqua, Clásicos Castellanos, nueva serie [unnumbered] (Madrid: Espasa-Calpe), pp. 490-551.

VEGA, Carlos Alberto, ed., 1991. '*La vida de San Alejo*': *versiones castellanas*, Textos Recuperados, 2 (Salamanca: Universidad de Salamanca).

VEISBERGS, Andrejs, 1997. 'The Contextual Use of Idioms, Wordplay, and Translation', in *Traductio: Essays on Punning and Translation*, ed. Dirk Delabastita, Collection Langues et Littératures, 2 (Manchester & Namur: St Jerome Publishing and Presses Universitaires de Namur), pp. 155-76.

VÉLEZ-SAINZ, Julio, 2002. 'Boccaccio, virtud y poder en el *Libro de las claras e virtuosas mugeres* de Álvaro de Luna', *La Corónica*, 31 (Fall): 107-22.

——, ed., 2009. Álvaro de Luna, *Libro de las virtuosas e claras mugeres*, Letras Hispánicas, 647 (Madrid: Cátedra).

VIERA, David J., 1980. *Bibliografía anotada de la vida i obra de Francesc Eiximenis (1340?-1409?)*, Publicacions de la Fundació Salvador Vives Casajuana, 61 (Barcelona: Fundació Salvador Vives Casajuana).

———, 1991. 'Vincent Ferrer's Sermon on Mary Magdalene: A Technique for Hagiographic Sermons', *Hispanófila*, 34.2 (January, 101): 61-66.

VITZ, Evelyn Birge, 1986. 'Rethinking Old French Literature: Orality, Literacy, and the Octosyllabic Rhymed Couplet', *Romanic Review*, 77: 307-21.

———, 1987. 'Vie, légende, littérature: traditions orales e écrites dans les histoires des saints', *Poétique*, 72: 387-402.

———, 1991. 'From the Oral to the Written in Medieval and Renaissance Saints' Lives', in *Images of Sainthood in Medieval Europe*, ed. Renate Blumenfeld-Kosinski & Timea Szell (Ithaca: Cornell University Press), pp. 97-114.

WALKER, Roger M., 1971. 'Oral Delivery or Private Reading? A Contribution to the Debate on the Dissemination of Medieval Literature', *Forum for Modern Language Studies*, 7: 36-42.

———, ed., 1977. *Estoria de Santa María Egiçiaca*, 2nd ed., Exeter Hispanic Texts, 15 (Exeter: University). First edition published as EHT, 1 (Exeter: University, 1972).

WALSH, Christine, 2007. *The Cult of St. Katherine of Alexandria in Early Medieval Europe: Church, Faith and Culture in the Medieval West* (Aldershot: Ashgate).

WALSH, John K., 1992a. *'La vida de Sant Alifonsso por metros' (ca. 1302): edición y estudio*, Supplement to *Romance Philology*, 46:1 (Berkeley: University of California Press).

———, 1992b. *Relic and Literature: St Toribius of Astorga and his 'Arca Sancta'*, Fontaine Notre Dame, 2 (St Albans: David Hook).

———, & B. Bussell THOMPSON, ed., 1987. *La leyenda medieval de Santo Toribio y su 'arca sancta', con una edición del texto en el MS. 780 de la Biblioteca Nacional*, Pliegos Hispánicos 4 (New York: Lorenzo Clemente).

WARDROPPER, Bruce W., 1967. *Poesía elegíaca española*, Biblioteca Anaya, 80 (Salamanca: Anaya).

WEBSTER, Jill R., 1993. *'Els menorets': The Franciscans in the Realms of Aragon from St. Francis to the Black Death*, Studies and Texts, 114 (Toronto: Pontifical Institute of Medieval Studies).

WEISS, Julian, 1991. 'Álvaro de Luna, Juan de Mena and the Power of Courtly Love', *Modern Language Review*, 106: 241-56.

———, 2006. *The 'Mester de clerecía': Intellectuals and Ideologies in Thirteenth-Century Castile*, Colección Támesis, A231 (Woodbridge: Tamesis).

WILTROUT, Ann E., 1971. 'Hacia algunas interpretaciones dramáticas de la leyenda de Santa Bárbara', *Filología*, 15: 251-65.

WINSTEAD, Karen A., 1997. *Virgin Martyrs: Legends of Sainthood in Late Medieval England* (Ithaca: Cornell University Press).

WOLF, Kirsten, 1997a. *The Icelandic Legend of Saint Dorothy*, Studies and Texts, 130 (Toronto: Pontifical Institute of Medieval Studies).

——, 1997b. 'The Severed Breast: A Topos in the Legends of Female Virgin Martyr Saints', *Arkiv för Nordisk Filologi*, 112: 97-112.

WRIGHT, Roger, 1997. 'Translation between Latin and Romance in the Early Middle Ages', in *Translation Theory and Practice in the Middle Ages*, ed. Jeannette Beer, Studies in Medieval Culture, 38 (Kalamazoo, MI: Medieval Institute Publications, Western Michigan University), pp. 7-32.

WYATT, Carmen Joy, 1983. 'Representations of Holiness in Some Spanish Hagiographic Works: The Thirteenth through the Seventeenth Centuries', PhD thesis (Stanford University). *Dissertation Abstracts International*, 44 (1983-84): 2787A.

YALOM, Marilyn, 1997. *A History of the Breast* (New York: Alfred A. Knopf).

ZAMORA VICENTE, Alonso, ed., 1946. *Poema de Fernán González*, Clásicos Castellanos, 128 (Madrid: Espasa-Calpe).

ZANIBONI, Maria, 2007. 'Lucia, la Santa Siracusana', in *Éthnos: Quaderno di Etnologia*, ed. Corrado di Pietro (Siracusa: Centro Studi di Tradizioni Popolari Turiddu Bella), pp. 8-11

ZARCO CUEVAS, Julián, 1924-29. *Catálogo de los manuscritos castellanos de la Real Biblioteca de El Escorial*, 3 vols (Madrid: Imprenta Helénica).

——, 1927. 'Sermón de pasión predicado en Murcia por San Vicente Ferrer', *La Ciudad de Dios*, 148: 122-47.

ZELECHOW, Bernard, 1993. 'The Myth of Translatability: Translation as Interpretation', in *Translating Religious Texts: Translation, Transgression and Interpretation*, ed. David Jasper, Studies in Literature and Religion (London: Macmillan), pp. 122-39.

ZUMTHOR, Paul, 1984. 'The Text and the Voice', *New Literary History*, 16: 57-92.